Global Governance on the Ground

Global Governance on the Ground

Organizing International Migration and Asylum at the Border

Nele Kortendiek

OXFORD
UNIVERSITY PRESS

OXFORD
UNIVERSITY PRESS

Great Clarendon Street, Oxford, OX2 6DP,
United Kingdom

Oxford University Press is a department of the University of Oxford.
It furthers the University's objective of excellence in research, scholarship,
and education by publishing worldwide. Oxford is a registered trade mark of
Oxford University Press in the UK and in certain other countries

Published in the United States of America by Oxford University Press
198 Madison Avenue, New York, NY 10016, United States of America

British Library Cataloguing in Publication Data

Data available

Library of Congress Control Number: 2024939993

ISBN 9780198889120

DOI: 10.1093/oso/9780198889120.001.0001

Printed and bound by
CPI Group (UK) Ltd, Croydon, CR0 4YY

For Asma

Acknowledgments

How do international organizations make a difference in world politics? Who governs in international organizations, and how? Curious about what lies behind organizational mandates and boundaries, I ventured down the winding road of researching global governance on the ground. This intellectual journey would not have been possible without the support of many institutions, colleagues, and friends. I would like to sincerely thank them all.

My first "intellectual homes" while working on this book were the Cluster of Excellence "The Formation of Normative Orders," funded by the German Research Foundation, and the Technical University (TU) of Darmstadt. I am grateful to both institutions for supporting my work financially and enabling me to conduct the field research on which this study builds. My special thanks go to Jens Steffek at TU Darmstadt, who supervised the dissertation on which this book is based: without his continuous support and trust in my work, this book would not have been written. I have benefited greatly from our discussions and his deep insights into the processes of global governance. I also learned a great deal at our research seminar in Darmstadt and am grateful to Leonie Holthaus, Miranda Loli, Johannes Klassen, and Gianna Schlichte, among many others, for reading many of my chapter drafts. My heartfelt thanks also go to Leonard Seabrooke who not only became the second supervisor of my dissertation but whose intellectual curiosity, breadth of knowledge, and open ear profoundly shaped my thinking and writing.

When my PhD scholarship in Darmstadt ended, I began working with Lisbeth Zimmermann, first briefly at Peace Research Institute Frankfurt (PRIF), then at Zeppelin University Friedrichshafen, and now at Goethe University Frankfurt. I am deeply grateful for her mentorship throughout this time and the freedom to complete this book. I also would like to thank everyone I worked with at PRIF, in Friedrichshafen, and in Frankfurt. These everyday encounters often end up shaping the big picture; as I hope to show the reader in this book. At Goethe University, I would like to thank everyone at the "RiesiKo" international relations (IR) research seminar, especially Nicole Deitelhoff, Christopher Daase, Tobias Wille, Hanna Pfeiffer, Ben Christian, Alexandros Tokhi, Hande Abay, Anjo Peez, Fabian Rasem, and, once again, Lisbeth Zimmermann. The process of finalizing the book manuscript has benefited greatly from the engaged discussion of my key arguments in this forum.

I am grateful for TU Darmstadt's equal opportunity fund which enabled me to travel to Oxford in 2016 and spend a term at the University of Oxford's Centre on Migration, Policy and Society (COMPAS). I thank Franck Düvell for hosting me and Federica Infantino and Nick van Hear for all their valuable insights and feedback. Thanks to Michael Zürn, I also found scholarly sanctuary at the WZB Berlin Social Science Center in spring 2018. I drew much inspiration from the many discussions at both places, which provided an exceptional intellectual environment.

Thanks are also due to all the colleagues who, at different times and in different contexts, read drafts of the book and its chapters, provided me with valuable insights into their research strategies, or discussed the central arguments I present. This includes Alice Chessé, Anna Triandafyllidou, Antonia Witt, Benjamin Faude, Bud Duvall, Catherine Liu, Corinna Frey, David Welch, Felix Anderl, Frank Gadinger, Friedrich Kratochwil, Ian Hurd, Jannik Pfister, John Karlsrud, Jutta Joachim, Klaus Dingwerth, Maren Hofius, Mariam Salehi, Mark Raymond, Michael Barrett, Mirko Heinzel, Monique Beerli, Nele Marianne Ewers-Peters, Nina Hall, Nina Reiners, Ole Jacob Sending, Peter Groenewegen, Sara Kalm, Stephanie Hofmann, Tine Hanrieder, and Yf Reykers. I deeply appreciate the numerous excellent ideas they provided in workshops, conferences, email exchanges, and conversations. Of these many inspiring encounters, I would like to highlight the AGORA IV workshop organized by Len Seabrooke and Ole Jacob Sending at Warwick University in 2014. This was my first workshop as a first-year PhD student, and discussing my initial ideas with brilliant scholars, including Kate Weaver, Alex Kentikelenis, Stephen Nelson, Susanna Campbell, Sarah Bush, Nina Hall, and Jean-Frédéric Morin, set me (probably without them realizing) on the path to writing the dissertation that now comes to fruition in this book.

I am especially indebted to the practitioners I interviewed for this project and who helped me navigate the complicated institutional landscape of governing migration and asylum, both at headquarters and in the field. Although they cannot be mentioned by name here, they have been indispensable. I hope that by highlighting and conceptualizing their work, I can do justice to their resilience, expertise, and helpfulness.

Transforming the dissertation into a readable manuscript has been a challenging task and I would like to thank Pauline Helms for her research support during this process as well as Nancy Du Plessis for her dedicated work as language editor. My thanks also go to Dominic Byatt and his team at Oxford University Press who not only commissioned excellent reviews but made the entire process of publishing the book a very smooth and enjoyable experience. I would like to expressly thank the reviewers whose careful reading and insightful suggestions helped get this book over the finish line. I gratefully acknowledge permission by Wiley to reproduce parts of "How to Govern Mixed Migration in Europe. Transnational Expert Networks and Knowledge Creation in International Organizations" (*Global Networks*, 21(2), 320–38).

Last but not least, I would like to thank my family and friends, who have supported me in many ways: My heartfelt thanks go to Beate Kortendiek for always supporting me in my studies and research. She has appreciated nothing more than the value of an education that she herself was denied for a long time. I would also like to thank Philipp Kortendiek who has been by my side for as long as I can remember and has always challenged my views and convictions. Kurt Walter, "Querkopf" and free spirit, taught me to think and ask questions—the foundations for everything. I would also like to thank Lotte Kirch, Paula van Aken, and Mia Wyszynski as well as Dorit Schulte, Luise Baar, and Charlotte Noltenius, without whose friendship and solidarity I would not have been able to complete this book. Most of all, I would like to thank Max Lesch, my partner in everything, and of course our daughter Alma, who spent many days sleeping on my chest, writing the book with me.

Finally, my greatest respect and gratitude goes to the people on the move who I met during my research. While not part of this study, they are of course very much at the heart of it. I cannot escape the thought that while I have the privilege of writing this book from the safety of my home, the main social and political struggles of our time are being fought on their backs. We all only have this one life. I dedicate this book to them.

Contents

List of Figures, Tables and Boxes

Figures

Tables

Boxes

List of Abbreviations

AU	African Union
AVRR	assisted voluntary return and reintegration
CCAC	Closed Controlled Access Centre
CCCM	Camp Coordination and Camp Management
CEAS	Common European Asylum System
CESRT	Chios Eastern Shore Response Team
CoP	communities of practice
DG ECHO	Directorate-General for European Civil Protection and Humanitarian Aid Operations
DG HOME	European Commission's Directorate General for Migration and Home Affairs
DMM	Department of Migration Management
DOE	Department of Operations and Emergencies
DRC	Danish Refugee Council
DTM	Displacement Tracking Matrix
EAC	European Asylum Curriculum
EASO	European Asylum Support Office
ECCHR	European Center for Constitutional and Human Rights
ECRE	European Council on Refugees and Exiles
EU	European Union
EUAA	European Union Agency for Asylum
EURODAC	European Dactyloscop
Eurojust	European Union Agency for Criminal Justice Cooperation
Europol	European Union Agency for Law Enforcement
FAO	Food and Agricultural Organization
FRO	fundamental rights officer
Frontex	European Border and Coast Guard Agency
FRS	First Reception Service
GAMM	Global Approach to Migration and Mobility
GATS	General Agreement on Trade in Services
GCM	Global Compact for Safe, Orderly and Regular Migration
GCR	Global Compact on Refugees
GFMD	Global Forum for Migration and Development
GLC	Global Learning Centre
GMG	Global Migration Group
HLA	Humanitarian Leadership Academy
HRC	Hellenic Red Cross
IAMSAR	International Aeronautical and Maritime Search and Rescue
IASC	Inter-Agency Standing Committee

ICMC	International Catholic Migration Commission
ICMPD	International Centre for Migration Policy Development
ICRC	International Committee of the Red Cross
IDP	internally displaced person
IFRC	International Federation of the Red Cross
IGO	intergovernmental organization
ILO	International Labor Organization
IMF	International Monetary Fund
IMO	International Maritime Organization
IMRF	International Maritime Rescue Federation
IO	international organization
IOM	International Organization for Migration
IR	international relations
LIBE Committee	European Parliament's Committee on Civil Liberties, Justice and Home Affairs
MADE	Migration and Development Civil Society Network
MDM	Médecins du Monde
MHUB	Mixed Migration Hub
MICIC	Migrants in Countries in Crisis Initiative
MMC	Mixed Migration Centre
MMTF	Mixed Migration Task Force
MOAS	Migrant Offshore Aid Station
MRCC	Maritime Rescue Co-ordination Center
MSF	Médecins sans Frontières
NATO	North Atlantic Treaty Organization
NFI	non-food item
NGO	non-governmental organization
NRC	Norwegian Refugee Council
OAS	Organization of American States
OCHA	UN Office for the Coordination of Humanitarian Affairs
OHCHR	Office of the High Commissioner for Human Rights
OLAF	European Anti-Fraud Office
PA	principal-agent
PHAP	International Association of Professionals in Humanitarian Assistance and Protection
ProCap	Protection Standby Capacity Project
RCP	Regional Consultative Process
RIC	Reception and Identification Center
RIS	Reception and Identification Service
SAR	search and rescue
SAR Convention	International Convention on Maritime Search and Rescue
SCI	Save the Children International
SFOR	Stabilization Force in Bosnia
SIMN	Scalabrini International Migration Network
SMH	Salvamento Marítimo Humanitario
SOLAS	International Convention for the Safety of Life at Sea

SoP	standard operating procedure
UASC	unaccompanied and separated children
UK	United Kingdom
UN	United Nations
UN DESA	United Nations Department of Economic and Social Affairs
UNDP	United Nations Development Program
UNHCR	United Nations High Commissioner for Refugees
UNICEF	United Nations Children Fund
UNMEER	UN Mission for Ebola Emergency Response
UNMIL	United Nations mission to Liberia
UNODC	United Nations Office on Drugs and Crime
US	United States
WASH	water, sanitation, and hygiene
WHO	World Health Organization
WTO	World Trade Organization

1
Introduction

Governing International Migration and Asylum on the Ground

How do international organizations (IOs) govern disputed, crisis-ridden, and emerging issues in global politics? Confronted with issues too new to have been formally addressed by international policy-making, contentious questions that are hard to regulate, or matters that have been severely disturbed by crises, IOs[1] must improvise collective action. In policy fields ranging from finance, public health, and climate change to peace and security, we observe IOs testing various ways to address public challenges in practice. When established institutional frameworks are missing or incomplete, IOs use their personal contacts and professional skills to devise provisional solutions. These ad hoc solutions either stabilize into new organizational routines or, once the initial urgency has subsided, are forgotten—meaning that IOs will have to improvise again. With epistemic and political uncertainty inherent to global politics, IOs are continuously navigating the unsettled spaces between formal international institutions.

This book is about this specific mode of governance that is widespread in practice but neglected in international relations (IR) theory. Through its in-depth look at the case of mixed migration, the book suggests that IOs not only govern global issues through law, expertise, numbers, standards, and rules but also *through practice on the ground*. The main theoretical argument that I advance in this book is that governing on the ground is a distinct mode of governance that works through *informal networks* spanning the boundaries of multiple organizations and *interactive loops* interleaving IO fields and headquarters. In Chapter 2, I develop a model of global governance on the ground that is rooted in sociological approaches to IOs centered on knowledge and professions. I connect these approaches with the literature

[1] I use the term "international organization" to broadly refer to intergovernmental organizations (IGOs) and non-governmental organizations (NGOs) as well as regional agencies because they often perform similar tasks when governing public issues. I focus on the professionals working for these organizations and take their practices as the main unit of analysis. For a conceptual discussion of IOs, see Chapter 2.

Global Governance on the Ground. Nele Kortendiek, Oxford University Press. © Nele Kortendiek (2024).
DOI: 10.1093/oso/9780198889120.003.0001

on street-level bureaucracy and the implementation of international politics to outline a conceptual framework that accounts for interorganizational and cross-level dynamics in global governance.

Two processes lie at the heart of this conceptual framework: *situated learning* and *stabilization.* "Situated learning" takes place in the field—in the spaces where IOs are confronted by global problems. The term describes IO field staff developing impromptu solutions to these challenges as they play out in everyday life at the frontlines of global governance. In contrast to negotiators in official policy arenas in New York, Washington, Geneva, Brussels, and Nairobi, field staff are directly confronted with the exigencies of global issues and cannot avoid making at least provisional decisions. I use "stabilization" for the process by which these tentative practices and the experiential knowledge undergirding them become consolidated in wider organizational repertoires and diffused across operations. Situated learning and stabilization are both deeply embedded in organizational environments and open ended: Global governance through practice works in nested feedback loops (see Section 1.2 and Chapter 2). Because these processes open up or restrict possibilities for action by the final addressees of global politics, I view them as a form of governance.

Mixed migration—the unauthorized movement of asylum seekers, climate refugees, victims of trafficking, low-skilled migrant workers, and other types of (unclassified) migrants across international borders, by simple means of travel, and often facilitated by smuggling networks (van Hear 2011; Crawley and Skleparis 2017)—serves as the empirical case for this book. Because the migration-asylum nexus is one of the most salient and contested global challenges of the 21st century (Börzel and Risse 2018; Seabrooke and Tsingou 2019), its analysis is particularly well-suited for drawing attention to the means of governance IOs rely on when confronted with novel, politicized, or crisis-stricken issues. Although mixed migration is arguably one of the most obvious examples of global governance on the ground, similar conditions are present in conflict resolution and peacebuilding (Autesserre 2014; Bode and Karlsrud 2018), humanitarian aid and disaster relief (Gross Stein 2011; Sending 2015a; Beerli 2018), democratization and state-building (Kurowska 2014), public health (Yang 2021; Kreuder-Sonnen and Tantow 2022), environmental protection (Biermann and Siebenhüner 2009a; Maertens 2018), and finance (Broome et al. 2015; Kentikelenis and Babb 2019). In these areas, too, we can expect IOs to work outside their officially defined spheres of competence to respond to unforeseen circumstances, using their access to the field and blurring the boundaries with other IOs to govern (see Section 1.4 on the case selection and scope conditions).

The empirical analysis of global mixed migration governance, which is at the center of this study (see Chapters 3–5), is based on ethnographic fieldwork at the European Union's (EU) external border during the migration and refugee crisis of 2015 and 2016, as well as extensive document analysis and expert interviews at the headquarters of seven organizations (see Section 1.4 on the research design).[2] The case study illustrates the analytical value of my theoretical argument, and helped develop it. As often happens in qualitative research, I developed the model outlined in Chapter 2 in an iterative process, going back and forth between the empirical material and theoretical literature, although the book, the outcome of this circular research process, is structured chronologically.

As a whole, the book sheds new light on how IOs govern. Conceptually, it uncouples global governance from the notion of authority and by suggesting a new, minimalist, definition of governance, calls attention to how IOs make collective decisions that operate at a very low institutional threshold. Unlike rational-choice institutionalist and social-constructivist approaches that focus on delegation and authority to explain IO agency and influence in global governance, it does not treat IOs as coherent collective actors or only consider them at the secretariat level. Instead, this work focuses on local communities of practice, addressing how their ways of knowing and doing things are translated across sites to develop an *interorganizational* and *cross-level perspective on global governance.* Unlike anthropological and practice-oriented approaches in IR that focus on field missions and the everyday of global governance, it moves beyond a micro-level view of international politics to link field dynamics with decision-making at headquarters. By focusing on the contents of governance and substantive professional skills, it moves beyond viewing practices as purely procedural.[3] In short, the book develops a novel approach to the way IOs exploit their room for maneuver during moments of contention and learn from crises (or not) to produce new ways of governing.

The book thereby deepens our understanding of informal, experimentalist governance. It offers a dynamic account of how IOs use and create knowledge—beyond expertise—to govern open and contentious issues in world politics. By outlining ways of harnessing the innovative capacity of global governance through practice while simultaneously mitigating its accountability risks, it helps advance the normative debate on who has the right to make "rules for the world."

[2] I do not view this "crisis" as a problem caused by movements of large numbers of people but rather as a crisis in governance. See Section 1.4 and Chapter 3.

[3] See the discussion of contemporary research on IOs and global governance in Section 1.3.

The remainder of this Introduction presents the book's central empirical and theoretical building blocks. In the first section, I lay the groundwork for my theoretical and analytical arguments by outlining the main dilemmas in governing novel, uncertain, and contested global issues. I present the book's research puzzle, namely that IOs have been able to govern mixed migration despite many policy, institutional, and knowledge gaps. In the second section, I introduce the book's key argument: IOs govern mixed migration and similar contentious, crisis-ridden, and emerging issues at the frontlines of global governance—through practice on the ground. I outline the theoretical model and illustrate it with some of the key findings of the case study. In the third section, I discuss how my argument contributes to and differs from existing accounts of IOs and their governing practices. I explain the case selection and present the strategies for data collection and analysis in the fourth section. In the fifth and final section, I introduce the book's structure and preview the chapters.

1.1 Governing International Migration and Asylum: Key Questions

During an interagency meeting in early March 2015, the secretary-general of the International Maritime Organization (IMO) stated that,

> The issue of mixed migration by sea, including irregular migration, has been a serious concern for decades—if not longer. But, in recent years, it has reached epidemic proportions, to the extent where the whole system for coping with such migrants is being stretched up to, and sometimes beyond, its breaking point. (IMO 2015)

The following year saw another drastic increase in the number of people fleeing war, persecution, environmental degradation, and poverty. Between April 2015 and June 2016, over two million people irregularly crossed sea and land borders into Europe (Frontex 2016d: 6). In Southeast Asia, Central America, Northern and Eastern Africa, too, large populations were displaced by violence and conflict, unemployment and inequality, droughts and natural disasters. In response, then UN (United Nations) Secretary-General Ban Ki-Moon (2016) called for an international summit to "address large movements by migrants and refugees." International migration and asylum was recognized as one of the most pressing issues of our time, and led to the adoption of the Global Compact for Migration and the Global Compact on Refugees in late 2018.

Despite the newly acknowledged necessity of finding joint international solutions to problems such as the rising deaths at sea and overstretched reception capacities that are posed by mixed migration, policy-makers have continued to fight about how to define the key issues and public goods at stake: Is it about protecting people on the move[4] or securing national borders? For example, while the two compacts were being negotiated, some countries began to dispute that migration even existed and the most prominent among them—the United States (US) and Hungary—refused to sign the Global Compact for Migration that states, "Migration has been part of the human experience throughout history" (GCM 2018: 2). They would not accept that migration is an acknowledged fact, and Hungary's foreign minister took the phrase to mean that the compact's main premise is "that migration is a good and inevitable phenomenon." He disagreed: "We consider migration a bad process, which has extremely serious security implications" (Reuters 2018). This shows how difficult it is to reach even minimal agreement on baselines for governing migration and asylum. As a result, there are still no comprehensive and legally binding norms and no IO has been formally tasked with dealing with mixed movements.

A related outcome of the politicization of mixed migration is that responsibilities for international migration and refugee politics are spread across different international actors and arenas: Several intergovernmental organizations (IGOs) hold partial mandates but there is no integrated system. For instance, the UN High Commissioner for Refugees (UNHCR) has a strong normative mandate to protect asylum seekers, returnees, and refugees. But low- and unskilled migrant workers, climate refugees, and people fleeing gang violence fall outside the scope of the quite narrow refugee definition entrenched in international law by the 1951 UN Refugee Convention. They are thus outside the UNHCR's formal jurisdiction. Victims of trafficking are the official concern of the UN Office on Drugs and Crime (UNODC), the guardian of the UN Convention against Organized Crime and its protocol on human trafficking. The International Organization for Migration (IOM) is charged with supporting migrants who are unlikely to receive asylum, including through assisted voluntary return and reintegration (AVRR) programs. Regional agencies like the European Border and Coast Guard Agency (Frontex) register incoming migrants, return rejected asylum seekers, and set up border control systems—also outside the EU. To this list must be added the high number of international non-governmental organizations (NGOs)

[4] I use the generic term "people on the move" to not distinguish between "migrants" and "refugees." I only do that when an actual asylum procedure is involved. These legal categories are often instrumentalized in public discourse to justify particular border and asylum policies. Because they perform an important political function, they cannot be used purely descriptively, see Crawley and Skleparis (2017) and Chapter 3.

that offer humanitarian aid to displaced people. Myriad organizations govern migration and asylum, creating both overlaps and institutional gaps (see Chapter 3 for an overview of the international mixed migration governance architecture).

In addition to political contestation and organizational fragmentation, knowledge gaps and misconceptions of mixed migration persist. Its clandestine nature makes obtaining reliable information on motives, figures, and patterns difficult. The UN's main body in charge of migration data, the Department of Economic and Social Affairs (UN DESA), relies on official census data to estimate the number of international migrants. It does not measure migrant flows or movements, let alone *unauthorized* movements (Koser 2009). Other organizations gauge irregular flows by compiling apprehension statistics or work with country case studies on regularization programs but do not collect data on migrant networks and decision-making (ILO 2004; Vespe et al. 2017; IOM DTM 2018). Thus, knowledge of the extent and mechanisms of mixed migration remains limited.

Beyond these policy, institutional, and knowledge gaps, mixed migration is typically dealt with as a crisis. Its deep political contestation makes reaching agreement on long-term institutional solutions hard. That said, mixed migration has been a stark empirical reality throughout modern history (Czaika and Haas 2015; Haas et al. 2019). Emergencies develop whenever large mixed migration movements occur without the necessary institutional schemes in place (for an overview, see Menjívar et al. 2019). Usually, migration and displacement must be addressed in great haste.

How is mixed migration governed under these conditions of political and epistemic *uncertainty* as well as organizational *complexity* and *urgency*? This question becomes particularly pertinent because it clearly *is* governed (see Chapters 4 and 5). As the case study shows, IOs organize collective action on migration and displacement. From search and rescue (SAR) to camp management, asylum interviews, family reunification, and returns, IOs develop and perform routines that bring some degree of order to spontaneous, undocumented migration and the turmoil it causes at transit and destination sites in the absence of safe and legal migration pathways. These IO practices both restrict possible behaviors and enable new courses of action for people on the move, thereby creating immediate regulative impacts on their lives. *They represent a form of governing* (Chapter 2 presents a conceptual discussion of global governance). The fact that IOs govern mixed migration in practice is puzzling because they lack the most common parameters for global governance: formal mandates, explicit types of expertise, standards, norms, rules, and policies. To account for mixed migration's *de facto* governance, I argue that IOs rely on a specific mode of global governance: They govern international migration and asylum *through practice on the ground*. That they do so is troubling from a normative perspective because this governance mode's broad margin of discretion opens the door to arbitrariness, failure, and the misuse of power.

Against this backdrop, the major analytical-conceptual goal of the book is to develop a theoretically sound explanation of global governance on the ground. Its main normative-theoretical ambition is to reconstruct why this mode of governance is normatively alarming and to outline how it can be democratically recaptured.

1.2 The Argument: Global Governance on the Ground

The book analyzes how international migration and asylum is governed on the ground—starting from the observation that this governing practice differs from other modes of governance and has not yet been accounted for in the literature.

1.2.1 Modes of Global Governance

A number of global governance modes have been investigated in great detail by IR researchers (see Risse 2018). Many authors have demonstrated how laws (Sell 2003), policies (Reinalda and Verbeek 1998; Park and Vetterlein 2012; Pouliot and Thérien 2023), standards (Abbott and Snidal 2001; Mattli 2001; Dingwerth 2007; Bartley 2018), benchmarks (Sending and Lie 2015; Broome et al. 2017; Robinson 2018), indicators (Kelley and Simmons 2020; Martin de Almagro 2021), goals (Kanie and Biermann 2017), formal and informal rules (Stone 2011; Graham 2015; Pouliot 2021), best practices (Broome and Seabrooke 2012; Bernstein and van der Ven 2017), frames and social norms (Keck and Sikkink 1998; Price 1998), and soft law (Abbott et al. 2000) function as governing tools. They have reconstructed how these modes work as both processes and outputs of global governance. For example, experts usually create benchmarks, indicators, and rankings to measure performance by different governance addressees, mostly states. They seek to steer behavior and achieve common goals by formulating targets and publicly displaying their achievements.

Other researchers have focused more extensively on the formal and informal processes that lie behind the development of governance outputs, such as advocacy and agenda setting (Carpenter 2010; Hall 2022), deliberation and persuasion (Risse 2000; Deitelhoff 2009; Jepsen et al. 2021), bargaining (Stasavage 2004), brokering (Goddard 2009), law-making (Johnstone 2005; Brunnée and Toope 2010; Venzke 2011; Reiners 2022), and multistakeholder consultations (Agné et al. 2015; Nasiritousi et al. 2016). Whether the focus is on procedures or products, these governance modes are mostly analyzed in terms of their degree of bindingness and whether they are driven by public or private actors. And while these authors generally focus on secretariat-level activities, some have turned to direct enforcement (Eilstrup-Sangiovanni and Bondaroff 2014; Karlsrud 2015) and street-level decision-making (Autesserre 2014; Honig 2018; Schettler et al. 2018) to investigate how IOs operate in the field. As a result, we know a lot about the different governance modalities that various international actors employ: We know what they do in the field and at headquarters and how they use formal and informal means to influence decision-making on global issues. However, we still lack a concept that integrates all four dimensions. How are formal and informal practices in the field linked with formal and informal decision-making in global arenas and how does this shape how the content of global issues is treated? As it stands, we have no concept for governing dynamics in the field that return to the global level and shape governing activities beyond specific local contexts. Below I set out a five-step model of global governance on the ground that conceptualizes that governance mode and allows us to analyze how IOs use the practical knowledge that emerges in operational spaces to govern global issues on-site at locations worldwide.

To develop this model, I draw on the works of Leonard Seabrooke and his colleagues on the networks of transnational professionals (Seabrooke 2014; Seabrooke and Tsingou 2014, 2015; Henriksen and Seabrooke 2017; Seabrooke and Sending 2019). I follow their assumption that IOs have porous boundaries and that transnational professionals working for different IOs form interorganizational networks which largely control how global issues are treated. I combine their concepts with insights from sociological approaches to work, learning, and knowledge in organizations (Lave and Wenger 1991; Yanow 2004; Nicolini 2013) as well as street-level bureaucracy in international politics (Côté-Boucher et al. 2014; Kurowska 2014; Cooper and Cornut 2019) to reconstruct how individual actors in IOs apply their professional expertise and competencies to govern contentious and emerging issues through practice on the ground.

This shift in theoretical perspective means that organizational boundaries lose their ontological significance, and transnational professionals and their practices become the main unit of analysis. This makes it possible to include several types of IOs—ranging from IGOs, NGOs, and regional agencies to transnational volunteer networks and professional associations—into the analysis and not exclude important (private) actors on conceptual grounds prior to the empirical study (see Chapter 2). This view contrasts with most conceptions of IOs which make a sharp distinction between IGOs and NGOs (see for example Roger 2020: 26). Classical IO studies typically consider public organizations only, i.e. those that have been founded by states, because only those can make publicly binding decisions in the form of international law. Since I consider formal rule-making but one mode of global governance, I do not need to make this distinction here. In fact, it would prove counterproductive for investigating how underregulated issues are governed.

1.2.2 The Five Steps of Global Governance on the Ground

To reconstruct how it was possible that IOs governed migration and asylum during the crisis of 2015–16, I theoretically argue and empirically show that IOs govern on the ground. IO actors stationed at the frontlines of global issues improvise collective action. Working in unpredictable environments with incomplete information and time constraints, they learn to cope with situational challenges through trial and error—developing provisional practices that determine how issues are *de facto* governed in the field. In the process of learning to govern new and contested issues in operational spaces, they also stake out claims to competence for their professions and organizations. For their part, headquarters staff enter this process when they devise scripts for on-site practice and train fieldworkers. They consolidate and diffuse frontline practices and practical knowledge that concretize or replace formal policies and mandates.

This argument is based on five main propositions, which I discuss in greater detail and situate in the theoretical literature in Chapter 2. These propositions match the five ideal-typical steps of global governance on the ground (see Figure 1.1).

The first three steps (improvising, negotiating competence, and routinizing practice) take place in the field and together constitute *situated learning*. Steps four and five (consolidation and diffusion) constitute the process of *stabilization* and connect the field with headquarters. I sketch and illustrate each step using findings from the case study.

Improvising. International norms and rules are necessarily vague because international policy-making either cannot anticipate every possible course of action related to transnational affairs or shies away from regulating highly

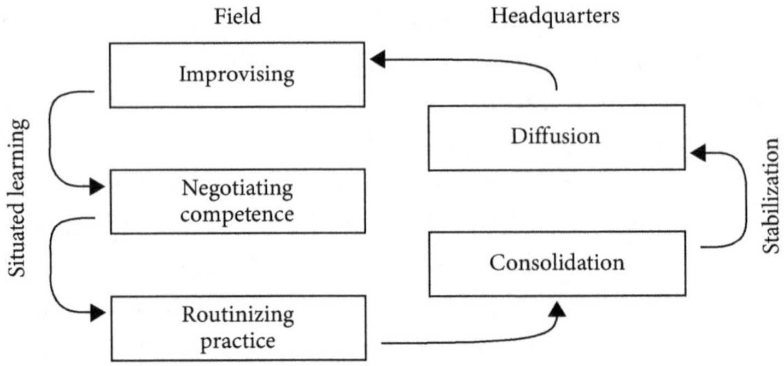

Fig. 1.1 The five steps of global governance on the ground

politicized topics. That means that those responsible for implementing them often face ambiguous situations. At the same time, because they are positioned at the interface between IOs and target populations in spaces where global challenges physically manifest, they are pressured to close the policy gaps. Crises exacerbate the initial situation. Those addressing emerging or contested global issues in practice will always have to improvise to reconcile unclear policy frameworks with local realities and unforeseen events, but in moments of crisis, uncertainty and the acute need for action become even greater. I argue that IO operational staffers make practical judgments, deviate from existing international agreements, and creatively adapt to novel situations. They develop the initial practical knowledge needed to govern new, contested, or crisis-ridden issues at the frontlines of global challenges through learning by doing.

To do so, *professional knowledge* is a major resource. So are personal *interorganizational networks*. Professional skills and expertise enable IO fieldworkers to deal with indeterminate situations and address new tasks. Because most international issues (especially those that are emerging, contested, or crisis ridden) are seldom addressed by a single organization, they are likely to engage with professionals employed by other IOs who are also working on the ground. Being closely bound up in a shared local work context reduces the importance of organizational affiliation. However, informal improvisation in everyday work relations across organizational boundaries is not *per se* cooperative. Fieldworkers learn to govern unsettled issues in practice through cooperation—as well as by competition and open conflict.

In the case of mixed migration governance at the EU's external border, it was mostly humanitarians, border and coastguards, lifesavers, asylum caseworkers, migration lawyers, and medical professionals who learned how to respond to the high pace and scale of people on the move by doing.

The lack of comprehensive, coherent international and regional migration and asylum policies caused them to complain: "Everything is just very scattered and confusing" (I-5, Annex II). At the same time, directly exposed to mixed migration dynamics, they "just cannot avoid the responsibility to attend to these people" (I-8, Annex II). Given the lack of policy guidance and fragmentary mandates, fieldworkers tried "to adjust as much as possible and be creative" (I-9, Annex II). In the process, they worked closely with transnational professionals from other IOs. Since they felt that they had to "take up the slack" created by the "lack of ownership" on the part of official policy-makers, they interacted closely on-site (I-15, Annex II). Although "people get protective of the niches that they carve out for themselves" (I-11, Annex II), in general, "everyone is fully committed and trying to be flexible [. . .] and cooperating regardless of different mandates" (I-9, Annex II).

In fact, many fieldworkers addressed the situation through the lens of their profession. For example, an IOM employee, whose "main work is AVRR" but who is a psychologist by training, contacted fieldworkers from the UNHCR and the NGOs Save the Children and the Norwegian Refugee Council (NRC) as soon as he started working at the external border "to provide support to people that had attempted suicide" (I-2, Annex II). Similarly, paramedics from a SAR NGO worked on Frontex patrol vessels to respond to possible medical emergencies (I-8, Annex II). Formal affiliations with the UNHCR, the European Asylum Support Office (EASO), the IOM, Frontex, and humanitarian NGOs did not prevent them from closely collaborating in the field to find provisional solutions to the challenges of mixed migration (see Chapter 4).

Negotiating competence. Improvisation goes hand in hand with the negotiation of competence. On-the-ground improvisers, I maintain, make implicit and explicit claims to "knowing well" when they experiment with new ways of organizing collective action for specific issues. Others assess the feasibility and appropriateness of these claims against existing views of how to do the work. I expect that fieldworkers negotiate what gets accepted as competent practice by collectively assigning meaning to doing and competing over how to do things well.

Such struggles over competence among transnational professionals have been observed in the issue areas of population politics (Seabrooke and Tsingou 2015; Sending 2015b) and peacekeeping (Karlsrud 2018; Laurence 2019). In migration and asylum governance during the crisis, disputes over how to respond to people irregularly crossing maritime borders into Europe are an example of competence negotiations. In such situations, boatswains, lifesavers, firefighters, and other rescue professionals first noticed the unseaworthiness of the boats people were traveling in and perceived the potential loss of life at sea as the main problem. They responded with their specific skills—maneuvering, emergency steering, rigging, mooring, towing, and crowd control, as well as "taking on board survivors from any lifesaving appliances or other floating objects and from the water" (IMRF 2011: 7–11; Frontex 2017a: 314; SOS Méditerranée 2019). In contrast, law enforcement officers and border guards perceived the irregular crossing as the central issue—and responded using their experiential knowledge of patrolling, screening, and debriefing. They employed their know-how of using "physical force safely" (Frontex 2017b: 144), applying "cognitive interviewing techniques" (Frontex 2018a: 26), conducting body and luggage searches, and similar competencies to intercept people on the move, determine their nationalities, and gather intelligence on migration routes and smuggling networks.

Thus local practitioners with different professional backgrounds had varying approaches to the same situation, which sometimes clashed. However, because they operated in the same physical locations (the sea, beaches, and ports), they had to come to an agreement on how to handle such situations. Through cooperative, competitive, and conflictual sense-making processes, they negotiated the meaning of large numbers of people crossing maritime borders without valid travel documents, in rubber dinghies, wearing defective life jackets—and how to respond in a professional manner. In the words of an SAR rescue professional who challenged Frontex personnel, other NGO workers, and volunteers: "I usually ask, '*This* is a professional service?!' Because this is *not* a professional service because *it is not well done*" (I-8, Annex II). By quarreling over how to appropriately respond to irregular crossings, they established, for example, local SAR, disembarkation, and registration procedures that included ensuring the safety of people on the move as well as their official registration and accommodation (see Chapter 4).

Routinizing practice. Once an improvised way of doing has become accepted as competent, it is likely to slowly become an on-site routine. Repetition reduces uncertainty and provides field staff with a repertoire for handling things. I therefore expect them to establish informal protocols and on-the-job training to routinize their practice. In the case of governing mixed migration at Europe's external border, the local community of practice established telephone chains and virtual logbooks, defined referral pathways and reporting protocols, introduced systems for shadowing experienced fieldworkers, and organized simulations and collective exercises to routinize what they had learned during the crisis, and pass it on to newcomers. Otherwise, "Any knowledge that had been accumulated [would have been] lost, which [would have been] very foolish" (I-7, Annex II).

Improvisation, competence negotiation, and routinization lead to new *practices*—patterned actions that become meaningful against the background of practical knowledge in a particular social context—emerging incrementally or changing. During the European migration and refugee crisis of 2015–16, to work out how to govern mixed migration at the border, fieldworkers improvised, negotiated competence, and routinized their doing and knowing across organizational divides and against the background of different professional bodies of knowledge. Because this global issue has not (yet) been formally regulated, they "just kind of stepped into that role" (I-7, Annex II) and determined through practice on the ground what mixed migration means as a public challenge and the response needed. Adapting existing policies and mandates to local demands while working outside organizational boundaries to fill governance gaps, they established how to conduct land and sea patrols, SAR, first reception on arrival, transportation, screening, registration, and debriefing, as well as how to manage camps, protect and monitor, interview asylum seekers, and organize legal aid, relocation, and returns. In other words, they developed and performed practices that have a direct regulative impact on the lives of migrants and refugees. For example, the way asylum interviews and SAR missions are conducted greatly influences the life choices of people on the move (see Chapter 4). In short, because frontline practices define how existing policy frameworks play out in the lives of the governed—or substitute for lacking policies—I argue in this book that they are a form of governance.

Consolidation. Practices developed in the field do not necessarily stay local. IO officers tasked with training operational staff are critical connections between the field and headquarters. One of their core tasks is to design and update learning material, which, I argue, positions them to translate practical knowledge from the field "upwards." By putting that into manuals, best practice handbooks, templates for face-to-face training sessions and similar tools, they are effectively gatekeepers in intra-organizational networks and disproportionately influence the skills and practices that are regarded as relevant and become stabilized in organizational training schemes. While fieldworkers often creatively work around institutional restraints and venture out into new issue areas, I assume that headquarters staff continue the process of global governance through practice by consolidating frontline practices in learning programs.

Most of the organizations that operated at the EU's external border during the crisis have training units at their headquarters (see Annex II for a brief discussion of the IOs' different training mandates and learning programs). Their staff members describe their role as a "bridge function because we need to channel information from the headquarters to the field and vice versa" (I-35, Annex II). Usually, they create learning material that is "based on existing policies and existing law" (I-33, Annex II). Their job is "to find a way to translate them to make them practical" (I-35, Annex II). At the same time, they try "to learn from the operations and see what works in practice and what doesn't" (I-32, Annex II). They "try to capitalize on as much information as possible that we can gather from [...] our target audience"—that is, the fieldworkers (I-34, Annex II). Through briefing and debriefing, pilot projects, workshops, on-the-job training and similar activities, they have developed detailed guidelines for providing psychosocial support for people on the move (IASC 2008; IOM 2009b; IASC and CCCM 2014), providing shelter and managing a camp (CCCM 2015; UNHCR 2017; Sphere 2018), screening migrants (Frontex 2014b, 2018b), and interviewing asylum seekers (EASO 2014), to give just a few examples. The practical guidelines spell out how to govern migration and asylum in practice, and in some cases, substitute for formal policy guidelines: "Normally the training is about something which already exists. But indirectly, and quite often, the training content becomes guidance as such because in many situations, there is not really a pre-existing guideline" (I-22, Annex II) (see Chapter 5).

Diffusion. Finally, I assume that consolidated frontline practices get translated "downwards" and circulated across sites through training. Officers in IO programs and operational units seek to standardize and professionalize on-the-ground practices by training fieldworkers. Of course, this can never fully streamline on-site practice. But through training, headquarters staff join the process of staking out how specific global issues are treated in practice.

Headquarters staff training EU asylum experts working at external border "hotspots" is an example of using training to shape mixed migration governance. Asylum caseworkers deployed by EASO receive detailed training on how to interview asylum seekers and gather information about their displacement experiences. Headquarters staff meticulously instruct them about how to speak to asylum seekers, assess personal details, and draft decisions regarding applications for international protection. They teach how to check for inconsistencies in a person's story, assess the credibility of individual statements, examine supporting documents, and identify factors such as traumatic experiences that could cause distortions (see EASO 2015: 3). However, despite comprehensive training, detailed flowcharts, and other practical guidance, EASO experts are regularly confronted with situational challenges requiring them to make spontaneous decisions and deviate from established practices. For example, after the EU-Turkey Statement was signed in March 2016 and Turkey was declared a "safe third country" to which all asylum seekers—except for "vulnerable people"—who had reached Europe by crossing its territory could be returned, it was unclear at first *who exactly* was meant. After first leaving this to the discretion of caseworkers in EU hotspots like Moria and Vial, headquarters staff started to draft a "vulnerability catalogue" with concrete indicators and checklists (see Chapters 4 and 5).

Overall, the case study shows that governing migration and asylum on the ground is the dynamic interplay between IO staff working in the field and at headquarters. By continuously struggling over how to deal with mixed migration, they not only define what this issue means as a policy problem but also create and control the professional competence needed to address it at the border.

It goes without saying that this mode of governance will sometimes fail: Either fieldworkers succumb to the messiness of new, politicized, or crisis-ridden issues and don't manage to develop local governing practices or trainers fail to translate. In other cases, however, they develop stable organizational skills and routines that fill governance gaps. And sometimes these practices even precede formal policy-making or lead to IO mandates being extended. This happened to EASO: In mid-January 2022, EASO—which "had already been operating at the very limits of its mandate"—became a "fully-fledged asylum agency" with a permanent asylum reserve pool of 500 operational staff members (EUAA 2022). The IOM is similarly expanding its humanitarian policy portfolio as a result of its operational work (Betts 2013).[5] It is likely that new practices and mandates will be applied and adapted in new rounds of governing global issues in practice during moments of uncertainty, urgency, and complexity. Because global issues are never fully ordered, I posit that global governance on the ground is irreducibly dynamic and works in loops.

1.3 Agency and Influence of International Organizations in Global Governance

The argument of global governance on the ground contributes to two ongoing debates about the role of IOs in world politics: The "rationalist-constructivist" debate on the sources of IO agency and influence on global governance and the "IOs in the everyday" debate on the power of practitioners in anthropological and practice-oriented IR studies.

[5] Chapter 2 discusses the caveats and possible outcomes of global governance through practice in more detail.

1.3.1 Governing at Headquarters: Authority and Mission Creep

IR theorizing about IOs' ability to govern hinges on the concept of authority. The two main theoretical approaches to IOs in IR, rational-choice institutionalism and social constructivism, are centered on how IOs obtain, exercise, and extend authority to account for the way they govern. Rational-choice approaches, and principal-agent (PA) frameworks in particular, focus on states formally *delegating competence* to IOs to explain how they become global governors. They analyze why and how states decide to outsource tasks to IOs and turn to institutional design processes to study IOs' agency and influence (Nielson and Tierney 2003; Hawkins et al. 2006a; Voeten 2008; Cooley 2010; Johnson 2014; Hooghe et al. 2017; Green 2018). Social-constructivist approaches, specifically those that define IO secretariats as bureaucracies, concentrate on the *social relations* between governors and governance addressees. They stress IOs' legal-rational capabilities to explain why the governed (be it states, non-state actors, or individuals) have reason to recognize IO claims to authority and, accordingly, how IOs become autonomous actors in international politics (Barnett and Finnemore 2004; Biermann and Siebenhüner 2009a; Avant et al. 2010a; Bauer et al. 2017; Herold et al. 2021; Liese et al. 2021). Although their explanations regarding authority sources differ, both approaches subscribe to the general assertion that authority—broadly defined as the legitimate right to rule (Hurd 1999; Buchanan and Keohane 2006; Lake 2010)—positions IOs to govern.

In line with this fundamental assumption, governing is almost universally equated with the exercise of authority (see Rosenau 2002; Ruggie 2004; Zürn 2018). To understand how issues are governed, the vast majority of researchers examine the *organizations* that hold authority on the subject matter. It follows that new or contested issues for which no competence has been established tend to disappear from IR scholars' field of vision. I seek to rectify this by starting with the *issue* of mixed migration. With this book, I offer the conceptual tools for analyzing how regular people who work for different IOs use their practical professional knowledge to informally organize collective action with respect to emerging transnational challenges.

The way IOs push into new issue areas to expand their spheres of influence has of course been studied. Studying "mission creep," both rationalist and constructivist authors have probed the conditions that allow IOs to move beyond their mandates (Babb and Buira 2005; Hall 2016; Hooghe et al. 2019; Littoz-Monnet 2021). PA scholars have studied how IOs use "agency slack" to exploit the discretion they need from states because of incomplete contracts. They have been particularly successful in explaining why it is hard for state principals to effectively control IO agents (Gutner 2005; da Conceição-Heldt 2010, 2017; Gutner and Thompson 2010; Graham 2014). For their part, constructivist scholars have focused on how, in the legitimation game, IOs use knowledge as a token to claim jurisdiction over new issues. They have put a lot of effort into reconstructing how IOs renegotiate their epistemic authority to control emerging topics (Boswell 2008; Sending 2015b; Littoz-Monnet 2017c, 2020). This book furthers this debate by theorizing and empirically examining the governing activities of IOs operating below even informal authority expansions that take place between them and their target populations—rather than between IOs and states.

Both research strands have also started to analyze informal dynamics in IOs and international law (Lipson 1991; Koremenos 2013; Stone 2013; Westerwinter et al. 2021). This work has significantly helped identify the factors involved in creating informal institutions that states use to further international cooperation without establishing secretariats (Vabulas and Snidal 2013; Roger 2020) and the informal provisions in organizations that allow states to control the choices of particular IOs, such as the International Monetary Fund (IMF) (Stone 2011) or the EU (Kleine 2013). They have done a lot to account for the way innovative institutional settings and actor constellations, such as government clubs, public-private partnerships, transnational networks, and roundtables, emerge despite the existence of formal IOs (Brassett et al. 2012; Abbott and Faude 2021). However, researchers largely focus on the causes of informal governance, analyzing state interests, domestic constraints, or potential efficiency gains to explain informality and institutional experiments. They either take states as central units of analysis or, when studying IO bureaucrats (for example Nair 2020), focus on their relations with state actors (see Chwieroth 2013; Kentikelenis and Babb 2019; Pouliot 2021 for important exceptions). In contrast, this book does not treat informal governance as an outcome or institutional form and makes a novel contribution to the debate by analyzing how it shapes the way issues are treated. This allows us to address the ensuing normative questions, as Jonathan White (2022) recently urged us to do, for example.

Besides its focus on organizations, another central implication of the authority perspective is that IOs are conceived as *coherent collective actors*: either agents of state principals or bureaucracies to which states and other international actors defer because of their moral standing, specialized knowledge, or problem-solving capacities. This means we understand very well how IOs and their secretariats function. However, less attention has been paid to the way the different bodies within IOs engage with the external environment (see Neumann and Sending 2010; Hanrieder 2014; Johnson 2014). While rationalists and constructivists increasingly discuss interorganizational relations, including beyond the analytical distinction of intergovernmental and non-state organizations (Abbott et al. 2015; Grigorescu 2020; Pantzerhielm et al. 2020; Green and Hadden 2021), most scholars continue to study how IOs as a whole interact. For example, the research agendas on regime complexity (Alter and Meunier 2009; Gehring and Faude 2013; Gómez-Mera 2016; Green 2022) and the opening up of IOs (Steffek 2013; Tallberg et al. 2013; Anderl et al. 2021) usually seek to explain the causes and consequences of interactions between single IOs, defined as unitary actors. I build on this research, which has significantly helped to explain the increasing complexity of global governance. But I use transnational professionals affiliated with different organizations as my analytical starting point. This shift in perspective allows me to describe how they govern emerging or open issues without letting organizational boundaries guide the analysis—offering new insight into how IOs actually govern.

A final analytical corollary to the authority perspective is the neglect of field dynamics. Since rationalist scholars primarily study institutional design processes and their effects (Koremenos et al. 2001; Johnson and Urpelainen 2014; Búzás and Graham 2020) and constructivists as well as organizational sociologists focus on the internal, cultural dynamics of IO secretariats (Cox and Jacobson 1974; Reinalda and Verbeek 2006; Babb 2009; Chorev 2013; Kentikelenis and Seabrooke 2017), they direct their attention to processes at headquarters. Surprisingly, even anthropological studies of IOs usually investigate processes and practices in the meeting rooms or conference corridors of global offices (Müller 2013; Niezen and Sapignoli 2017; Eckl 2021). Apart from a few important exceptions (Hanrieder 2015), regional offices or field missions go unconsidered. While some have studied the implementation of international norms and rules in domestic contexts (Joachim et al. 2010; Betts and Orchard 2014; Bartley 2018; Eckhard and Parizek 2020) and assessed the discrepancies between "talk" at headquarters and "action" in the field (Weaver 2008), scholars of IOs and global governance in IR and sociology have not sufficiently researched how IOs exploit the room for maneuver they get from field access. Avoiding a secretariat-only or a top-down perspective, this book offers an interactive account of how knowledge creation on the ground is embedded in processes at headquarters and vice versa.

1.3.2 International Organizations in the Field: Everyday Governance

IO scholarship typically analyzes collective actors and their authority. Two newer IR research strands draw attention to how IOs govern in the field and in practice. Anthropological approaches to international politics, particularly in the area of peacekeeping and interventions (Carvalho et al. 2011; Autesserre 2014; Daho et al. 2019; Witt 2022; Ruffa and Rietjens 2023), humanitarianism (Smirl 2015; Hor 2022), and development (Fechter and Hindman 2011; Mosse 2011a; Lie 2015; see also Honig 2018; Heinzel 2022), have started to investigate how local actions of IOs influence international policy-making. In detailed case studies, the authors have shown that policies and mandates need to be interpreted and extensively adapted during operations.

Similarly, IR practice approaches (Adler and Pouliot 2011; Bueger and Gadinger 2015) demonstrate how quotidian interactions of international lawyers, diplomats, economists, and bureaucrats shape world politics (Neumann 2005; Bode 2015; Sending et al. 2015; Block-Lieb and Halliday 2017; Adler-Nissen and Drieschova 2019; Louis and Maertens 2021; Pouliot and Thérien 2023). In this context, increasing attention is paid to IO "foot soldiers" (Broome and Seabrooke 2015: 957) and how their everyday practices—rather than abstract policy frameworks and organizational structures—determine governance outcomes on the ground (Côté-Boucher et al. 2014; Hofius 2016; Cooper and Cornut 2019).

These approaches further our understanding of the leeway enjoyed by those responsible for implementing international politics but tend to lose sight of how local governing modes are connected to decision-making at headquarters. They concentrate on how local life worlds "create everyday spheres of action autonomous from the organizing policy models" (Mosse 2011b: 10) and are usually constrained by their focus on the inner logics of "aidland" and "peaceland." Aside from analyses of organizational learning in peacekeeping (Howard 2008; Benner et al. 2011; Hirschmann 2012; Goetze 2019), feedback effects and links within organizations are rarely studied (but see Beerli 2018; Bode and Karlsrud 2018; Karlsrud 2018). Yet studies of organizational learning are geared to identifying factors that explain policy failure and make peacekeeping more effective; they are generally less interested in IOs and global governance. Unlike these approaches, this book is not primarily concerned with improving organizational performance in particular policy fields. Instead, it offers a conceptual framework for studying how on-site practice is linked to headquarters dynamics and influences the way issues are governed across operational spaces.

Lastly, investigations of how practices order global governance usually exhibit bias toward the procedural aspect of world politics. Authors contributing to this debate mostly analyze speechwriting, joint declaration drafting, conference hosting, NGO accrediting, and similar "technical" governing practices. Or they analyze personal social skills and how they enable international practitioners to navigate social milieus and position themselves as skillful, and therefore powerful, actors in organizational settings

(Neumann 2007; Adler-Nissen and Pouliot 2014; Pouliot and Thérien 2018). This is why authors like Ole Jacob Sending (2015b) and Tim Bartley (2018) have called for new approaches that focus on the *contents* of governance. They have set out to develop *substantive* theories of global governance. I seek to contribute to their endeavor by outlining how transnational practitioners' professional knowledge shapes perceptions of global challenges and disputes over the appropriate responses.

In sum, attempting to bridge the divide between headquarters and field perspectives, I build on and expand the four accounts of IO agency and influence on global governance outlined above. I propose a dynamic approach to global governance linking organizational levels and reorienting attention from collective actors (and how they become governors) to issues (and how they are governed on a substantive level). This seemingly subtle shift allows me to analytically open up IOs and observe what individual actors with different organizational affiliations actually do in practice at local and global sites that are not hierarchically, but rather conceptually, ordered. The book's research design and structure reflect this emphasis on vertical (cross-level) and horizontal (interorganizational) integration.

1.4 Case Selection and Data

This book is the fruit of a problem-driven research strategy. It starts from the puzzling observation that IOs governed mixed migration at the European external border during the crisis in 2015–16 despite having no clear legal-political frameworks for the migration-asylum nexus. The governing dynamics during this crisis, which have affected the lives of millions of people on the move and caused institutional upheaval within the EU and at the UN are themselves relevant. Furthermore, the case of mixed migration governance at Europe's external border provides an empirically rich source for theorizing professional practice on the ground as an informal, experimentalist mode of global governance that cuts across organizational levels and boundaries.

At the same time, this raises the question of generalizability to other IOs and issues in global governance. The case study is of course exceptional because the issue area of mixed migration exhibits a strong degree of underregulation, a high number of organizations responding on the ground, and large leeway for people working at the border. Yet, it is not too dissimilar from other issues in global politics, which also have become unsettled by political disputes, crises, or emerging challenges. In fact, recent research points out that we find similar patterns to the ones I describe in this book in UN peacekeeping operations (Bode and Karlsrud 2018; Campbell 2018; Laurence 2019; Ruffa and Rietjens 2023), humanitarian missions, for example after earthquakes or the outbreak of epidemics such as the Ebola crisis in West Africa (Kamradt-Scott 2016; Beerli 2018), development aid (Mosse 2011b; Honig 2018; Sondarjee 2021), finance (Moschella 2011), protection of the environment (Maertens 2018), and maritime security and ocean governance (Bueger and Edmunds 2021). These studies provide initial empirical evidence for UN peacekeepers, North Atlantic Treaty Organization (NATO) naval officers, World Health Organization (WHO) medical professionals, IMF development finance experts in country teams as well as humanitarian workers employed by international NGOs such as Oxfam and Médecins sans Frontières, the UN Office for the Coordination of Humanitarian Affairs (OCHA) or the International Committee of the Red Cross (ICRC) facing uncertainty, urgency, and organizational complexity in their daily work—and improvising across organizational divides in the field to cope with these challenges and devise provisional solutions which then change organizational practice from the bottom up. They are similar in terms of the issue structure (uncertainty and urgency stemming from novel, unforeseen events and the lack of clear policy instructions) on the one hand, and organizational structure (field presence and overlapping mandates) on the other.

The case of the European migration and refugee crisis is thus not only useful for establishing the dynamics behind governing on the ground (situated learning and stabilization) but also revealing with regard to the conditions that make it more likely: When IO staff are (a) *stationed in the field*—i.e. removed from headquarters oversight and in close physical proximity with fieldworkers from *other IOs*—and (b) encounter *novel situations* to which existing mandates and policies cannot easily be applied, they are likely to improvise to adapt and extend policy instructions. Crises, especially “fast-burning” ones (Seabrooke and Tsingou 2019), amplify these conditions by functioning as catalysts because they intensify the uncertainty about which rules apply to a given situation and which IO is in charge as well as the level of urgency to address that situation. However, fieldworkers will encounter unpredicted challenges and organizational complexity in their daily work in more or less stable times too, meaning that governing on the ground is likely to happen during all IO operations in the field, albeit to different degrees and with different outcomes (see Chapter 2).

The book's case study is located at two levels (field and headquarters) and includes eleven organizations: the IOM, the UNHCR, Frontex, EASO, NRC, Save the Children International (SCI), the International Federation of the Red Cross (IFRC), Médecins du Monde (MDM), Salvamento Marítimo Humanitario (SMH), the Chios Eastern Shore Response Team (CESRT), and Drops in the Ocean. Since the messy organizational landscape of governing migration and asylum (see Chapter 3) and this book's theoretical framework (see Chapter 2) defy the logic of a comparative case study design, the organizations are not studied as closed, separate entities. Instead, the case study begins on the ground at Europe's external border on the Greek island of Chios, with all the transnational professionals who worked on migration and asylum during the crisis (see Chapter 4). This prevents me from excluding important actors and interactions due to formal organizational features and *a priori* analytical distinctions such as public/private or humanitarian/security. To then trace how transnational professionals' ways of knowing and doing become embedded in wider organizational contexts, the second part of the case study is located in the IO operations and training units in Warsaw, Valletta, Geneva, Brussels, and Budapest (see Chapter 5).

The way these inter- and intra-organizational networks organized migration and asylum on the Greek islands in the Eastern Mediterranean is useful for studying how IOs with an operational branch govern under uncertain, urgent, and complex conditions. While the Aegean Islands have always been important migration transit zones, the second half of 2015 and first half of 2016 witnessed a dramatic increase in the number of people crossing the border into Europe there. During this period, 1,048,171 people were registered as having reached the EU along the Eastern Mediterranean, with the overwhelming majority (1,015,100) arriving on the islands of Lesvos, Chios, Samos, Leros, and Kos (Frontex 2016b: 16, 2016d: 8; UNHCR Regional Bureau for Europe 2016: 1). This mixed migration route thus became the most frequented one in the world (see Figure 1.2).[6]

Because long-term strategies and institutional responses to migration and displacement were lacking, the "international community was unprepared for such large numbers of people" (UNHCR and IOM 2016: 8) and a humanitarian crisis developed along the border (see Chapter 3). In response, the European Commission adopted the European Agenda for Migration,

[6] In 2015, the IOM and UNHCR counted 850,000 people traveling through the Aegean Islands to Europe, with as many as 12,500 people per day (UNHCR and IOM 2016: 8). Most were Syrian, Iraqi, and Afghani nationalities, with high or *prima facie* recognition rates as refugees. Among the other nationalities recorded were Iranian, Pakistani, Somali, Algerian, and Nigerian. Thus migration across the Eastern Mediterranean border qualifies as "mixed."

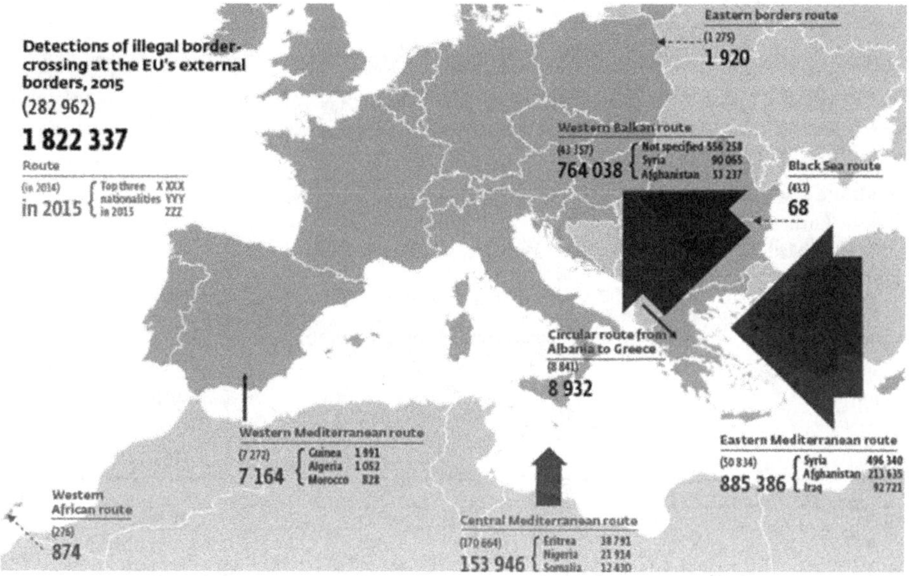

Fig. 1.2 Migration along the Mediterranean routes in 2015

Source: Frontex (2016a: 16).

devised its "Hotspot Approach" and deployed Migration Management Support Teams consisting of Frontex, EASO, and other EU agencies to Greece. The IOM, the UNHCR, humanitarian NGOs, and transnational volunteer groups also started working there. In comparison with other global borders—"the main economic, demographic, political, geographical, cultural and environmental fault lines of the world" along which "international migration is particularly intense" (Wihtol de Wenden 2012: 76)—the Eastern Mediterranean qualified as the mixed migration site where (1) migratory pressure was exceptionally high, (2) a crisis resulted from the lack of an institutional infrastructure, and (3) a high number of IOs responded to it in the field (see Table 1.1). These strong conditions of uncertainty, urgency, and complexity make the governing activities on the Aegean Islands a useful case for studying how IOs with access to the field govern new, contentious, or crisis-ridden issues through practice on the ground that promises to be the "richest in information" (Flyvbjerg 2006).[7]

The primary evidence for the first part of the case study consists of 530 hours of participatory observation I made while volunteering on the Greek island of Chios in March, April, and May 2016. These were recorded in

[7] For recent research on governing dynamics at the American and Australian borders, see Williams and Boyce (2013); Macdonald (2015); Little and Vaughan-Williams (2017); Squire (2017).

Table 1.1 Case selection

Global borders	Routes	Irregular border crossing points
USA/Mexico		
Australia / Southeast Asia		
Russia/China		
Europe / Middle East and North Africa	Western Mediterranean	
	Central Mediterranean	
	Eastern Mediterranean	Lesvos
		Chios
		Samos
		Leros
		Kos

field notes and include over sixty conversational interviews. Another sixteen recorded interviews lasting between thirty and ninety minutes were conducted with practitioners from different professional groups and all the IOs present. Although Lesvos is the biggest of the five main Aegean Islands where most people arrived, thus *prima facie* promising the densest data points, I selected Chios for my fieldwork because it received less media coverage and thus afforded me better access. The intense media attention on Lesvos attracted a huge number of NGOs and volunteer groups and created widespread volunteer fatigue. Chios, the second largest Aegean island, presented very similar conditions in terms of the migratory challenge, the crisis moment, and the presence of multiple IOs. But there I was able to more deeply immerse myself in the local community of practice, which was crucial for collecting first-hand data on the creation and performance of frontline practices (see Yanow 2009; Adler-Nissen and Drieschova 2019; Adler-Nissen and Eggeling 2022).

As a member of the CESRT, I participated in shore patrol, helped with beach landings and port disembarkations, entered the Vial Hotspot, worked in the Souda and Dipethe open campsites, attended weekly coordination meetings at the townhall, participated in local seminars and working groups on protection, child protection, and communication with communities, took part in a SAR training exercise, drank coffee on a Frontex ship after a night shift, lunched with EASO staff, and went to a local bar with UNHCR, NRC, and Save the Children staff (see Annex I for my reflections on methods and ethics). I complemented my field notes and interviews with formal and informal organizational documents, such as IO reports, meeting minutes, and WhatsApp chat groups, to provide greater insight into how IO field staff were struggling to define the challenge at hand and organize collective responses. Press releases and official statements from EU institutions and UN documents provided background information on formal migration and asylum policy development during that period. Finally, I have used reports by other volunteers and researchers as well as academic secondary literature on mixed migration governance at the European external border to cross-check and contextualize my fieldwork findings.

Interviews and training documents served as primary sources for the second part of the case study. Aiming for organizational balance and diversity, I spoke with twenty-five training and operations experts from the UNHCR, the IOM, Frontex, EASO, and several NGOs. As is typical for elite interviews, interviewee selection was based on purposive and snowball sampling (Littig 2009: 101). Interviews lasting between thirty and ninety minutes were conducted in the interviewees' offices, IO secretariat cafeterias, and using Skype in February, March, and May 2017 (see Annex II on the interview partners). The semi-structured interviews combined factual questions with in-depth discussions of organizational processes (King and Horrocks 2010: 25). In addition, I coded 119 training documents retrieved from IO homepages or obtained during interviews to analyze the skills and routines for governing migration and asylum at the border that become consolidated and diffused. The interviews mainly serve to reconstruct *processes* of stabilization; learning materials were the most direct sources of evidence for the *content* of training.

1.5 Outline of the Book

There are three parts to the book. The first develops concepts and theory, the second is devoted to the empirical analysis, and the third revisits the key assumptions on IOs and global governance and discusses the theoretical, normative, and institutional implications of the case study. In Chapter 2, I provide the book's theoretical framework. In an initial step, I discuss why I deem it useful to not conceptually equate governance with the exercise of authority. I propose a more minimalist definition of global governance to capture fast-moving, informal governing dynamics.

In a second step, and in contrast to the common collective actor perspective, I propose taking transnational professionals as the starting point for analyzing IOs. This shift draws attention to the organizing strategies of professional actors in IOs that cut across organizational boundaries. It allows me to consider several IOs without *a priori* excluding certain types of organizations, most importantly NGOs and regional agencies.

I finish Chapter 2 by developing a five-step loop model of global governance on the ground. The main theoretical argument that I advance here is that governing on the ground is a unique mode of governance that nests the field and headquarters and functions on the basis of practical professional knowledge. In short, I posit that, faced with complexity, uncertainty, and urgency, transnational professionals stationed on the ground improvise to respond to global problems. They use their skills and expertise to negotiate which ad hoc responses will eventually be accepted as competent ways of handling things and routinized for on-site practice. The frontline practices thus generated become consolidated and diffused through training by headquarters staff who seek to standardize how issues are addressed in practice. Given the irreducible messiness of global affairs, once such a loop is completed, it is likely to start again. My key claim is that transnational professionals who are embedded in inter- and intra-organizational networks govern transnational challenges in the spaces where they occur without first going through formal decision-making channels or renegotiating their authority. Although they require mandates and funds to act, institutional factors do not determine how professional actors in IOs make use of the room for maneuver that opens up during episodes of crisis and contention and the discretion that comes from their position at the organization's periphery. In Chapter 2, I offer conceptual tools for studying how they do that and to what effect.

The following three chapters contain the book's empirical core: the extensive case study of organizing international migration and asylum at the European external border. Chapter 3 sets the stage by briefly discussing the current architecture of global migration and asylum governance. It reconstructs how the notion of "mixed migration" gradually became recognized as an analytical and political category, and demonstrates that the public goods its governance should provide remain poorly understood and contested. Next it outlines the main actors and institutions and shows that the formal institutional framework for governing mixed migration is riddled with loopholes and inconsistencies. It traces these gaps and overlaps to the politicized nature of international migration and shows how they create emergencies like the recent European migration and refugee crisis. The chapter introduces the basic parameters of the crisis and briefly discusses European and international policy initiatives that were launched in response. It also introduces the Aegean island of Chios as a central border crossing point and hotspot of the crisis.

Chapter 4 then studies the operational response to the crisis at the European external border in Greece. Drawing on ethnographic fieldwork on

Chios, I analyze how border and coastguards, camp managers, humanitarians, doctors, paramedics, social workers, psychologists, lifesavers, firefighters, lawyers, and asylum caseworkers made sense of the high number of people crossing without authorization from Turkey. It reconstructs how, in the thick of things, IO field staff negotiated a response. The chapter first shows that despite being formally affiliated with the UNHCR, the IOM, EASO, Frontex, the NRC, the IFRC, Save the Children, MDM, and SMH, or working in volunteer teams, IO staff interacted closely on a daily basis. They relied on their personal networks and professional stocks of knowledge to try out how to handle large movements of migrants, asylum seekers, and refugees. Surprisingly, not only did organizational boundaries fade into the background but no main cleavage emerged between humanitarian and security professionals: Those working at the border were highly committed to finding provisional solutions—and distinguished themselves from officials in charge in Athens, Brussels, and New York (and their representatives, such as local authorities and European Commission envoys visiting the hotspots). They operated outside their formal mandates—often as private persons but in a self-perceived public capacity—to address the issues at hand.

Chapter 4 demonstrates that fieldworkers assumed responsibility for managing mixed movements and fought over how to do it *well*. They used their professional judgment to evaluate spontaneous ways to cope with migration and displacement, and argued about suitability. Interestingly, they explicitly shied away from claiming authority for their organizations and instead felt compelled to find feasible and acceptable practical solutions. In competitive, confrontational, and cooperative interactions, they negotiated how to competently deal with mixed migration in the everyday.

Chapter 4 traces how IO staffers routinized their on-the-ground practices, gradually determining how to spot and safely land migrant boats, register and accommodate people on the move, record identities and asylum claims, interview and assess asylum applications, organize relocations and returns—and how to protect peoples' rights during the procedures. By defining how to perform these far from straightforward practices and deciding which to include in the governance of mixed migration, they introduced some degree of order to the unauthorized movements, restricting or enabling new courses of action for people on the move: They governed migration and asylum at the border.

Chapter 5 turns to processes of stabilization and shows that governing at the border is embedded in larger inter- and intra-organizational expert networks. IO staff charged with training and learning—in the UNHCR Global Learning Center, Frontex's Capacity-Building Division, EASO's training unit in the Department of Asylum Support, and interagency initiatives, such as the International Maritime Rescue Federation (IMRF) or the Global Camp Coordination and Camp Management Cluster that the IOM runs with the UNHCR and the NRC—consolidate local practices in training tools. They devise detailed scripts for best practices and compile rosters of international trainers to teach fieldworkers how to, *inter alia*, search and rescue, manage camps, conduct asylum interviews, and handle relocation and returns. The chapter analyzes who drives stabilization dynamics and which content gets consolidated and diffused, thereby determining how mixed migration is governed in the absence of formal regulation.

Chapter 6 has two main ambitions: to evaluate the conceptual and theoretical arguments put forward in Chapter 2 and to outline the practical and normative implications that follow from the analysis. This concluding chapter begins by briefly reviewing the definition of governance proposed in Chapter 2. I reassess the claim that it makes sense to conceptually uncouple authority and governance. I argue that focusing on authority and its disengagement from the nation-state has resulted in global governance theory neglecting physical spaces. Adopting the "spatial turn" in peace and conflict studies, I sketch how to include spaces in analyses of IOs and global governance. The chapter thereby connects the loop model of global governance on the ground to current IR debates on territory, practice, and authority. Chapter 6 ends by discussing the promise and pitfalls of global governance on the ground. It identifies factors and institutional solutions for redressing the concerns of failure and arbitrariness in this governance mode, namely high-quality professional training, better job incentives, and latitude for fieldworkers—and ombudsmen, individual complaint mechanisms, and similar instruments of direct accountability for the governed.

2

Governing on the Ground

Unexpected situations and crisis moments force international organizations (IOs) to experiment with new ways of regulating an issue—often right where the emergency erupted. Eventually, these local experiences stabilize into new governing practices. In one instance, during the global financial crisis of 2007–9, the International Monetary Fund (IMF) tentatively agreed to capital controls for Iceland and Cyprus, a measure that had previously been unacceptable in international financial policy-making. As a consequence, the IMF changed its view of legitimate operational policy options (Moschella 2015). Similarly, the conflict in the Democratic Republic of Congo became a laboratory for the United Nations (UN) to test new peacekeeping practices, slowly but drastically redefining what "impartiality" in conflicts means (Laurence 2019: 10). In the issue area of migration and asylum, several IOs spontaneously organized collective action on mixed migration to Europe during the 2015–16 crisis. Faced with significant regulatory voids and authority gaps, on-site experience and innovation in practice that later became consolidated in organizational routines and professional competencies determined how IOs handle migration and displacement (see Chapters 4 and 5).

As I argue in this book, these are instances of a unique mode of global governance: *governing through practice on the ground.* This phenomenon has been overlooked by International Relations (IR) scholars because of a division of labor between approaches that analyze processes at headquarters and those studying field dynamics. The dominant theoretical predisposition of "secretariat approaches" focuses on studying relations between bureaucracies and member states to understand how IOs, defined as unitary collective actors, gain authority and agency. As a result, what IOs do *on the ground* has received little attention. In turn, the anthropological inclination of "field approaches" means that local IO practices are well-studied but their effects on global governance beyond concrete local sites remain largely unexplained (see Section 1.3).

As a result, with respect to informal global governance based on practical professional knowledge, studies of IO secretariats limit their analyses to mission creep. They typically either examine how bureaucratic entities incrementally extend the boundaries of their mandates by exploiting institutional

Global Governance on the Ground. Nele Kortendiek, Oxford University Press. © Nele Kortendiek (2024).
DOI: 10.1093/oso/9780198889120.003.0002

loopholes or how they renegotiate their authority by demonstrating expertise on emerging issues to state actors (Barnett and Finnemore 2004; Babb and Buira 2005; Hawkins et al. 2006a; Steffek 2013; Hall 2016; Hooghe et al. 2019; Littoz-Monnet 2020). In contrast, studies of field practices limit their analyses to local decision-making and reconstruct how the operational staff's local embeddedness transforms international mandates and policies during implementation (Mosse 2011a; Autesserre 2014; Smirl 2015; Hor 2022). The instances of governing new, contested, or crisis-ridden issues briefly presented above do not, however, conform to these patterns. On one hand, they describe a very direct form of governing between IO field staff and target populations that eschews lengthy authority renegotiations, while on the other, they describe local practices that do not stay put: They are consolidated and travel across operational spaces—guiding the governance of transnational issues elsewhere. They are not more of the same but rather are ontologically different from both authority-based and local modes of governance.

To account for this distinct mode of global governance, the chapter proceeds in three main steps. It first addresses the notion of governance itself. After briefly reviewing the IR literature on IOs and global governance, I develop a minimalist definition of governance that does not rely on the concept of authority. I propose to understand global governance as the *organizing of collective action on public issues that results in the opening up or restriction of possibilities for action by the addressees of global governance on the part of entities acting in a public capacity*. This allows us to account for governing dynamics that operate at a very low institutional threshold that would otherwise fly under the radar of IR scholars but whose political and normative implications warrant our critical assessment.

Following these general conceptual reflections on governance, Section 2.2 suggests a shift in analytical perspective on IOs. A change in IO staffing and hiring practices brought the role of transnational professionals in global governance to the fore (Momani 2005; Cooley 2010; Seabrooke and Sending 2019). A large percentage of IO staff is now hired on consultant contracts and financed through project funds, subjecting the image of the international civil servant who is loyal to one IO throughout her career (Sending 2015; Steffek 2021) to critical scrutiny—and with it, the view that IOs are coherent unitary actors. If staff members are not thoroughly socialized into the organizational cultures of IO bureaucracies and can avoid sanctions and controls by their principals because of their short-term contracts, should IOs continue to be treated as closed systems? Building on the works of organization scholars (Aldrich and Pfeffer 1976; Scott and Davis 2007), several authors in IR's rational-institutionalist and sociological-constructivist tradition have argued that it makes more analytical sense to treat IOs as open systems: composite entities with several sub-units that independently engage with actors in the organizational environment (Neumann and Sending 2010; Graham 2014; Hanrieder 2014; Johnson 2014; Seabrooke and Tsingou 2015).

Given these considerations and drawing on the professional networks literature, I propose using *transnational professionals* affiliated with different organizations as the analytical starting point. It follows that, in contrast to most conceptions of IOs in IR scholarship that converge on the theoretical assumption that IOs have relatively stable and fixed boundaries, I understand IOs as having *porous boundaries.* This shifts attention from coherent, collective actors (whether bureaucracies or agents) and their relations with states to transnational professionals and how they work to control issues in global governance. This shift in perspective also allows analysis of how these professionals are deployed to various field missions, country offices, and regional bureaus and how their knowledge travels across sites. In other words, it prepares the theoretical grounds for an *interorganizational* and *cross-level perspective* on global governance that integrates several (types of) IOs, as well as headquarters and field dynamics. This makes it possible to understand how on-site improvisation that cuts across organizational boundaries during moments of contention leads to the informal development and diffusion of professional practices that determine how transnational challenges are governed in practice.

After laying the theoretical groundwork in Sections 2.1 and 2.2, the remainder of the chapter conceptualizes practice on the ground as a specific mode of global governance. In Section 2.3, I develop a *loop model* of governing on the ground that is rooted in sociological approaches to work, learning, and knowledge in organizations (Lave and Wenger 1991; Yanow 2000; Nicolini 2013). I develop a basic typology of knowledge and translate central concepts from the study of organizations in sociology, public administration, and management studies to the field of international politics. I combine these insights with research on street-level decision-making in global politics (Côté-Boucher et al. 2014; Kurowska 2014; Cooper and Cornut 2019) to model how experimentation on the ground, at the "organizational periphery," and training at headquarters—in the "organizational center"—shape the governance of new or contentious issues.

The loop model outlines five ideal-typical steps, which take place at two levels: Together, the first three steps—improvising (1), negotiating competence (2), and routinizing practice (3)—constitute *situated learning* and take place in the field. Steps four and five—consolidation (4) and diffusion (5)—happen at headquarters and together constitute a mechanism that I call *stabilization.* Situated learning means that transnational professionals working for different IOs learn by doing against the background of their skills and expertise. In everyday work relations that span several organizations, they create new experiential knowledge which they use to govern unsettled issues on the ground. In brief, IO field staff confronted with novelty, contestation, and crises develop provisional practices that are both feasible and acceptable to their peers. Stabilization describes the process of consolidating and streamlining these practices. When training and operations officers at headquarters design learning programs, they integrate practical knowledge from the field into organizational repertoires—that they diffuse through training field staff in order to standardize what colleagues are already doing on the ground. Once such a loop is completed, it is likely to start again. Practical knowledge can never be fully codified and global governance is never finally ordered (see for example Ikenberry 2018), which means that global governance on the ground works in nested feedback loops.

These assumptions yield a loop model of global governance that is at the core about transnational professionals' knowledge and practice. Yet formal and cultural organizational features continue to influence how IOs govern on the ground. For example, operating plans signed with host countries, resource allocation to field missions, and reporting requirements *vis-à-vis* project managers, state representatives, and donors significantly enable or constrain fieldworkers' leeway. Transnational professionals work in the shadow of state laws, bureaucratic hierarchies, and donor interests (see for example Graham 2017; Stroup and Wong 2017; Honig 2019; Patz and Goetz 2019; Thorvaldsdottir and Patz 2021). Notably, this also implies that organizational boundaries do not become obsolete. Although I consider an IO's collective agency and the boundaries drawn around it as an ongoing organizational achievement (see Hanrieder 2015: 32), these boundaries do not vanish—not least because IO staff reassert them when seeking project funding (see Cooley and Ron 2002; Krause 2014). Finally, professional and organizational cultures often overlap (Biermann and Siebenhüner 2009b: 342), which points to the fact that an IO's rules, rituals, and beliefs also inform how transnational professionals adapt to situational challenges. Thus, notwithstanding the analytical primacy of transnational professionals' knowledge and practice, organizational structures and cultures remain important. However, here they are understood as starting points rather than key explanatory factors for reconstructing how IOs govern.

How to study global governance on the ground is the topic of this chapter's final section, which concludes with some methodological reflections. It also briefly discusses the broader applicability of my argument to the study of IOs in global governance.

Generally, with the theoretical account that I develop in this chapter, I seek to make a threefold contribution to the scholarly debate about how IOs govern. First, I offer a dynamic account of how IOs use and create *knowledge* to govern. Given its overriding interest in expertise (Sending 2015; Littoz-Monnet 2017c, 2020; Zürn 2018; Liese et al. 2021), the IO literature does not spell out all the implications of other forms of knowledge for global governance (but see for example Adler-Nissen and Pouliot 2014; Julian et al. 2019). To be sure, these works have been highly instrumental in shifting the debate from state actors to how multinational companies, non-governmental organizations (NGOs), epistemic communities, intergovernmental organizations (IGOs), and other public and private actors become global governors. They show that these actors use expertise to influence policy-making and construct global authority. However, largely missing from the discussion of epistemic authority is how practical skills and competencies shape the way global issues are treated.

Second, by offering a cross-level and interorganizational approach to IOs, I respond to the challenge of accounting for the normative consequences of *informal* and *experimentalist* global governance (see White 2022). Despite renewed interest in interorganizational relations, accounts of informal interactions and their effects, especially in the field, are rare (Biermann and Koops 2017: 10). Studies of informal or experimentalist governance in turn usually focus on single IOs or adopt strong top-down perspectives—and do not address questions of *legitimate* governance (Chwieroth 2013; Búrca et al. 2014; Westerwinter et al. 2021). In addition, research on the local lives of IOs often neglects intra-organizational links, tending to only analyze what happens at specific local sites (Autesserre 2014; but see Beerli 2018; Bode and Karlsrud 2018; Karlsrud 2018). This is unfortunate because informal local action can have global repercussions.

Third, by reconstructing how actors draw on their professional knowledge (for example, as border guards, humanitarians, and migration lawyers) to govern specific issues, the chapter balances the usual procedural bias in practice approaches to global governance. Students of international practices have pushed IR's boundaries by showing that the "everyday 'doing' of international politics" reproduces and changes the international order (Adler and Pouliot 2011; Bueger and Gadinger 2015; Schindler and Wille 2015: 331). However, they tend to foreground technical governing practices like speech-writing, negotiating, cooperating, conference-hosting, and accrediting NGOs (for example Neumann 2007; Pouliot and Thérien 2018; Adler-Nissen and Drieschova 2019)—and neglect the *contents* of governance (see Sending 2015; Bartley 2018). Practices are of course relational and procedural but, as I argue in this book, they are not "empty": For example, addressing mixed migration with patrolling, screening, and debriefing serves to define it as a security threat.

2.1 Thinking beyond Authority: Defining Governance

To capture the mode of governance that I describe in this book, governance is not conceptually equated with the exercise of authority. This view contrasts with most IR theories of global governance that commonly define it as "the *exercise of authority* across national borders as well as consented norms and rules beyond the nation state, both of them justified with reference to common goods or transnational problems" (Zürn 2018: 3–4; emphasis added).

Early accounts of global governance follow the logic that because public issues have become globalized and de-territorialized since the end of the Cold War, the authority to deal with them—now dispersed across networked arrangements of public and private actors and institutions located in local, regional, national, and international settings—has, too (Florini 2000; Kahler and Lake 2003; Ruggie 2004; Dingwerth and Pattberg 2006; Büthe and Mattli 2011). Starting from the assumption that the international system is anarchical because, unlike the domestic polity, it lacks centralized enforcement mechanisms, first-generation global governance scholars argued that for collective decisions to be complied with, rule addressees need to voluntarily defer to global governors and their norms, rules, and procedures. Therefore, global governors must have authority, a form of political power that, unlike coercion, works on the basis of social recognition. In other words, to organize collective action on international issues, IOs must be able to create binding rules and therefore need to be socially accepted as legitimate. Otherwise, it is conceptually inconceivable that they could claim obedience. Since this understanding of global governance ultimately describes authority relations of prescription and deference, it rests on legitimacy beliefs (Hurd 1999; Buchanan and Keohane 2006; Steffek 2007; Lake 2010).

More recently, scholars like Michael Zürn, Nico Krisch, Ole Jacob Sending, Nicole Deitelhoff, and Christopher Daase have started to promote a more dynamic understanding that does not emphasize structural changes of the global order or the emergence of new governors. They have begun to reconceptualize global authority as "liquid" and "reflexive" and turned to practices of legitimation, contestation, and recognition instead of considering legitimacy beliefs as given (Sending 2015; Krisch 2017; Zürn 2018; Deitelhoff and Daase 2021). These authors are more interested in how different actors in world politics are able to induce deference in concrete social relations and practices, for example by making "requests" (Zürn 2018) or competing for peer recognition (Sending 2015). Yet they continue to treat authority as the "founding principle" of global governance, which first must be understood before governing can be examined.

I suggest turning this train of thought on its head: Instead of treating authority as the starting point for thinking about global governance, I propose viewing it as a possible outcome of governing dynamics. The reason behind this conceptual proposition is that if we assume, for example, that (1) IOs are public administrations that employ experts (actor type) and therefore (2) hold epistemic authority in a particular domain (authority type), then (3) we only perceive the governing activities based on exercising this type of authority. We are analytically blind toward the doings that also "affect [...] the daily lives and fortunes of people" (Ruggie 2004: 499) but stem from other sources. If, however, we begin at the opposite end of the conceptual equation and investigate the IO activities that have governing effects on the lives of target populations and trace them to their origins, we can be analytically receptive toward other sources of IO agency and influence besides authority. To push the boundaries of the lively scholarly debate on global authority and IOs, I propose understanding governance as a series of activities that have the same effects as the exercise of authority—instead of treating governing as the result of a particular type of authority that flows from a particular type of actorness (see Sending 2015: 14–18; Seabrooke and Henriksen 2017a: 3–5).

What, then, *is* global governance? I submit that two elements are central to defining it: a constraining or enabling effect, and publicness. Following the assumption that it "can only be determined on the basis of outcomes" (Strange 1996: 91, as quoted in; Baumann and Dingwerth 2015: 107), I contend that the activities "coordinating and constraining individual behavior" (Abbott and Snidal 2001: 345) amount to governing. In addition, global governance always "involves an element of 'publicness'"—whether driven by public or private actors (Zürn 2018: 4). It does not just pertain to issues affecting individuals: It relates to loosely defined common goals and involves organizing collective action. That is, governing happens when *organizing collective action on issues deemed public results in opening up or restricting courses of action for the final addressees of global politics by entities acting in a public capacity*. This decidedly minimalist definition is open to different *modi operandi* (laws, norms, rules, standards, numbers, or practice) and sources of agency. It is guided by Zürn's notion that authority relationships "may, in some cases, emerge spontaneously—for instance, in crisis situations" (2017: 8). Zürn acknowledges the ad hoc, improvisational side of global governance, arguing:

> If there is a fire in a theater, a few may turn out to coordinate the exit movement without any such pre-assignment. If the same group of people that spend the evening in the theatre would sit in an airplane and an emergency evolves, it would be likely that the passengers look at the same people asking for injunctions. (Zürn 2017: 8, fn. 6)

This thought experiment illustrates how competent people organize collective action and make decisions that have enabling or restraining impacts on the lives of others without being formally tasked or authorized to do so. Whereas Zürn is mainly interested in how such spontaneous relations of deference stabilize over time, the definition of governance I propose here conceptually takes these spontaneous interactions *themselves* seriously.

The conceptual advantage of this definition is that it does not blind us to those forms of global governance which, "though highly consequential, do not operate through formal, legal tools" (Krisch 2017: 4–5). It takes into account that some actors may govern *de facto* and "circumvent formal circuits of authority" (Seabrooke and Henriksen 2017a: 5), for example, by using their access to the field and drawing on their substantive professional know-how. At the same time, this definition is not fundamentally at odds with more traditional understandings. James Rosenau (1990: 9) already pointed out that institutions "connote the presence of authoritative principles, norms, rules, and procedures, thereby running the risk of obscuring the informal, non-authoritative dimensions that are so essential to the functioning of international orders and regimes." In short, the definition I propose seeks to supplement existing conceptions of global governance. I do not seek to eliminate authority from thinking about global governance. What I want to do is highlight the governing dynamics that take place *before* authority relations have been established and the governing dynamics that are *beyond* formal mandates.

Having clarified my general understanding of governance, I now turn to the question of *who* governs. I briefly outline my theoretical approach to IOs in the following section before developing the loop model of governing on the ground, addressing *how* they govern through their access to the field.

2.2 Transnational Professionals in Global Governance: Toward an Interorganizational and Cross-Level Perspective

With a few exceptions, not only do most IOs work to advocate policy change, establish standards, make rules, and negotiate treaties in global arenas but they also have an operational presence on the ground.[1] However, in IR theorizing on IOs and global governance there is a disconnect between approaches that provide analytical tools for studying the influence IOs exert through processes at the secretariat level (Joachim 2003; Price 2003; Barnett and Finnemore 2004; Hawkins et al. 2006a; Betsill and Corell 2008) and those focused on the discretionary power of IO fieldworkers (Mosse 2011a; Autesserre 2014; Krause 2014). This dominant debate has also neglected the fact that people who work for IOs often move through revolving doors (Seabrooke and Tsingou 2021) and rotate across missions (Lundgren et al. 2022). While the focus on *collective actors* and *authority* that most theories of IOs and global governance share has successfully explained how IOs become governors that are autonomous of their member states (Avant et al. 2010a) and why their levels of authority differ (Hooghe et al. 2017; Zürn et al. 2021), it neglects what IO staffers do in the gray areas between mandates and sites. It thus hinders analysis of how the issues are governed for which no IO has established competence.

To account for the way still-unclaimed global issues are governed, I suggest taking transnational professionals as the analytical starting point. As Leonard Seabrooke and his colleagues have argued (Seabrooke and Tsingou 2014; Seabrooke and Wigan 2015; Seabrooke and Henriksen 2017b; Seabrooke and Sending 2019), this shift in analytical perspective makes it possible to conceptualize IOs as open systems of linked institutional ecologies, in which professional actors whose behavior is not completely determined by their organizational memberships coordinate and compete over how to define transnational issues (Seabrooke 2014: 50; Seabrooke and Tsingou 2015: 7). From this viewpoint, an IO's mandate or effective claim to authority is not equivalent to its control over a particular issue (Seabrooke and Henriksen 2017a: 5). Likewise, before an empirical analysis is made, the boundaries between an IO's inside and outside are not used as analytical categories (Sending and Neumann 2011: 231; Sending 2015: 3–4). Instead, attention

[1] For example, NGO scholars distinguish between "service" and "advocacy" NGOs to account for these different types and functions, see Beer et al. (2012). IGO scholars speak of "normative/functional" or "regulatory/ operational" organizations to account for these differences, see Gehring and Faude (2013); Hall (2016).

is focused on how transnational professionals employed by different public and private IOs effectively draw boundaries around who is best equipped to deal with a transnational issue. In short, and in line with my definition of governance, this perspective reverses the "causal logic of much work in transnational governance [which is] that organizations have a type of authority that enables them to engage in rule making" (Seabrooke and Henriksen 2017a: 3). Assuming "this may overplay the importance of recognized authority coming from organizations as entities" (Seabrooke and Henriksen 2017a: 5), the transnational professionals perspective starts with professionals and their strategies and investigates how they exploit organizational opportunities to control transnational issues. I borrow from this perspective to theoretically and empirically reconstruct how migration, border, and humanitarian professionals working for different organizations (IGOs, NGOs, or regional agencies) with limited mandates and competencies define what mixed migration is and how it needs to be governed in and through practice.

In addition, since looking through the lens of the transnational professionals' framework allows us to recenter attention from IOs as global authorities to individual actors and their practices, we can look beyond secretariats, intergovernmental assemblies, and executive committees to understand how IOs govern. It thus paves the way for including operational spaces into our analysis and reconstructing how professional knowledge is used and developed to define tasks and claim competence. However, by focusing on struggles for control, the framework concentrates on organizational and professional elites and underestimates the problem-solving component of professional knowledge (see Evetts 2003; Young and Muller 2014). In addition, it is agnostic regarding the creation of professional knowledge. In the following, I therefore combine key insights from the literature on transnational professionals with practice-oriented approaches to work, knowledge, and learning in organizations to account for processes of professional knowledge production. I also link it to research on street-level bureaucracy in international politics to expand the dominant focus on headquarters dynamics.

In short, I propose adopting an interorganizational, cross-level perspective on global governance. From this angle, IOs are conceived as having permeable boundaries and existing at multiple sites. This allows me to conceptualize global governance on the ground with a view to the specific professional competence that shapes how international issues are governed *de facto* at the frontlines of global challenges.

2.3 A Loop Model of Global Governance on the Ground

This section provides a model for analyzing how IOs govern emerging, contested, and crisis-ridden issues in international politics. In keeping with my general theoretical assumptions on global governance and the nature of IOs outlined in the previous sections, the model focuses on professional knowledge creation through processes of organizational learning at different levels of global governance or, rather, at different global and local sites.[2] It outlines how practical knowledge is created in interorganizational networks and nested feedback loops and is used to define particular transnational issues and their regulation.

To set the stage, I briefly introduce the conceptual distinction between tacit and explicit knowledge. This serves to develop a basic typology of knowledge that is important for understanding how professional practical knowledge emerges, functions, and is used to claim jurisdiction. The remainder of this section is divided into the five steps of the loop model. The first three (improvising, negotiating competence, and routinizing practice) constitute *situated learning* and take place in the field (Section 2.3.2). The last two (consolidation and diffusion) break down the process of *stabilization*, which links the field to headquarters (Section 2.3.3). These five steps should be understood as Weberian ideal types that very likely overlap. Whether, at which point, and how extensively they occur must be examined empirically, case by case. This distinction is analytically useful, however, because it helps us reconstruct the mechanisms of governing on the ground.

2.3.1 Knowledge in International Organizations: Expertise and Competence

The political functions of knowledge have been researched extensively in IR, with the literature divided over whether knowledge should be viewed as a resource for problem-solving or for furthering experts' standing in power struggles. Research on epistemic communities, for instance, has investigated how experts use "an authoritative claim to policy-relevant knowledge" (Haas 1992: 3) to inform and rationalize international policy-making (Haas 1990; Davis Cross 2013). Studies of IO bureaucracies, particularly

[2] See Chapter 6 for a conceptual discussion of space in global governance.

the seminal work by Martha Finnemore and Michael Barnett (2004), have shown that IOs' access to specialized bodies of knowledge puts them in a position to define problems, fix categories, and shape how international actors perceive their own interests (Boswell 2012; Busch and Liese 2017). More critical approaches have often borrowed from science and technology studies or Foucauldian understandings of knowledge to analyze how framing political debates in technical, scientific, or quantitative terms serves to insulate international policy-making from contestation and constitute "governance objects" that thereby become "governable" (Sending and Lie 2015; Kennedy 2016; Allan 2017; Littoz-Monnet 2020). Hence, authors argue that, in functional terms, IOs use knowledge to make policy prescriptions and advise policy-makers. Beyond this narrow understanding, constructivist researchers claim that IOs use knowledge to give meaning to international issues and structure possible responses. Critical scholars maintain that expertise is not simply "out there" or objectively constructed but is relational and enmeshed with experts' personal interests and claims to influence.

Despite these differences, these studies share a focus on *expertise*, usually understood as codified or reliable knowledge produced by specialists and presented as neutral and apolitical (Boswell 2017; Littoz-Monnet 2017b: 2). This interest in expert knowledge can be explained by the specific status that it provides: Those who dispose of expertise usually have superordinate social positions and can make interpretations, judgments, and decisions to which others defer (Sending 2015; Zürn 2018: 52; Herold et al. 2021). There is an inherent link to authority, so it is indeed appropriate to focus on expertise when studying how knowledge puts organizational actors in positions to govern. However, the downside of this focus is that other forms of knowledge, most notably practical knowledge, have not been studied enough. Only recently have scholars sought to understand how practical knowledge or *competence*[3] influences international politics (for example Kustermans 2016). Very generally speaking, the concept of competence draws attention to how skills and experience are used to make things known and shape policy-making on transnational issues (Adler-Nissen and Pouliot 2014; Bueger 2015), including by people who are not deemed experts according to established criteria (Julian et al. 2019).

These newer research endeavors draw on the fundamental distinction between tacit and explicit knowledge first introduced by Michael Polanyi (2009 [1958]) to conceptualize what knowledge is and does. Polanyi stresses

[3] These notions are used interchangeably because they pertain to the same conceptual core. For an overview of the terms subsumed under expertise and competence, see Table 2.1.

that knowledge is both an intellectual disposition and an inarticulate, bodily way of knowing how to do things (see also Yanow 2000: 259; Reckwitz 2002: 246; Nicolini et al. 2003; Pouliot 2008). He famously gave the example of cycling to illustrate the two dimensions of knowledge: After learning to ride a bike, without explicitly knowing *how*, we ride. We cannot formulate the physical laws of bike-riding but have the tacit—practical—knowledge of how to do it (Polanyi 2009 [1958]: 4; see also Collins 2001: 116–17). This distinction draws attention to the fact that action itself does epistemic work: Knowing is something we do in the social and physical world. Not only can it be mobilized as an external resource and used in action, but it is also part of an action (Schön 1983: 49; Blackler 1995; Cook and Seely-Brown 1999: 382–3; Orlikowski 2002: 250–1). It is therefore often described as competent participation in practice or termed "practical knowledge" (see Table 2.1 for an overview of the various designations). Here, practical knowledge is understood as "a skill acquired through experience. It ensures that we know how to go on, it enables us to handle situations" (Kustermans 2016: 11; see also Zahle 2012: 52–3).

Professional knowledge distinguishes professionals from lay people. It provides them with the tools to define and process the uncertainties of modern life. Professions are "essentially the knowledge-based category of occupations which usually follow a period of tertiary education and vocational training and experience" (Evetts 2003: 397; see also Adler et al. 2008; Young and Muller 2014). This definition stresses that professional knowledge encompasses both expertise and competence. Professionals are "individuals with abstract higher level learning and specific skill sets to address tasks" (Seabrooke and Henriksen 2017a: 10). While the expertise of transnational professionals has been extensively researched (Haas 1992;

Table 2.1 Two types of knowledge

Expertise	Competence
Explicit knowledge	Tacit or background knowledge
Theoretical or abstract knowledge	Practical, experiential, concrete, or local knowledge
"Know that"	"Know-how"
Knowledge (noun)	Knowing (verb)
Intellectual capacity	Practical skills
Intellectual disposition	Inherently linked to doing
Mental process	Bodily experience
Cognitively acquired knowledge	Knowledge learned in action, interactively derived

Barnett and Finnemore 2004: 24; Quack 2007), the way they apply their practical professional skills to influence global governance has received little attention. In light of this gap, the book's main theoretical ambition is to outline how practical professional knowledge is used and produced to govern new or contentious issues in operational spaces.[4]

2.3.2 Situated Learning

How do IOs create knowledge, especially on emerging topics? In line with the focus on expertise discussed above, most theories of IO knowledge seek to explain how they employ it to enhance their epistemic authority (Boswell 2008; Avant et al. 2010b; Busch and Liese 2017; Liese et al. 2021). Knowledge is commonly understood as a strategic resource in interorganizational competition for control (Sending 2015; Ban et al. 2016; Littoz-Monnet 2017a; Kranke 2022). Very little attention has been paid to how knowledge is created and by whom (Bueger 2015: 1–3; but see for example Esguerra and van der Hel 2021; Martin de Almagro 2021; Littoz-Monnet 2022). In contrast, IR's neighboring disciplines of public administration, organization, and management studies have made great efforts to understand processes of organizational learning and explain how organizations create, retain, and transmit knowledge (Nonaka and Takeuchi 1995; Argote 1999; Patriotta 2003). I draw on social learning theories in these research strands (Lave and Wenger 1991; Seely-Brown and Duguid 1991; Wenger 1998; Cook and Seely-Brown 1999) and research on street-level bureaucrats in IR (Côté-Boucher et al. 2014; Kurowska 2014; Cooper and Cornut 2019) to conceptualize global governance on the ground as the use and development of practical professional knowledge at the frontlines.

Improvisation

Moments of crisis disrupt established ways of doing and knowing (Hofius 2016: 952). They cause uncertainty because it is unclear if—and which—rules and regulations apply. They bring missing policy guidelines to the fore and engender a sense of urgency in light of looming harm or damage (see Natorski 2016: 647). During crises, IO staff thus have to improvise: To remain capable of acting, especially those working where crises are unfolding, such as borderlands, conflict zones, and embassies, are compelled to

[4] Having said that, I do not want to downplay the centrality of expertise. Instead, I would like to stress that expertise and competence are two complementary and mutually enabling forms of knowledge. I therefore set out to conceptualize how their interplay in social interactions can generate new governing practices.

try out how to deal with the issues that arise (see also Cornut 2018 whose argument is similar, but from a Bourdieusian standpoint). In their everyday work, they have to interpret new and ambiguous situations, make practical judgments, and act on them (Wagenaar 2004; Honig 2018). By trial and error, they develop the practical knowledge that enables them "to do their job" (Wenger 1998: 47) in the face of confusion, disorder, and need for action.

While these conditions are amplified by crises, they are very likely found in all work contexts, even in relatively "ordinary" times because those who put policy into practice always encounter unforeseen events and need to cope with situations left open by formal policy-makers (see Chapter 1). This means that the field—understood here broadly as operational sites where transnational professionals carry out operative work (as opposed to campaign and advocacy or administrative and programmatic work at headquarters or persuasion and bargaining in negotiating forums)—becomes an informal arena for improvisation. Learning by doing most likely occurs in the field, not only because it is more exposed to global governance's substantive problems and ultimate addressees but also because of its distance from the tight organizational cultures in IO secretariats and trade-off requirements in official decision-making arenas (see Seely-Brown and Duguid 2001: 203).

To learn by doing, fieldworkers rely on their professional expertise and skills. For trained and experienced professionals, knowledge is a key resource for handling indeterminate situations and addressing new tasks (Evetts 2003: 397). By applying this knowledge to real-world problems and interacting with other professionals in their social environment (Seely-Brown and Duguid 1991: 47–8; Nicolini 2013: 80–3), they learn to cope with challenges that can be neither delegated nor deferred.

Thus the processes of sense-making and experimenting in the field span several IOs. Especially in emergent and contentious issue areas or where IO mandates overlap and uncertainty prevails about organizational responsibilities, IO staffers closely interact with the transnational professionals who also populate this field, including those working for other IOs. Organization scholars have shown that in uncertain environments, professionals engage with other professionals in their immediate physical surroundings to cope with complex novel challenges (Blackler 1995; Adler et al. 2008: 359; Mørk et al. 2010: 578; Eyal and Pok 2015: 38). They have also demonstrated that the chances of a single profession or organization being able to take control are limited when issues have not been clearly defined. In turn, "the shared experience of interconnected action" through improvisation across organizational and professional boundaries can be an important driver for innovation in practice, even without the conscious intention to create new forms of knowing and doing (Czarniawska-Joerges 1992: 188; see also Gherardi 2000: 214; Quack 2007: 647, 660; Block-Lieb and Halliday 2017: 27; Furrusten 2017).

In that sense, these boundary-spanning dynamics are akin to what communities of practice (CoP) approaches in IR (Bicchi 2011, 2022; Græger 2016; Hofius 2016) study under "a sense of joint enterprise." Based on Emmanuel Adler's (2005, 2008) reading of Etienne Wenger's work, these scholars stress that organizational belonging fades into the background if "a group of people works really well together and comes up with innovative solutions to shared problems" (Bicchi 2022: 24). I concur with the view that being bound up in a shared work context can equal a form of self-organization that is "based on sociality among practitioners and the sharing of practical activities" (Corradi et al. 2010: 267) rather than organizational membership. However, these authors tend to emphasize socialization and the community-building dimension of joint practice. I focus instead on the *practical knowledge* it changes and creates and, following Wenger, do not assume that those who partake in moments of situated learning constitute steady, integrated social groups (Lave and Wenger 1991: 98; Wenger 1998: 96).

Finally, *disputes* are part of on-the-ground improvisation (see Kurowska 2014). Shared work can be but is not *per se* collaborative.[5] Briefly, in informal everyday work relations in operations, interorganizational and interprofessional conflict and competition, along with problem-oriented cooperation, drive situated learning—which is prompted by moments of complexity, urgency, and uncertainty and generates new, provisional ways of doing and knowing (see Seely-Brown and Duguid 1991: 54; Wenger 1998: 56; Marshall and Rollinson 2004). Therefore, the first proposition of the loop model of global governance on the ground reads:

> *(P1) When confronted with complexity, uncertainty, and urgency, IO field staff use their professional expertise and competence to improvise provisional ways of doing and knowing in informal interorganizational relations, which can be cooperative, competitive, or conflictive.*

This first proposition resonates with but differs from research on IO emergency politics (Kreuder-Sonnen 2019; Conceição-Heldt and Mueller 2021; Heupel et al. 2021). Like these authors, I investigate how IOs use crises to govern. But instead of focusing on exceptional times and the self-empowerment that leads to sudden and extensive leaps in authority

[5] For a general critique that CoP approaches overly focus on cooperation, see Fox (2000); Roberts (2006).

in response to international emergencies (such as terrorist attacks, the outbreak of infectious diseases, or the imminent collapse of the international financial system), I examine the everyday dimension of governing in moments of crisis. I propose analyzing how IOs navigate uncertainty, which I treat as an irreducible element of international politics that can be exacerbated by crises (see also Best 2012; Katzenstein and Seybert 2017). This redirects attention from actors and institutions to the way global issues become ordered as a result of managing such situations in practice.

Negotiating Competence

The dynamics of muddling through that initiate the process of situated learning are accompanied by the negotiation of competence. Improvisation is driven by impromptu actions informed by prior professional knowledge. Importantly, it goes hand in hand with claims of "knowing well" (see Adler-Nissen and Pouliot 2014: 909; Seabrooke 2014: 52). At the same time, spontaneous actions are assessed in terms of their suitability for solving specific problems: Should they pass practitioners' processes of trial and error, they are accepted as appropriate. Fieldworkers improvise in "situations characterized by novelty, deep uncertainty, and the requirement to act on the situation to find some kind of resolution that is both feasible and acceptable" (Wagenaar 2004: 649). Situated learning thus involves a reflexive as well as a strong social component (see Orlikowski 2002: 249; Bueger and Gadinger 2014: 19; Bode 2018). In brief, ad hoc improvisation is embedded in intersubjective struggles over meaning and competence, which can be summarized as my second proposition:

> *(P2) IO field staff improvise ways of knowing and doing, then assess their feasibility and appropriateness through functional and normative judgments: They collectively negotiate what they'll accept as competent practice.*

To be clear, in this understanding, what "is considered 'competent' at any moment in time and space is a normative judgment" (Gross Stein 2011: 90) and not only an assessment of expediency or practicality. Competence cannot be established by an external, functional yardstick: It must be negotiated among the professionals involved who collectively give meaning to their doing (Duvall and Chowdhury 2011: 338; Nicolini 2013: 78; Pouliot 2021: 4). In doing so, they draw on existing understandings of what counts as *good* (feasible) and *right* (appropriate) practice that stem from their work experience and their professional view of the world. By implication, frontline practice can also be viewed as ineffective or harmful (see below).

Routinizing Practice

Once a new way of doing is accepted as competent, it is likely to be repeated. Routinization reduces the burden of having to test and negotiate how to handle things that is imposed on frontline workers because they are immediately exposed to global challenges (see Friesendorf 2018). It follows that fieldworkers establish informal protocols, standard operating procedures, briefings, and on-the-job-training programs to routinize their practice.

Ultimately, on-site improvising, competence-negotiating, and routinizing results in the creation of *practices*, usually defined "as socially meaningful patterns of action, which, in being performed more or less competently, simultaneously embody, act out, and possibly reify background knowledge and discourse in and on the material world" (Adler and Pouliot 2011: 4). Practices are socially standardized, patterned actions organized around an end. They are inherently linked to knowing because that is what gives meaning to a practice. Practices empower certain courses of action over others, thereby steering behavior (Nicolini and Monteiro 2016). They emerge and change in and through practice on the ground (see also Hopf 2018; Cooper and Cornut 2019; Stappert 2020; Bueger and Edmunds 2021; Sondarjee 2021a). In line with these basic assumptions, the third proposition reads:

> *(P3) When an improvised way of doing and knowing has been accepted as competent and is routinized in the field, new practices emerge and existing ones are adapted.*

Why do practices matter? Because transnational professionals determine how global issues are treated by performing and developing practices in the field. When formal policy instructions are ambiguous, incomplete, or lacking, practices substantiate and, in some cases, replace them. The obvious implication is that the field is not just the place where decisions made elsewhere are carried out (see Autesserre 2014: 25; Bartley 2018). Because practices change—or substitute—global norms and rules (see Côté-Boucher et al. 2014: 197–8; Kentikelenis and Babb 2019; Laurence 2019; Pouliot 2021), their creation and performance are a form of policy-making in their own right. Students of street-level bureaucracy (Lipsky 1980; Hupe et al. 2015) have long called frontline workers the "ultimate policy-makers." Since they are positioned at the boundary between the state and citizens and removed from the supervision of higher-ups in organizations, they inevitably have decision-making autonomy in their jobs and enjoy wide latitude to decide which rules to follow, bend, or ignore. Their frontline status affords them considerable discretionary power in realizing policy (Maynard-Moody and Portillo 2011: 252–61). Frontline practices determine how existing policies play out in the lives of target groups and fill governance gaps where formal agreements are missing.

2.3.3 Stabilization

How are the practices that emerge at the frontlines of international challenges normalized and disseminated? How do headquarters staff get involved in shaping frontline practices? This section explores the second stage of global governance on the ground: the process of translating practices from the organization's periphery to its core and circulating it across operational sites.

Consolidation

Organization scholars have shown that practical knowledge produced at the organization's periphery is often ignored by managers high up in an organization's hierarchy who mostly conceive of knowledge as a commodifiable object. They either are unaware of or disregard local forms of knowing that are socially embedded in working and diverge from the Cartesian image of what counts as (valuable) knowledge (Seely-Brown and Duguid 1991; Yanow 2004: 11).[6] Similarly, students of organizational learning in UN peacekeeping have demonstrated that the circulation of knowledge in IOs is often obstructed by the lack of regular job rotations. Short-term contracts and limited jobs at headquarters result in experiential knowledge from the field often getting lost in translation (Benner and Rotmann 2008: 56; Goetze 2019: 352). I therefore expect that if learning from local experiences takes place at all, it happens in IO units that train fieldworkers (see also Benner and Rotmann 2008: 59; Bueger 2015: 16).[7]

Due to the work of educational sociologists who have demonstrated that knowledge flows from the world of work to the world of education mainly function through the concept of "required competences" (Pavlin et al.

[6] In Dvora Yanow's conception, "local" and "peripheral" do not necessarily pertain to geographical sites. They describe the peripheral workers outside of formal organizational decision-making centers who interact daily with people beyond the organization's formal boundaries: suppliers, customers, clients, and so on. "Local" knowledge describes practical knowledge that emerges from the close working relations of street-level practitioners and their intimate understanding of how the work is done (Yanow 2004: 15). In line with the definition of the field outlined above, I consider operative sites as the IOs' "periphery." This is where they deliver services, confront operational problems, and interact with citizens, customers, and clients: migrants and refugees, people in conflict or post-coup situations, those afflicted by global epidemics, or domestic civil servants who receive international loans and manage structural reform programs or legal reforms. This terminology does *not* imply any hierarchical ordering (see Chapter 6 for a discussion of space in global governance).

[7] Ernst and Peter Haas (1995: 262) cautioned us early on that "organizational learning is rare."

2010: 101; Young and Muller 2014), it is now widely acknowledged that abstract professional knowledge contributes little to effectively performing daily tasks at work. Thus, institutions tasked with professional training are increasingly focusing on *practical* professional knowledge and devising their learning material accordingly. One current central concern of curriculum development is professional judgment: the ability of professionals to reason, judge, and act in complex and unpredictable work situations (Winch 2014: 58). In other words, while formal, technical training remains key to professional education, practical knowledge in the form of know-how, skills, and competencies are a significant part of organizational capacity-building (see Broome and Seabrooke 2015).

This means that practices and the inherent professional practical knowledge generated in field-level operations are a central resource for staff in IO training units that design learning material. They thereby stabilize what has been learned on the ground. Translating knowledge from the field to headquarters, in turn, makes them gatekeepers in intra-organizational networks: They control the content of training tools and decisively influence how frontline practices become consolidated in organizational repertoires (Kortendiek 2021). This is why the fourth proposition reads:

> *(P4) IO staff design training programs by drawing on the practices and related practical knowledge developed by IO fieldworkers—and thereby control how frontline practices get consolidated.*

To be sure, practical knowledge cannot simply be "uprooted and repackaged for circulation" (Seely-Brown and Duguid 1991: 54; see also Gherardi and Nicolini 2016). Organization scholars stress that practical knowledge is not a fixed, static object that can be stripped from its context. And yet, as Andrew Abbott (1988: 104) himself emphasized, the professions need to perform a properly balanced abstraction of practical knowledge: To be effective, professional knowledge has to strike an equilibrium between extreme abstraction and extreme concreteness. This means it is possible to debrief fieldworkers and assist them in the process of reflecting about their on-site actions and then to translate their tacit knowledge into how-to manuals, textbooks, standard operating procedures, and other learning tools (Nicolini et al. 2003: 3, Yanow 2004: 16; see also Nonaka 1994, Lam 2000, Bernstein and van der Ven 2017). Wenger, too, points out that reification is possible for codifying knowing in practice—that is, points of focus must be created—around which the negotiation of competence becomes organized:

> Writing down a law, creating a procedure, or producing a tool is a similar process. A certain understanding is given form. This form then becomes a focus for the negotiation of meaning, as people use the law to argue a point, use the procedure to know what to do, or use the tool to perform an action. (Wenger 1998: 58–9)

Wenger stresses that although consolidation necessarily strips away some of a practice's contextualized, socially negotiated meaning, its codification in training material informs new cycles of interaction and meaning-making (as I discuss in more detail below).

This fourth proposition is related to but also differs from IR research on IO knowledge management systems (Svenson 2017; Rietig 2021) and organizational learning (Haas and Haas 1995; Hardt 2018). Like this book, both of these research strands seek to explain how knowledge is produced, retained, and transmitted in IOs. Ernst Haas (1990) was one of the first to argue that IOs need to learn to create knowledge. Following him, several authors have analyzed how IOs can learn to improve their performance, mostly in peacekeeping (Howard 2008; Benner et al. 2011; Campbell 2018). Often, they focus on barriers to successful learning whereas I am less concerned with organizational pathologies and more with how learning dynamics define issues. I also draw on different theories on learning. I see learning as a participative, situated process, whereas existing accounts mostly understand knowledge creation as the intellectual activity of structuring information about causes and effects. They regard cognitive forms of knowledge creation as "infinitely superior to trial-and-error-learning" (Haas and Haas 1995: 260). The ambition of this book is to not dismiss social learning and practical knowledge too quickly and to show that they indeed affect how global issues are governed.

Diffusion

When practical knowledge is consolidated in learning tools, it gets diffused and re-enacted across sites through fieldworker training. IO training programs not only serve to create competence but also seek to standardize the operational staff's work. Organization scholars James Faulconbridge and Daniel Muzio (2012: 143) have shown that training programs are important venues for creating transnational professional standards. They describe how global professional service firms like Clifford Chance (law), PricewaterhouseCoopers (accounting), Aedas (architecture), and Arup (engineering) use global recruitment and training schemes to guarantee consistency in their services. IOs similarly seek to professionalize the behavior of their operational staff through face-to-face training sessions, workshops, pre-deployment briefings, handbooks, and certification schemes. They aim to create uniform professional norms that enable fieldworkers to work together according to the same global standards (see also Horii 2012; Maertens 2019).

Thus, training serves as a form of top-down translation in which practices, skills, and competencies circulate across organizational sites. IO training and operations unit officers instruct fieldworkers how to govern on the ground in the absence of clear policy guidance. Through their epistemic and standard-setting practices they exert considerable influence over global governance in the field. The fifth and final proposition reads:

(P5) Through fieldworker training, IO staff in operations and learning units diffuse practices and the related practical knowledge across operational sites and instruct colleagues on the ground how to govern in practice.

Of course, training does not conclusively control or harmonize practice on the ground (see for example Weaver 2008: 4, fn. 102; Honig 2019). Just as some practical knowledge is inevitably lost, skewed, distorted, or suppressed when recorded in learning tools, training does not close off situated learning processes. Improvising, negotiating competence, and routinizing, as well as updating learning material and training are likely to continue given the precarious nature of practical knowledge, the irreducible discretionary power of frontline practitioners, and the fact that global governance is never completely ordered. I therefore propose a *loop* model of global governance on the ground (see Figure 2.1).

The loop model suggests that global governance on the ground is not concluded after passing through these five steps: Most likely it starts again. In nested cycles or feedback loops, newly emerging practical knowledge from the field—that draws on prior professional expertise and competencies—is

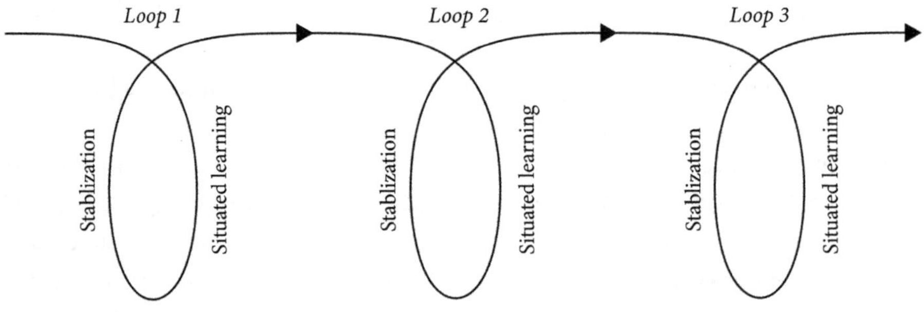

Fig. 2.1 Loops of global governance on the ground

consolidated in learning schemes. These in turn form the basis for training future cohorts of professionals deployed to missions and projects worldwide (see also Quack 2007: 644–6; Campbell 2008: 22). Once on the ground, they will have to make sense of situational circumstances and adapt their ways of knowing and doing to local demands. Situated learning on the ground cannot be foreclosed by training; nor can translation completely stabilize what has been learned in the field. Governing on the ground is an ongoing, dynamic process that responds to the immanent messiness of global affairs.[8]

One of the central caveats concerning global governance on the ground is thus that it does not inevitably happen under urgent, uncertain, or complex conditions—nor is it necessarily productive. Very possibly, when confronted with new crises, those at the frontline will ignore everything that has been learned earlier and start again from scratch. Similarly, many fieldworkers will completely fail to respond to new and ambiguous situations. As Peter Katzenstein and Lucia Seybert have demonstrated, "protean power"—the power derived from agile actors' ability to "handle the unexpected with improvisation and innovation" (2018: 81)—is not equally distributed among organizational actors. Not all fieldworkers will be able to creatively cope with uncertainty and as a result, there may be no situated learning. Or training could be poorly institutionalized in IOs and headquarters staff may choose to disregard frontline knowledge for various reasons (see for example Autesserre 2014: 72). In other words, global governance on the ground is not a progressive, unidirectional process in which practical knowledge simply accumulates. To the contrary, its provisional, informal nature makes it a governance mode that is very prone to fail. However, when successful, it determines how issues that are emerging or in a state of upheaval are governed by inter- and intra-organizational networks in practice. In some cases, it might even lead to formal institutional or policy change, such as new treaties, regulations, or mandates. Because crises often reveal the regulatory failures that have contributed to their emergence, developing new institutional solutions to redress them could become a policy priority (see Moschella and Tsingou 2013: 407; Natorski 2016).

[8] In that sense, my account is akin to socio-legal studies of globalization in sociology and international political economy that stress the iterative nature of global law-making. Halliday and Carruthers (2007), for example, prominently stressed "the recursivity of law," underlining that international norms emerge and evolve through "diagnostic struggles" among professionals, situated in different domestic and IOs, who fight over how to implement specific laws and how experiences in practice should feed back into formal law-making. Edelman and colleagues (1999) similarly emphasized the "endogeneity of legal regulation" to stress that the meaning of international norms is dependent upon what organizations and professions "do" with them.

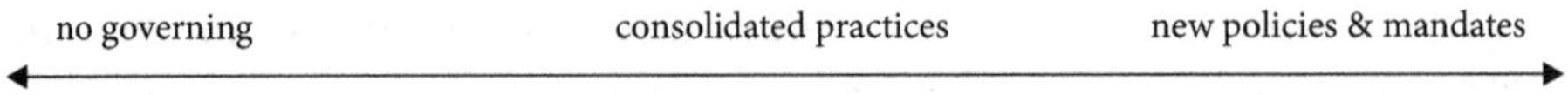

Fig. 2.2 Outcomes of global governance on the ground

In conclusion, with the loop model, I try to avoid deterministic approaches to complexity, uncertainty, and urgency—and the ensuing governing dynamics. Rather, there are several conceivable outcomes that can be placed on a continuum ranging from no governance at all, through different gradations of more or less stable and coherent organizational routines, to the formalization of practices in new policies and mandates (see Figure 2.2).

Empirical case studies are needed to determine whether global governance through practice fails to occur, whether the waves of "ad hocism" that characterize situated learning consolidate into stable governing practices that concretize and substitute formal policies, or whether practice precedes official policy-making and the extension of IO mandates. Such case studies are also needed to carefully assess *which kind* of practices come out of these instances of governing on the ground. The model developed in this chapter provides several propositions to guide these analyses. It draws attention to the power of frontline workers, translators, and trainers in IOs and provides the conceptual tools to examine whether and how they govern through practice on the ground when confronted with crises and uncertainty.

2.4 Conclusion: Studying Global Governance on the Ground

Based on the professional networks literature, knowledge- and practice-oriented approaches to organizations, and research on street-level bureaucracy in international politics, this chapter theorizes the dynamics of governing global issues at the frontlines of global challenges. It emphasizes the agency of transnational professionals in IOs that comes from their skills and personal networks, and specifies the processes they use to define what emergent, contested, or ambiguous global issues mean as a policy concern: Through situated learning on the ground and stabilization in headquarters, they produce, consolidate, and diffuse practical knowledge and routines that determine how issues are treated and also create direct regulative impacts on the lives of governance addressees.

This dynamic account of global governance seeks to uncover the governing activities in the spaces in-between formal institutions that do not necessarily cause institutional changes such as extended mandates or new policies.

It seeks to understand how IOs make use of substantive professional knowledge to govern specific issues at operational sites. To achieve this, the loop model theorizes the different stages and mechanisms through which global governance on the ground works, but not the factors that determine the long-term trajectories. Its central argument is that practice on the ground itself has governing effects. The claim is not, then, that global governance on the ground is normatively better or more effective than other modes of governance: It is not difficult to think of cases where it has gone tremendously wrong. The spread of cholera in Haiti and the multiple cases of sexual abuse by UN peacekeepers are just two recent examples of the misuse of discretionary power in the field and the failure to learn from such experiences (see Pillinger et al. 2016; Hirschmann 2019). Nor do I claim that governing through practice on the ground is uncoupled from organizational opportunities and restraints, or occurs whenever global issues are in flux. It is one thing to argue that professional competence provides IO actors with agency and that moments of uncertainty and the peripheral location of fieldworkers create permissive environments. It is quite another to assert that global governance on the ground will always take place under these circumstances. The model provides the conceptual tools to examine empirically if, how, and with what outcome IOs govern on the ground.

How, then, can we study global governance on the ground? Its dynamic, often amorphous nature begs research strategies that afford us proximity to the knowing and doing of practitioners (Ybema et al. 2009; Bueger 2014; Adler-Nissen and Eggeling 2022). Observations with different degrees of participation, interviews with people who are experts in a particular practice, and texts that are close to the experience, such as diaries, reports, internal logs, protocols, and manuals, are all suitable sources. They make it possible to reconstruct meaning-making processes and explore the tacit knowledge that organizes work practices. Recently, these ethnographic research methods have made major inroads into the study of organizations in IR (Vrasti 2008; MacKay and Levin 2015; Nair 2021). They are especially compatible with case study designs that allow for in-depth observations and thick descriptions. The extended case study that follows in Chapters 4 and 5 is based on fieldwork at the European external border in Greece during the crisis of 2015–16. To "zoom out" of practice in the field and trace how they shape global governance at the macro level (Nicolini 2009b), my fieldwork in Greece is complemented with expert interviews at the headquarters of the IOs I encountered at the border (see Annexes I and II). The book also makes extensive use of training documents to analyze which skills and routines are consolidated and diffused across operational sites (see Chapter 1 on data sources).

The theoretical argument of global governance on the ground and the loop model outlined in this chapter will hence be illustrated in depth regarding the case of mixed migration at the European external border in the empirical analysis that follows this chapter. Accordingly, this book can only offer case-specific conclusions. However, I expect that similar dynamics are also at work in the issue areas of peacekeeping, state-building, humanitarianism, disaster relief, food security, global health, environmental protection, development, and finance because the IOs that operate in these issue areas have an extended network of field offices and missions, face organizational complexity, and often have to manage unforeseen challenges and emergencies (see Chapter 1 on case selection and scope conditions).

Recently, other researchers have demonstrated that in these policy fields, experimentation and stabilization also shape IO responses to complexity, uncertainty, and urgency (e.g. Gross Stein 2011; Moschella 2015; Beerli 2018; Bode and Karlsrud 2018; Kentikelenis and Babb 2019; Laurence 2019; Maertens 2019; Bueger and Edmunds 2021). Following the Ebola outbreak in West Africa in 2014, for example, the International Organization for Migration (IOM), the World Health Organization (WHO), and Médecins Sans Frontières (MSF) deployed several hundred technical experts with various skillsets, including logistics, laboratory services, social mobilization, and clinical case management to Guinea, Liberia, and Sierra Leone. On the ground, they improvised to set up treatment centers, organize health screenings as well as case diagnosis, implement infection prevention and control measures such as sanitization and contact tracing, and find ways to organize safe and dignified burials. The fieldworkers' efforts in containing the virus were supported by UN peacekeepers as the UN Security Council extended the UN mission to Liberia (UNMIL). These on-site activities ultimately spurred institutional innovation in the form of the UN's first-ever public health mission (UN Mission for Ebola Emergency Response, or UNMEER) and—although having widely been criticized as insufficient—the response on the ground led to the institutionalization of new practices: the surveillance of population movements using so-called flow monitoring points by the IOM, to give just one example (Kamradt-Scott 2016: 404–7; Kreuder-Sonnen and Tantow 2022).

Interestingly, not only humanitarian NGOs like Oxfam and MSF, operational UN agencies such as the UN High Commissioner for Refugees (UNHCR), the IOM, the UN Office for the Coordination of Humanitarian Affairs (OCHA), UN peacekeeping, the UN Development Program (UNDP), the Food and Agricultural Organization (FAO), the UN Office on Drugs and Crime (UNODC), and other IOs with a strong decentralized structure like the WHO or the North Atlantic Treaty Organization (NATO) use their access to the field and move beyond organizational boundaries to respond to global challenges. Recent studies also point out that the staff in IMF country teams and the people working in the World Bank country offices form closer work relations with experts on the ground (e.g. economists in national bureaucracies and civil society actors) than their colleagues in the headquarters. In these local CoP, they experiment with new ways of governing which are then scaled up—e.g. new, inclusive ways of making policy decisions in consultation with civil society actors "trickled up" from Uganda to the World Bank office in Washington (Sondarjee 2021b). This research provides ample indications that governing on the ground occurs beyond the crucial case of mixed migration—suggesting that global governance on the ground is a salient empirical phenomenon for IR scholars to study.

3

Global Mixed Migration Governance

Between Institutionalization and Crisis

Mixed migration is an emerging issue in international politics. Since the 1990s, migration and displacement have increased, along with attempts to regulate the migration-asylum nexus. Mixed migration is becoming more and more acknowledged as a salient global issue but the purpose of its governance continues to be deeply contested and it is still not covered by existing mobility regimes. No legally binding treaty addresses the problems resulting from unauthorized movements in a world divided by borders, and no international organization (IO) is mandated to deal with them. Mixed migration is an issue area characterized by policy, institutional, and knowledge gaps—shortcomings that tend to trigger crisis situations whenever large movements of migrants and refugees occur.

This chapter introduces mixed migration as an empirical phenomenon and traces how it emerged as a new analytical category in order to acknowledge that migration and displacement are often difficult to separate. It offers conceptual distinctions between "mixed" and "irregular" migration, migrant smuggling, and human trafficking, and maps the migration and asylum institutional landscape, showing that it is marked by overlaps and inconsistencies. It then discusses how the absence of a clear legal-political framework exacerbates humanitarian emergencies. It ends by outlining the European migration and refugee crisis and the policy response to it.

The chapter is divided into three main parts. Section 3.1 introduces the concept of mixed migration. Section 3.2 presents the architecture of global migration governance, showing that despite recent attempts to address large migrant and refugee movements, such as the Global Compact for Migration (GCM) and the Global Compact on Refugees (GCR), mixed migration remains underregulated. Several intergovernmental organizations (IGOs), non-governmental organizations (NGOs), and regional agencies are involved in its governance, but it has no clear focal actor. Section 3.3 discusses how these regulatory voids and competence gaps lead to emergencies, and introduces the crisis at Europe's borders in 2015–16 as the most recent and far-reaching one. It outlines how the European Union responded to the crisis

Global Governance on the Ground. Nele Kortendiek, Oxford University Press. © Nele Kortendiek (2024).
DOI: 10.1093/oso/9780198889120.003.0003

and describes the "hotspots" along the Mediterranean Sea route as central sites for governing migration and asylum on the ground.

3.1 "Refugees, Migrants, Neither, Both": What Is Mixed Migration?

International migration has been increasing since the 1990s.[1] The proportion of migrants to the world's total population stagnated at around 2.3% in the 1970s and 1980s, then started to increase in the early 1990s and peaked at 3.6% in 2022 (Czaika and Haas 2015; McAuliffe and Triandafyllidou 2021: 23). In absolute numbers, 281 million people were international migrants in 2022, a considerable increase from an estimated 173 million in 2000 (McAuliffe and Triandafyllidou 2021: 40). That year, the number of people fleeing conflict and persecution exceeded 108 million: more forcibly displaced persons than the United Nations (UN) High Commissioner for Refugees (UNHCR) had registered in the seventy-two years since it was established in 1950 (UNHCR 2022: 2).[2] Both figures reveal that international migration and displacement are growing, although the vast majority of the world's population continue to live in their countries of birth.

Given these developments, many observers agree that we live in the "age of migration" (Haas et al. 2019). Yet no internationally agreed definition of "migration" exists. In its online glossary, the International Organization for Migration (IOM) explains that "migrant" is an "umbrella term, not defined under international law, reflecting the common lay understanding of a person who moves away from his or her place of usual residence, whether within a country or across an international border, temporarily or permanently, and for a variety of reasons" (IOM 2019a: 132). It further explains, "At the international level, no universally accepted definition for 'migrant' exists. The present definition was developed by IOM for its own purposes and it is not meant to imply or create any new legal category" (IOM 2019a: 132).[3] As I elaborate below, migration's deep politicization hinders legal-political agreement on its meaning.

[1] Heading title adapted from Crawley and Skleparis (2017).

[2] This number includes 62.5 million internally displaced people (IDPs): those forced to flee their homes who did not cross any international borders.

[3] The most widely accepted working definition of international migration is the rather technical one in the *1998 Recommendations on Statistics of International Migration* by the UN Department of Economic and Social Affairs (UN DESA). This definition views "any person who changes his or her country of usual residence" for at least three months to be a migrant (para. 32). This minimal definition is used to compile statistics on migration stocks and flows. The *1998 Recommendations* were recently revised by the UN Statistics Division and a task force of the UN Expert Group on Migration Statistics to better measure trends in temporary mobility, too. "Global mobility" usually refers to movements of people across international borders for any length of time or purpose, including less than three months.

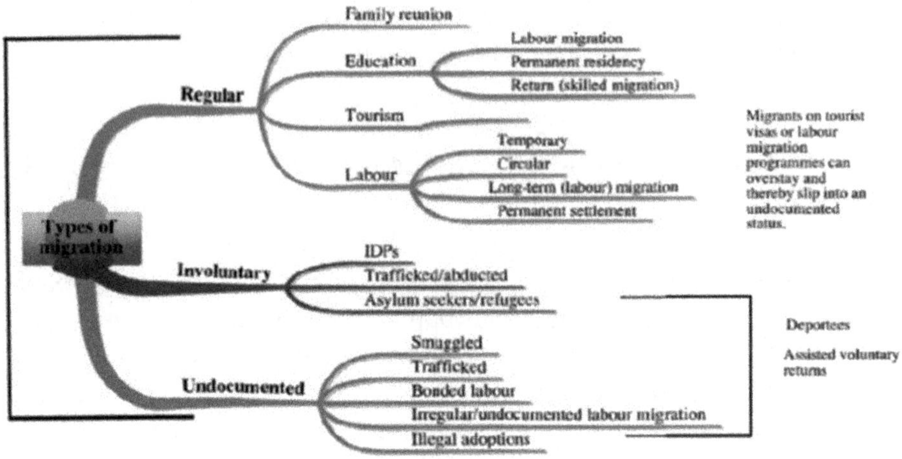

Fig. 3.1 Types of migration

Note: this figure is copyrighted by the UNDP and licensed under a Creative Commons Attribution 3.0 IGO license. For the legal code, please see <https://creativecommons.org/licenses/by/3.0/igo/legalcode>. No changes have been made to the original.
Source: UNDP (2010: 4).

Nonetheless, the UN broadly differentiates between regular, involuntary, and undocumented migration (see Figure 3.1).

It is important to stress that the largest proportion of international migration takes place voluntarily and through regular channels, including migrating to work (see Piper 2017; Ruhs 2017) and for leisure (see Koslowski 2011b; Oliver 2011), with most migrants coming from high- and middle-income countries. Yet many people leave their homes involuntarily or travel by irregular means. While the UN Department of Economic and Social Affairs (UN DESA) (2020: 6) observed that in 2020, asylum seekers and refugees accounted "for a relatively small share, 12 percent, of the total number of international migrants globally," it confirms the steady rise in the number of persons forcibly displaced across international borders. In addition, it attests that "undocumented migration is one of the fastest growing forms of migration in the world today" (as quoted in Düvell 2011: 78). In other words, migrants make up only a very small proportion of the world's population, the vast majority of whom travel by regular means. Yet both undocumented and forced migration are on the rise.

3.1.1 Mixed Migration as an Empirical Phenomenon

Undocumented and forced migration are increasingly hard to separate in practice. People unable to travel through humanitarian corridors or resettlement programs and those who cannot access labor migration programs and other regularized options clandestinely cross "green" borders or travel with false documents. They use simple means of transport, such as buses, trains, dinghies, and fisher boats—and travel long distances by foot. In many instances, they rely on smuggling networks to help them cross seas, rivers, mountains, and deserts without being apprehended by border police.

Examples of such unauthorized movements include mainly Syrians, Iraqis, and Afghans traveling through Turkey, Bulgaria, and the Balkans—or across the Eastern Mediterranean Sea—to reach Europe, as well as the "migrant caravan" in Central America with thousands of migrants mainly from Honduras, Guatemala, and El Salvador who walk over 4,000 kilometers to the US-Mexican border because they've lost their livelihoods to droughts or have been threatened with violence (Kingsley 2016). Another recent example is the mass exodus from Venezuela in 2018, when three million people fled political conflict, a rapidly collapsing economy, and severe food and medical shortages—mainly to neighboring Central and Southern American countries (Selee et al. 2019). East Africa is another hub of complex patterns of irregular migration (MMTF Somalia 2008; MMC East Africa & Yemen 2019), with many people traveling north from the Horn of Africa through Sudan to Libya and along the Central Mediterranean toward Southern Europe. They also move east, crossing the Gulf of Aden and the Red Sea to reach Yemen and then Saudi Arabia and Persian Gulf countries, whereas people fleeing civil war in Yemen have been moving west toward Eastern Africa. In Southeast Asia, many low-skilled migrant workers move from India, Pakistan, Sri Lanka, Nepal, and Bangladesh toward the Gulf mostly to work in construction or as domestics. Many Muslim migrant workers from Indonesia and Pakistan, as well as the politically persecuted Rohingya of Myanmar, travel to Malaysia irregularly. Indonesia is a major transit country for people from the entire region attempting to reach Australia by boat (MMC Asia 2019). In short, irregular migration movements occur in and connect all the regions of the world.[4]

A large percentage of people move irregularly to flee conflict and persecution and thus have legally recognized reasons to claim asylum. Although their *movement* is "irregular," on reaching the territory of a safe country they can obtain regular refugee status. Others, by contrast, are forced to leave home due to political strife, gang violence, forced conscription, or because they have lost their livelihoods through natural disasters or environmental

[4] It is important to stress that irregular (or mixed) migration—with its very complex patterns—is *not* primarily directed to Europe. Such a characterization is oversimplified and Eurocentric. See Haas (2008); Düvell (2012).

degradation. Still others seek economic betterment. The manifold reasons for irregular migration often interlink.

Motives and experiences often change en route. Many irregular travelers experience abuse while on the move: UN agencies and NGOs report that irregular migrants are kidnapped and extorted, detained and tortured in prison-like camps, with many, especially females, raped by state officials, armed groups, smugglers, and traffickers. Some are brutalized or sexually assaulted by border police or private militias; others are left in unseaworthy boats or left to die in the desert without food or water. Other forms of abuse and exploitation include unlawful killings, forced labor, and forced organ harvesting (IOM 2017a; UN General Assembly 2017; UNSMIL and OHCHR 2018; MMC Asia 2019: 8–9). The term "mixed migration" was conceived to cover the various intricate drivers and patterns of irregular migration movements that straddle the "forced/voluntary" distinction.

3.1.2 Mixed Migration as an Analytical Category

The term mixed migration first emerged as an analytical concept in the late 1990s, primarily to soften the dichotomy of "forced" and "voluntary" migration that has structured the academic and public discourse, as well as policy regimes on international migration, since the 1950s (van Hear 2011: 2–3). The distinction between those forced to flee and all other types of migrants was instituted with the refugee regime established after the Second World War (Karatani 2005; Long 2013). In the late 1990s, researchers started to criticize the stark distinction between refugees and migrants as a legal-political construct that does not accurately reflect much of contemporary human mobility (van Hear 1998).[5] In the following years, scholars and international practitioners such as Jeff Crisp, the UNHCR's head of Policy Development and Evaluation Service at the time, started to rethink the asylum-migration nexus (Türk 2002; Crisp 2008) and coined the term "mixed migration."

"Mixed" refers to two dimensions (see Sharpe 2018). First, it denotes the fact that *motives* for migrating cannot be neatly separated into categories such as economic objectives on the one hand and experiences of human rights violations, oppression, and persecution on the other. The reasons for irregular migration include a spectrum of motives—from forced to voluntary. Second, refugees, asylum seekers, stateless persons, returnees, victims of trafficking, unaccompanied children, low-skilled migrant workers,[6] "climate refugees,"

[5] On the politics of labeling people on the move, see Zetter (2007); Koch (2013); Crawley and Skleparis (2017); Meyer and Boll (2018); Mourad and Norman (2020).

[6] In fact, *low-skilled* labor migrants are usually just *low-paid*. Many have very specific skill sets that are poorly remunerated. In addition, many high-skilled migrants and refugees often work in low-skilled

and other (non-classified) types of migrants often travel together with no official authorizations to cross borders and rely on the same brokers and agents to help them pass. Irregular migration *flows* are also mixed (IOM 2008: 2; van Hear 2011: 2).

These descriptions indicate that mixed movements are a specific form of undocumented or *irregular* migration, which is typically defined as a "cross-border flow of people who enter a country without that country's legal permission to do so" (Vollmer 2011: 1). However, the term "irregular migrant" also refers to migrants who have entered a country legally but slipped into illegality by overstaying their visa or residence permits, working without permits, or being born to undocumented immigrants (Düvell 2008: 486–8; Fargues 2009; Anderson and Ruhs 2010: 176–7; LeVoy and Geddie 2010: 87). In contrast, mixed migration always involves illegal border crossing. A second important conceptual difference is that while the term "mixed" always refers to migrants who *enter* a country irregularly, such persons can become regularized by claiming asylum and obtaining refugee status or subsidiary protection.[7]

Mixed migration also cannot be equated with *migrant smuggling*. Although mixed migrants regularly rely on smuggling networks, they could in fact have made the entire journey on their own. Finally, for analytical clarity, mixed migration must be differentiated from *human trafficking*, which is defined as the transportation of persons by means of threat, coercion, abduction, fraud, or deception for the purpose of exploitation. This definition excludes voluntary agreements between a migrant and a smuggler (Triandafyllidou and Maroukis 2012: 4–7). Although trafficking victims may have been or might become part of mixed movements at some point along their journey, trafficking is a small and very specific part of mixed migration.

3.2 Falling between the Cracks: Mixed Migration in Global Governance

As the previous section clarifies, legal-political distinctions characterize mixed migration as an empirical phenomenon and an analytical category. At the same time, mixed migration is not part of established migration regimes (see Figure 3.2): existing regulations negatively define mixed migration without explicitly addressing it.

and low-paid jobs despite their educational and professional qualifications. See Ruhs and Martin (2008); Newland and Riester (2018).

[7] The terms "illegal migration" and "illegal" migrant have largely been removed from the political and analytical vocabulary for being discriminatory. Committing an illegal act does not make someone "illegal." See Anderson and Ruhs (2010).

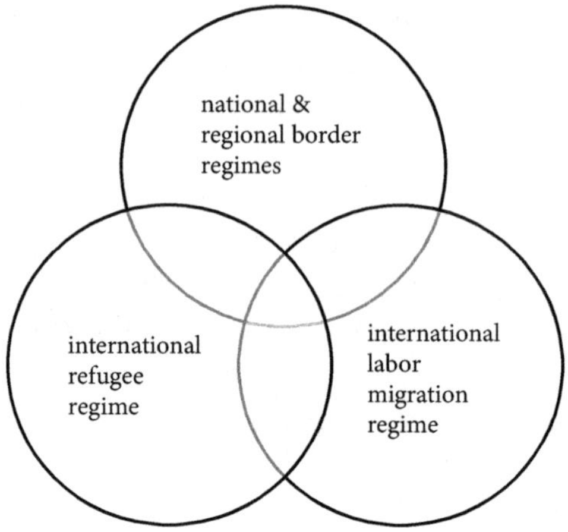

Fig. 3.2 Migration regimes

Source: My own, based on Koslowski (2011a)'s conceptualization of mobility regimes.

Mixed migration is not covered by the three main regimes that regulate global mobility: the border, labor migration, and refugee regime (Koslowski 2011a). It either contradicts their central provisions or falls outside their scope. First, it runs counter to the national and regional ***border regimes*** that set the rules for entering a state's territory.[8] They determine which types of identity and transit documents, such as passports and visas, are required for passing through official border crossing points. Increased (irregular) migration has led to more complex border control systems that rely on sophisticated security technology, such as e-passport and satellite communication systems, drones, and electronic databases (Andersson 2016; Zaiotti 2016b). Most states and the EU (Directive 2001/51) have introduced carrier sanctions that oblige railroad, shipping, and commercial aviation companies to control travelers' documents at the point of embarkation—effectively turning the staff into private first-line immigration officers (Rodenhäuser 2014). In addition, border controls at unofficial entry points have been reinforced (Lutterbeck 2006) through intricate physical walls and "virtual fences" made of camera towers, radars, ground sensors, and aerial surveillance. They also exploit natural barriers like deserts, rivers, and the sea (Koslowski 2011c: 1). Many border surveillance and patrol measures aim at intercepting and

[8] The border regime is sometimes called the "travel regime." Importantly, *national* border regimes always involve *international* cooperation. See Koslowski (2011b) and Fine (2018). On the increasing trend of fostering international partnerships to "externalize" borders, especially the joint European border that delineates the Schengen Area, see Lavenex (2004, 2015).

returning undocumented migrants before they reach a state's physical border and try to deter all attempts to cross (Boswell 2003; Gammeltoft-Hansen 2014; Little and Vaughan-Williams 2017). Thus, national and regional border regimes mainly aim to facilitate the smooth processing of "bona fide travelers" while detecting and preventing irregular movements. However, research shows that more sophisticated and restrictive border control systems do not curb irregular movements (Czaika and Hobolth 2016; Triandafyllidou 2018). Border regimes define mixed migration *ex negativo* by prohibiting those movements but they can neither stop them nor do they offer any institutional solutions to the public challenges they pose.

What about the ***international labor migration regime***? With some 60–70% of all international migrants being migrant *workers* (IOM 2017c: 28; McAuliffe and Triandafyllidou 2021: 11), a "thin layer of multilateralism" emerged, especially around the World Trade Organization's (WTO) General Agreement on Trade in Services (GATS) and the Global Forum for Migration and Development (GFMD) (Betts and Cerna 2011: 62; Toksöz 2018). In addition, several regional and bilateral programs, often negotiated with the IOM's help, regulate labor migration (Betts and Cerna 2011: 64–6; Kuptsch and Martin 2011: 42): An international labor migration regime is in the making. However, it mainly concerns high-skilled labor—"professional, technical, kindred and related workers" with higher education diplomas and specialized expertise, such as health professionals, IT specialists, and engineers (Martin et al. 2006). High-income states are often reluctant to formally cooperate on international migration but are "competing for a relatively small pool of highly qualified workers willing to migrate" (Ruhs and Martin 2008: 254) and thus agree to legal migration pathways like "Green Cards" in the US and "Blue Cards" in the EU for this group. Bilateral labor migration programs available to low-skilled workers, such as guest worker programs or temporary labor agreements for seasonal workers, complement the high-skilled labor migration schemes but accord fewer rights and protection mechanisms *vis-à-vis* recruiters, employers, and the host state (Ruhs 2017). That means that low- and unskilled workers often cannot access legal migration channels and have scant protection from international conventions (Newland and Riester 2018: 3). While in 1990, the UN General Assembly adopted the International Convention on the Protection of the Rights of All Migrant Workers and Members of Their Families, which codifies rights for migrants, including those living and working abroad irregularly, thirty-four years later, only fifty-nine states—mostly in West Africa and Latin America—have ratified it. No high-income-receiving states in the Global North or Gulf States are parties to the convention. The international labor migration regime has a weak institutional base (Koslowski 2011a: 5) that is tailored to facilitate the movement of highly qualified professionals and does not address the broader issues regarding mixed migration.

Mixed migration also falls outside the boundaries of the ***international refugee regime*** that provides protection mechanisms for forcibly displaced populations and, in contrast to the labor migration regime, has a strong legal-institutional base. Its two cornerstones are the 1951 UN Convention Relating to the Status of Refugees and its 1967 Protocol and the UNHCR, the convention's "guardian." The almost universally ratified Refugee Convention defines a "refugee" as a person who is forced to flee

> owing to well-founded fear of being persecuted for reasons of race, religion, nationality, membership of a particular social group or political opinion, is outside the country of his nationality and is unable or, owing to such fear, is unwilling to avail himself of the protection of that country.

It also sets out a number of refugee rights, the most important of which is the right to non-refoulement: the right to not be returned to a country where you risk persecution. As a principle of customary international law, non-refoulement is understood to be binding on all states, who have "a duty to offer, at minimum, temporary protection to refugees on their territory" (Loescher and Milner 2011: 192). No one can be returned or rejected before their claim of being persecuted has been assessed individually. However, the convention only spells out rights for people "outside the country of their nationality"—it does not stipulate *how they got there*. That is why most asylum seekers travel through irregular channels. Some scholars call this the "asylum paradox": to be able to make use of the right to claim asylum, you first have to break the law by illegally crossing international borders (Endres de Oliveira 2016; Moreno-Lax 2017). This is a fundamental flaw in the international refugee regime, which fails to cover the complex challenges of mixed migration.

Further, the 1951 convention provides relatively few grounds for being recognized as a refugee. Although it outlines determination procedures and eligibility criteria for refugee status, providing crucial means to access international protection, the definition of an international refugee excludes war and other forms of violent conflict. It merely stipulates a direct—individual—threat. Regional refugee conventions of the African Union (AU) and the Organization of American States (OAS) have enlarged the refugee definition to include "external aggression, internal civil strife or events seriously disturbing public order" (AU 1969: Art. 1(2)) as well as "generalized violence" and the "massive violation of human rights" (OAS 1984: III, 3). The UNHCR has largely adopted the more extensive regional refugee definitions, acknowledging these as legitimate causes of forced displacement in its practice (Loescher and Milner 2011: 192). Yet this still excludes a large number of mixed migrants of UNHCR protection (see for example Koch 2013). Mixed migration continues to be a "missing regime" (Hollifield 2000; Ghosh 2007).

In sum, we can only see and know mixed migration if we understand how mobility is currently governed. National, regional, and international regimes negatively define it because mixed movements either happen in spite of existing rules or fall outside the scope of international conventions.

3.2.1 All and None: The Fragmented Mixed Migration Governance Architecture

Despite the lack of a formal regime, several organizations and policies *do* address mixed movements—at least partially. Below I sketch how the UNHCR, the IOM, and other IGOs, regional agencies, and non-state actors deal with mixed migration. I outline soft law initiatives and discuss how the Global Compact for Migration and the Global Compact on Refugees seek to foster international cooperation on migration and asylum.

Intergovernmental Organizations

Several IGO mandates touch upon questions of mixed movement: the ***UNHCR*** is explicitly mandated to protect refugees and find long-term solutions to their plight (Betts et al. 2012: 82). Its main task is to promote "improvement of the refugee situation" and to develop normative guidelines and treaties for protecting refugees (Barnett 2002: 247): the organization has a normative mandate with policy-making powers (Hall 2015). Yet, as discussed above, its jurisdiction is restricted to asylum seekers, refugees, and stateless people. It has no mandate for other types of migrants. In fact, the UNHCR has actively tried to maintain the separation between refugees and migrants, fearing that protection mechanisms for refugees and asylum seekers would be watered down if they were no longer treated separately (UNHCR 2007b; Crisp 2008). While it initially insisted that "refugees are not migrants" (Feller 2005) and argued that "by 'lumping' them together, refugees are at risk of being considered unwelcomed irregular movers who do not deserve the rights they are conferred under international law" (van der Klaauw 2010: 60), the UNHCR has begun to acknowledge the *mixed* nature of migration and displacement. Continuing to stress that it "does not consider itself to be a migration organization" (UNHCR 2007b: 1), the UNHCR recognizes that patterns of human mobility have become increasingly complex, that there are multiple reasons to flee, and that the organization can only fulfill its mandate by engaging with global migration. Although the only people of official concern to the UNHCR remain refugees, asylum seekers, and stateless persons, the agency now often refers to its constituency as "people on the move" (Crisp 2009: 74) because of "a broad consensus that the traditional UNHCR notion of 'people who are in need of protection' can no longer be restricted to refugees" (Crisp 2008: 7; see also van der Klaauw 2010: 61).

Without being explicitly authorized by member states to extend its mandate beyond the narrowly defined area of forced migration, the UNHCR slowly began to engage with mixed migration. In 2001, with other IGOs and NGOs, it led a consultative process to explore global protection mechanisms for mixed migrants (Türk 2002) and established an asylum and migration unit at UNHCR headquarters. In its operational activities, the UNHCR has been developing ways to protect migrants traveling irregularly and, for instance, provides shelter to all people on the move. It is also developing guidelines and training operational staff to implement protection and humanitarian assistance in mixed migration contexts (see Annex II for a description of IO training mandates and programs). However, one of the UNHCR's main activities remains identifying "legitimate" asylum seekers and refugees in mixed flows to ensure that they are treated separately from migrants not deemed to need international protection (UNHCR and IOM 2001; UNHCR 2007a). In short, the UNHCR is increasingly supporting vulnerable migrants, mainly by addressing their humanitarian needs, while also continuing to reproduce the legal-political distinctions between migrants and refugees that produce mixed migration in the first place.

The main IGO working on international migration, the ***IOM***, has also recognized that mixed migration poses a key challenge to its work (IOM 2008, 2009a, 2015). Founded in 1951 as a purely intergovernmental, projectized organization with no formal links to the UN system or any policy-making mandate, during the New York Summit in 2016 it joined the UN as a "related organization" (UN General Assembly 2016). Henceforth styling itself as the "UN Migration Agency," its new agreement with the UN did not fundamentally change the IOM's non-normative nature (Bradley 2021). The IOM was tasked with facilitating the intergovernmental negotiations on the Global Compact for Migration (see below) but was not endowed with a new mandate or organizational structure. Observers therefore consider the IOM and the UN to have "unfinished business" (Guild et al. 2017; see also Bradley et al. 2022: 36).

Since the IOM did not receive any formal policy-making powers on joining the UN, its core activities with respect to mixed movements remain logistical operations, such as assisted voluntary return and reintegration (AVRR) and border governance. In other words, it continues to mainly assist governments—not migrants. However, the IOM is doing more and more to support vulnerable people on the move, such as victims of trafficking or children who are unaccompanied or have been separated from their parents. The IOM provides these groups with direct services such as family tracking. Its Department of Operations and Emergencies also provides humanitarian assistance in post-conflict situations. Having entered the "humanitarian market place," it now provides support to various displaced communities, including refugees (Betts 2013): The IOM trains field staff to manage camps, provide psychosocial support to individuals in need, and assist refugees and internally displaced people (IDPs) in informal and urban settlements. It has been able to expand its tasks into the issue area of mixed migration because its constitution does not legally define the target populations (see Bradley 2021: 254).

The IOM has also set up a number of regional Migration Response Centers, including eight in Ethiopia, Somalia, and Djibouti, and with the UNHCR, chairs the Mixed Migration Task Force (MMTF) that coordinates the field missions of different IOs in East and North Africa (IOM 2017b; IOM Nairobi n.d.). In West Africa, the IOM tracks mixed migration movements through "Flow Monitoring Points"—for example in Mali, Niger, and Chad, which are central transit states and countries where mixed movements originate (IOM Regional Office for West and Central Africa 2018). It also established IOM Transit Centers, including one in the major migration hub of Agadez, Niger, that provide provisional shelter for people on the move and organize returns. Transit Centers also educate migrants about the dangers of irregular travel (IOM 2016). Often funded by receiving states, IOM information campaigns aim to protect migrants—mostly to prevent them from moving on (see Pécoud 2010). The IOM also collects data on mixed movements: its Displacement Tracking Matrix (DTM) gauges irregular migration by compiling apprehension statistics (IOM DTM 2018). Since 2014, the Missing Migrants Project has been recording people who have died or gone missing while migrating (Brian and Laczko 2014). These activities have gradually made the IOM a crucial actor for governing mixed movements.

Less central players for mixed migration governance include the International Labor Organization (ILO) and the Vienna-based IGO International Centre for Migration Policy Development (ICMPD). The ***ILO***'s main focus is labor migration and protecting migrant workers, including in contexts of mixed migration (UNHCR and ILO 2001; ILO 2016).[9] It also addresses regular and irregular crisis migration, as well as the link between migration and development. However, in comparison to the UNHCR and the IOM, the ILO's normative and operational activities are limited: as a UN agency with an independent mandate to set labor standards for the global workforce and an autonomous bureaucracy, it plays a minor role in global migration governance. This is mainly because as global mobility regimes were being instituted in the inter- and post-war years, powerful donor states acted to marginalize the ILO's role in migration. The US and the United Kingdom (UK) in particular refused to support a global migration bureaucracy—preferring bilateral agreements instead—and thus thwarted the ILO's plan to become the world's migration agency (Karatani 2005: 522–36; Piper 2017: 378). The ***ICMPD*** is a small IGO specialized in facilitating intergovernmental dialogue and cooperation on migration issues, as well as capacity building. Mostly working with European states, it concentrates on border governance and migration management. Like the ILO, ICMPD operations are limited; within the global mixed migration governance architecture, it mostly helps states receiving migrants to design and harmonize policies for streamlining entry controls, combat the root causes of undocumented migration, and control irregular movements. It helps states develop strategies to intercept, detain, and return unauthorized migrants and fight smuggling networks (ICMPD 2007; Hess 2010).

Other UN agencies and IGOs whose mandates deal with individual aspects of international migration—including the WTO, the World Bank, the Office of the High Commissioner for Human Rights (OHCHR), the UN Office on Drugs and Crime (UNODC), UN Women, the UN Children's Fund (UNICEF), and the International Maritime Organization (IMO)—have also become increasingly involved with mixed migration. In 2006, a UN forum, the ***Global Migration Group (GMG)***, was established to coordinate their activities on matters including organizing remittances, protecting migrants' human rights, and assisting border governance as well as female migrants and refugees, children on the move, and search and rescue (SAR) at sea. It pools

[9] The ILO adopted three conventions on migrant workers: the 1949 Migration for Employment Convention (No. 97), the 1975 Migrant Workers Convention (No. 143), and the 2011 Domestic Workers Convention (No. 189).

UN expertise and organizes joint initiatives on such topics.[10] Similar to the IGOs and UN agencies that cooperate in the GMG, institutionalized *intergovernmental* collaboration takes place in the ***Global Forum on Migration and Development (GFMD)***, which is informal, voluntary, and consultative. Both the GMG and the GFMD have purely coordinative functions. They create a thin layer of "facilitative multilateralism" on international migration, including mixed flows (Betts 2011: 11; see also Rother 2009; Kalm 2010a). They do not enhance operational cooperation on mixed movements and the tension within and between the two bodies (Kainz and Betts 2021: 76–7) exemplifies the contested nature of international migration.

Non-Governmental Organizations

The two main global forums stimulated new transnational NGO coalitions on mixed migration. Civil society actors have little formal access to the GMG and the GFMD (see Kalm 2010b) but they formed global umbrella organizations like the NGO Committee on Migration and MADE, the Migration and Development Civil Society Network, which grew out of the GFMD Civil Society Days (Rother 2009). These networks promote changes in migration policy and practices to protect the dignity and rights of *all* people on the move. Generally, humanitarian, refugee, and migration NGOs, such as the Norwegian Refugee Council (NRC), Save the Children, the Scalabrini International Migration Network (SIMN), and the International Catholic Migration Commission (ICMC), as well as SAR NGOs like Sea Watch and SOS Méditerranée increasingly advocate the protection of vulnerable migrants, irrespective of motive and legal status. They implement humanitarian projects to protect people in mixed flows and train staff to conduct SAR missions and provide humanitarian and legal assistance for all people on the move (Borton and Collison 2017). Finally, more and more migrants and refugees are organizing transnationally to represent themselves at the international level (Rother and Steinhilper 2019). These various activities indicate that the remits of humanitarian assistance, the protection of asylum seekers and refugees, and migration politics are increasingly overlapping in the advocacy and operational work of non-state actors.

Regional and "Soft Law" Mechanisms

Finally, regional initiatives, such as the state-led ***Regional Consultative Processes*** (RCPs) and actors like the European Asylum Support Office

[10] With the adoption of the migration and refugee compacts, the GMG was transferred into the UN Network on Migration (see below) that is now also tasked with overseeing their implementation.

(EASO)[11] and the European Border and Coast Guard Agency (Frontex) are also playing more important roles in mixed migration. RCPs are nonbinding, informal dialogues for building personal networks among government officials and foster common understanding of what global migration is and how to deal with it (Kneebone 2014; see also Lavenex and Piper 2019). They also serve as voluntary, confidential arenas for state representatives to discuss mixed migration challenges.

EASO and Frontex are expanding their operational functions in mixed migration governance (see Marchetti 2010; Lavenex 2015): ***Frontex*** deploys border personnel to the European external border to apprehend people traveling irregularly, register their information, and possibly return them. It collects data on mixed flows and trains European border guards to patrol borders, register, screen, and debrief people on the move, and conduct return operations. Frontex also trains actors outside the EU to do the same thing: For example, it teaches the Libyan Coast Guard how to intercept migrant smugglers and human traffickers (see Kalkman 2021: 168–9). ***EASO***, the EU agency that helps member states process asylum claims, deploys and trains European asylum experts, interviewers, and caseworkers. Under the EU's Global Approach to Migration and Mobility (GAMM) and European Neighborhood Policy, EASO is also strengthening the asylum and reception capacities of non-EU countries. Although created to only assist national administrators, EASO is becoming an important international actor in its own right: EASO directly influences EU asylum decision-making processes by providing information about asylum seekers' countries of origin (van der Kist et al. 2019). It also more or less autonomously processes asylum claims at the EU external border. Through bi- and multilateral agreements, EASO is becoming increasingly active in third countries, which means that like Frontex, it has impacts beyond Europe (see Tsourdi 2020: 507–8).[12]

New regional mixed migration institutions have also been created. At the Horn of Africa and in the Euro-Mediterranean region, the NGO Danish Refugee Council (DRC) founded the Mixed Migration Centre (MMC), while in Egypt, the Mixed Migration Hub (MHUB) brings together the DRC, the UNHCR, the IOM, and other UN agencies and NGOs such as Save the Children to collect data and draft policy recommendations.

These regional and interregional activities are viewed as building blocks for global migration governance and, particularly in the area of irregular migration, are "either a step towards the emergence of a global approach or a

[11] Now renamed the EU Agency for Asylum (EUAA); see Chapter 5.

[12] See Annex II for a full description of their training mandates and Chapter 5 for a discussion of how the general mandates of Frontex and EASO have expanded since the crisis.

facet of more or less coordinated global policies" (Düvell 2011: 79). Beyond that, several soft law mechanisms to protect mixed migrants have been created (Betts 2010; Martin and Callaway 2011: 233–9), including the Migrants in Countries in Crisis Initiative (MICIC), a consultative, state-led program facilitated by the IOM, which has developed guidelines to assist migrants who transit, live, work, or study in countries beset by conflict or natural disasters.[13]

The Global Compacts for Migration and on Refugees

The most recent and explicit attempt to tackle mixed movements at the global level came in response to the European migration and refugee crisis (see below). On September 19, 2016, the UN General Assembly convened the UN Summit for Refugees and Migrants in New York. Unanimously adopted, the outcome document—the "New York Declaration"—launched a two-year intergovernmental process of formal and informal consultations with state and non-state actors around the world. It resulted in the adoption of two compacts, one on migration, the other for refugees, in separate intergovernmental conferences held in December 2018 in Marrakesh (Ferris and Donato 2020; Micinski 2021).

The Global Compact on Refugees (GCR) focuses on burden sharing between countries close to displacement crises and states which, due to geographical distance, usually host fewer refugees. With the UNHCR overseeing the negotiations, it was not openly contested—largely because it does not fundamentally alter the international refugee regime. In the run-up to the New York Summit, the UNHCR was expected to also address the narrow definition of "refugee" in the UN Refugee Convention but did not. Despite acknowledging the rise in mixed flows and the need for more comprehensive protection mechanisms, the UNHCR preferred to not open the Pandora's box of the refugee definition (see Gammeltoft-Hansen 2019; Lavenex 2020: 681–3).

The ***Global Compact for Safe, Orderly and Regular Migration*** (GCM) is the first international agreement on migration and thus drew much greater attention from the general public than the GCR. Its twenty-three objectives range from relatively technical and uncontroversial issues, such as promoting better data collection on mixed flows and ensuring that migrants travel with valid documentation, to political topics, such as making people on the move less vulnerable and migration routes safer. The GCM is non-binding: governments are free to decide how to implement its objectives, leading Kathleen Newland to describe it as "at best, the softest of

[13] Due to its influence on such soft law initiatives, scholars like Bradley (2021: 267–8) question whether the IOM is "non-normative"; see also Bradley et al. (2022: 34–7).

soft law" (Newland 2018: 660). Despite its non-legal nature, various countries either dropped out of the negotiations or abstained from endorsing the final documents, most notably the US, Israel, Hungary, Poland, and the Czech Republic, as well as Australia, Singapore, Austria, and Italy—all citing concerns about sovereignty. Nonetheless, the compact managed to initiate institutional changes (Kainz and Betts 2021: 81), for instance, the New York Declaration commissioned the IOM to lead the GCM negotiations, a new political task for the organization, which was also tasked with overseeing the GCM's implementation. The IOM now chairs the UN Migration Network, which replaced the GMG in 2018, and coordinates implementation efforts among states, UN agencies, and other IGOs, including the World Bank.

In sum, these compacts are the first agreements to address asylum *and* migration. Their endorsement by most states means they are indisputably "landmark achievements" (Micinski 2021: 2; see also Newland 2018). However, drafting and adopting two *separate* compacts entrenches the distinction between migrants and refugees that the concept of "mixed migration" seeks to overcome (see Carling 2018; Costello 2018; Oelgemöller 2021). Two close observers of the negotiations conclude that we have "still-separate global regimes on refugees and migration" (Ferris and Donato 2020: 1) and, "[g]iven that a major global governance challenge is how to respond to *mixed* movements, it is striking that the two compacts largely sidestep this issue" (Ferris and Donato 2020: 128; emphasis added). In other words, despite recent regional and international efforts to deal with mixed migration politically, there are still no comprehensive, integrated, or binding solutions and no IO is explicitly mandated to manage mixed flows. Several IGOs and NGOs have started to work on some aspects of mixed migration but its governance remains complex and fragmentary. Different formal and informal norms and bodies coexist at different levels of governance, forming a "kaleidoscope of institutions" (Pécoud and Thiollet 2023: 1) "without a clear hierarchical ordering principle" (Kainz and Betts 2021: 66). There is still no robust multilateral framework on mixed migration.

3.2.2 The Politics of Mixed Migration: What's at Stake?

More generally speaking, the legal-institutional patchwork of mixed migration governance reflects the fragmented architecture governing international migration (see Koser 2010; Newland 2010; Micinski and Weiss 2017; Triandafyllidou 2017; Kainz and Betts 2021; Pécoud and Thiollet

2023). This trend to "work within the existing tapestry of international organizations" (Betts 2011: 15) instead of creating a dedicated agency for (mixed) migration can be traced to its highly politicized nature and uncertainty about what its governance should achieve. In the words of a UNHCR staff member:

> My personal view [is that] the global migration architecture does not work very well. I also think that that is partially deliberate because states don't know what migration is and what they want to get out of it. [...] I think a lot of the migration governance architecture has sort of sprung up to fill perceived gaps or to work on discrete projects and so it sort of has bubbled up a little bit everywhere, which is why we have so many different bodies. I mean [a] World Migration Organization has definitely been discussed before but there is no political will for it. [...] So I think this is a political rather than [...] an institutional question. [...] It's quite deliberate that there is not a strong and centralized mechanism. (I-33, Annex II)

This statement indicates that mixed migration is a complex challenge involving a plethora of societal and political issues. Its governance "faces a principle paradox of our time: whilst politics of globalization promote the free flow of goods, capital, and information, the flow of people is subject to myriad restrictions" (Düvell 2011: 101; see also Geddes 2021: 119). It conflicts with the deterritorialization of several policy fields like trade, finance, and communication on one hand and a state-based organization of the international system on the other. Reconciling the dynamics of globalization and the dissolution of boundaries with a sovereign ordering of the world is a major challenge. Because migration policy-making often presents fundamental questions about the global political order and claims high sovereignty costs, it is particularly difficult to agree on specific migration policies or create new organizational competencies.

In addition, mixed migration is linked to questions of economic development, security, humanitarianism, and human rights. Therefore, both the global public good that its governance should produce and its normative regulative principle are highly contested (Martin and Martin 2006; Macdonald 2015; Bauböck et al. 2022). Generally speaking, mixed migration involves two conflicting policy objectives: (a) the protection of people on the move and (b) the control, prevention, and combating of irregular migration (see Chapters 4 and 5). Some actors consider "the mass casualties of refugees and migrants in the course of their flight" and "a quasi-generalized regime of impunity, worsened by an absence of accurate data on the dead and missing" as the central issues (UN General Assembly 2017: 2). Other actors stress that mixed migration creates security threats: for example, irregular flows could harbor foreign fighters and terrorists. After the 9/11 attacks, migration became increasingly securitized (Huysmans 2000). No decision has been made about whether the global governance of mixed migration is supposed to provide international security and bolster public order by closely monitoring cross-border movements, provide migrants with individual rights to protect them from abuse en route and in host communities, or address the labor market needs of receiving states, ensure remittances to further develop the countries of origin, and reduce global social inequalities (see also Ghosh 2007; Cusumano 2019; Bauböck et al. 2022; Pécoud and Thiollet 2023: 3). These trade-offs prevent agreement on the political meaning of mixed migration.

Power asymmetries and diverging interests between states also often block international decision-making on mixed migration. All countries send, function as transit areas for, and receive migrants. But major power imbalances prevail between the low- and middle-income countries of the "Global South," where migration often originates, and the high-income countries in the "Global North," where migration is often directed (Betts 2011: 22). Poverty is deemed a primary cause of international migration, with emigration a way to alleviate the pressures of high unemployment (Thouez 2003: 5). Economic disparities are still considered to be essential drivers of mixed migration, which economically and politically powerful states often try to restrict. Exacerbating these political concerns are domestic opposition in receiving states, where migrants and refugees are perceived as economic or cultural threats (see Kortendiek and Oertel 2023). Domestic political debates on migration are often highly emotional, with state representatives having difficulty communicating why and what they are negotiating in international fora (Betts 2011: 21; Banulescu-Bogdan 2018). This explains why mainly bilateral return and readmission agreements regulating the deportation of rejected asylum seekers have been concluded and why mixed migration governance often boils down to fighting smuggling[14]—measures to limit the number of migrants to the "Global North" (see for example Geddes and Boswell 2011; Zaiotti 2016a; Oelgemöller 2021: 185). Development aid to fight the "root causes" of migration and financial and technical assistance to reinforce border regimes are other ways to prevent movement (Castles and van Hear 2011). High-income countries usually hinder negotiations on more

[14] For example, the EU's Council Directive 2002/90 of November 28, 2002, defining the facilitation of unauthorized entry, transit, and residence.

comprehensive governance arrangements that also address issues like safe routes and mobility for low-skilled labor (see Kainz and Betts 2021).

Finally, when it comes to defining and regulating mixed migration, there are competing organizational interests. As discussed, the UNHCR feared that its authority would be undermined if another agency received a robust mandate to protect migrants that was comparable to its own for refugees. Thus the UNHCR was not keen for mixed migration to be recognized as an urgent international question and tried to prevent other IGOs from gaining formal competence on the matter (see Feller 2005). While the UNHCR eventually gave up its strong opposition and adopted a strategy of issue linkage and interorganizational cooperation as a way of reinforcing its leading position in global migration and refugee governance (Betts 2013), its initial resistance demonstrates that not only states but also IGOs struggle to define their stance toward mixed migration flows. Humanitarian NGOs, which previously worked only in displacement crises, have also begun to address migration without, however, clearly understanding how to do that (see Borton and Collison 2017). A screenshot of the thematic page on migration of the website of PHAP (Figure 3.3), the International Association of Professionals in Humanitarian Assistance and Protection, from 2016 shows that many non-state actors had not yet defined their organizational interests in relation to migration.

In sum, these examples show that not only states but also IGOs and NGOs "don't know what (mixed) migration is and what they want to get out of it"— or as Andrew Geddes (2021: 1) put it, "Migration governance occurs in the shadow of uncertainty, where facts, values and beliefs elide." Mixed migration is difficult to pin down as a political category and despite its growing salience, continues to be marked by organizational complexity, political uncertainty, and knowledge gaps.

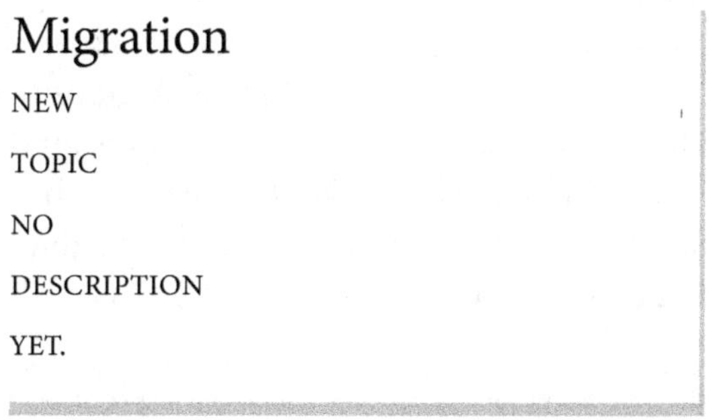

Fig. 3.3 PHAP website thematic page "migration"

3.3 The European Migration and Refugee Crisis

The fact that mixed migration is happening in violation of, and partly without, international rules and recognized organizational competencies means that mixed movements quickly become crises (see Menjívar et al. 2019). The most recent one that caused the greatest institutional upheaval both regionally and internationally was the European migration and refugee crisis of 2015–16 (Ferris and Donato 2020: 79).[15]

Between January 2015 and December 2016, nearly 2.5 million people reached Europe's borders (Frontex 2016d: 6, 2017d: 6). During the peak between July 2015 to March 2016, over one million migrants and refugees arrived by sea alone, most landing in Greece via the Eastern Mediterranean route. While not unprecedented, these were the largest numbers of people to irregularly reach Europe since World War II—fleeing protracted conflicts in Afghanistan, Iraq, and Syria. According to the UNHCR, the war in Syria alone displaced over five million people. Most of those forced migrants remained in Jordan, Lebanon, Turkey, and other countries within the region (Niemann and Zaun 2018: 3), where deteriorating conditions and their unclear legal status caused them to subsequently seek refuge in Europe. Syrian, Iraqi, and Afghan nationals accounted for the largest share of asylum seekers entering the EU in 2015 and 2016, but Iranian, Pakistani, Somali, Eritreans, Algerian, and Nigerian nationals also traveled the same routes (UNHCR and IOM 2016).[16]

The "international community was unprepared for such large numbers of people" (UNHCR and IOM 2016: 8). The dramatic increase in numbers and speed of people crossing the border into Europe exposed the systematic deficiencies in global migration and asylum governance architecture (see Bradley et al. 2022: 11) and EU cooperation on migration and asylum (see Trauner 2016). In June 2013, the EU had introduced a series of directives and the Dublin Regulation to create the Common European Asylum System (CEAS) featuring common protection standards and a clear distribution mechanism. CEAS determines which country is responsible for processing new arrivals' asylum claims and specifies procedural guidelines and safeguards. At the peak of the crisis, the Dublin system, which stipulates that a country of first entry is responsible for registering and processing asylum claims, broke down. Frontline states—mostly Greece, but also Italy and

[15] For a discussion of the politics behind framing and addressing migration as a "crisis," see Jeandesboz and Pallister-Wilkins (2015); Allen et al. (2018); Tsourapas and Zartaloudis (2022); Cantat et al. (2023).

[16] For a migrant- and refugee-focused account of the crisis, see Crawley et al. (2018).

Spain—were quickly overburdened, while other states refused to agree on refugee quotas or other responsibility-sharing mechanisms (Zaun 2018). As a result, asylum seekers were waved through and states lost control over their onward movement.

In addition, absent safe routes, 1,240 people drowned after their boats capsized (IOM 2019b). Those who did reach the Greek islands faced poor conditions because the Greek authorities did not implement the EU Receptions Conditions Directive. At best, new arrivals had limited access to medical care, psychosocial support, and humanitarian assistance. Particularly vulnerable groups like families with small children, unaccompanied minors, and sick and disabled people also had insufficient access to basic services like shelter and sanitary facilities—or none at all. The lack of accommodation for people on the move often led to many, including minors, being detained. Without effective screening and registration facilities in place, new arrivals could not claim asylum and no one knew for sure *who* was entering the EU. When put to the test, CEAS collapsed and Europe experienced a humanitarian emergency (see Niemann and Zaun 2018: 3–4).[17] The steep increase in arrivals to Europe did not in itself constitute a crisis, but the volume triggered a humanitarian emergency and a crisis in governance.

3.3.1 The European Union's Response to the Crisis

In response to the failure of CEAS and the ensuing crisis, the European Commission presented the European Agenda on Migration (EC 2015a) and outlined priority actions for implementing it (EC 2015b).[18] The first measure was the so-called ***hotspot approach***. A "hotspot" is a border region that "is characterized by specific and disproportionate migratory pressure, consisting of mixed migratory flows" (Avramopoulos 2015: 3). The Commission can deploy "Migration Management Support Teams" of Frontex, EASO, European Union Agency for Law Enforcement (Europol), and European Union Agency for Criminal Justice Cooperation (Eurojust) personnel to those regions to provide local authorities with on-the-ground

[17] Several European countries unilaterally responded by reintroducing border controls and effectively suspending free movement within the EU. This has led to scholars describing the additional "Schengen crisis": the system that stipulates border controls only at the EU's external border—delimiting "the Schengen Area"—largely broke down. See, for example, Schimmelfennig (2018).

[18] For an overview of measures taken by European member states in response to the crisis, see Kriesi et al. (2024).

operational support. Other member states are required to provide equipment and experts to staff the teams. The support teams are supposed to manage the high number of new arrivals by helping national agencies register, accommodate, interview, and relocate or return migrants and asylum seekers from within a single site (EP 2016: 26). For this purpose, new facilities were to be built (also called hotspots or hotspot centers; hereafter, I use hotspots for these facilities and not the regions). The central idea of the hotspot approach was "to swiftly identify, register and fingerprint incoming migrants" and "immediately channel" those claiming asylum into asylum procedures (EC 2015a: 6). It was designed to prevent autonomous secondary movements within the EU and guide people arriving at Europe's external border to a controlled relocation or readmission procedure.

To make that possible, the European Agenda for Migration also presented a ***relocation program.*** The agenda stipulates a "temporary distribution scheme for persons in clear need of international protection to ensure a fair and balanced participation of all Member States" (EC 2015a: 4). The Council also adopted means to relocate 160,000 people who belong to a nationality with a 75% recognition rate from Greece and Italy to other EU countries (EC 2015b: 2).

The third measure to stem the crisis was the EU-Turkey Statement of March 18, 2016 (Council of the EU 2016) that declared Turkey a "safe third country"—where, in principle, most migrants arriving in Europe could have accessed international protection.[19] As a result, their claims to asylum in the EU were "unfounded" or "inadmissible" and as of March 20, 2016, everyone crossing from Turkey to the Greek islands had to be sent back to Turkey. The EU-Turkey Statement introduced a new return procedure, the ***"fast-track border procedure"*** (Greek Law 2016: 4375/2016, Art. 60, 4).[20]

[19] Initially, Turkey was only considered a "safe third country" for *Syrian* nationals because Turkey has ratified the UN Refugee Convention but not its 1967 Protocol, meaning that it only grants asylum to people originating from Europe. Nonetheless, as part of the deal with the EU, Turkey pledged to provide international protection to Syrians and to refrain from deporting them to Syria—thus becoming a safe third country for Syrians. "In June 2021, the safe third country concept became the rule throughout the Greek territory for all asylum seekers originating from Syria, Afghanistan, Somalia, Pakistan, and Bangladesh, after the issuance of a Joint Ministerial Decision setting out a 'national list of safe third countries' including Turkey" Equal Rights Beyond Borders et al. (2022: 4).

[20] Additional measures outlined in the EU-Turkey Statement included a 1:1 resettlement mechanism. For every Syrian returned to Turkey from the Greek islands, a different Syrian had to be resettled to Europe. Turkey also promised to prevent the development of new sea and land routes from Turkey to Europe. In return for assisting Syrian refugees on its territory, Turkey received EUR 6 billion and visa liberalizations; see Niemann and Zaun (2018: 8). After the EU-Turkey Statement took effect, arrivals from Turkey dropped while the number of people crossing to Italy more than doubled. See Börzel and Risse (2018: 91).

The new procedure introduced three important changes to the hotspot system. First, it turned the hotspots into closed facilities.[21] Under Greek law 4375/2016, which transposes the EU-Turkey Statement into Greek legislation, arrivals to the islands after March 20, 2016, are subject to a "restriction of liberty" of up to twenty-five days, extendable to ninety days if Greek authorities have established a "risk of absconding." Until asylum seekers have been registered and the legality of returning them to Turkey established, they are not allowed to leave the islands. The statement also established a new interview procedure: the "admissibility interview" conducted by Greek caseworkers assisted by staff from EASO and the UNHCR. Conducted before asylum interviews, admissibility interviews are intended to find out if someone traveled through Turkey or is exempted from readmission because they belong to a "vulnerable group" or are a "Dublin case."[22] Third, the hotspot procedure shifted from relocating to returning. When the fast-track border procedure took effect, the new temporary relocation scheme was *de facto* suspended on the Aegean islands. As one of the legal professionals working in the hotspot on the Greek island of Chios observed:

> With the entering into force of the EU-Turkey Deal on 20 March 2016, the function of EU Hotspots fundamentally changed from relocation to return—which means deportations to Turkey. This is now the main purpose of the Hotspot procedure. The possibility of relocation is based on two Council decisions and these decisions actually stipulate that all persons who fulfill certain criteria and arrived in Greece or Italy before a certain date in September 2017 are eligible for relocation. Irrespective of these stipulations, however, everyone who arrived after 20 March 2016 on the Greek islands was no longer considered eligible for relocation. [...] The legal basis for this is completely unclear. In my opinion, there is none because the Council decisions explicitly stipulate the contrary and this practice—that only people who arrived in Greece before 20 March 2016 are eligible—is not stipulated. Still, nobody took legal action against this, which is also very difficult to do [...]. And it is also not documented if the European Commission is aware of this practice. So this is all very unclear. However, practically nobody who arrived after 20 March has been relocated. (I-16, Annex II)

[21] For a critique of the hotspot approach from a human rights and humanitarian perspective, see European Parliament (2016); Markard and Heuser (2016); Norwegian Refugee Council et al. (2016); Danish Refugee Council (2017).

[22] Greek Law (2016) (4375/2016, Art. 14, 8) stipulates that vulnerable people are "a) Unaccompanied minors, b) Persons who have a disability or suffering from an incurable or serious illness, c) The elderly, d) Women in pregnancy or having recently given birth, e) Single parents with minor children, f) Victims of torture, rape or other serious forms of psychological, physical or sexual violence or exploitation, persons with a post-traumatic disorder, in particularly survivors and relatives of victims of ship-wrecks, g) Victims of trafficking in human beings." "Dublin cases" are people who qualify for family reunification under the Dublin III Regulation. Under EU law, they must be relocated to the EU member state where one member of their nuclear family has applied for international protection because that country is also responsible for processing their asylum claim.

In short, the main policy initiative to manage the crisis at Europe's borders was the new readmission procedure in the hotspots.[23]

While the EU *did* respond to the crisis, its reply has been extremely weak. The European Agenda on Migration and the EU-Turkey Statement are brief and imprecise documents, with sketchy, unclear mechanisms. They outline "elusive" (Bousiou and Papada 2020) and "temporary solutions" (Bojar and Kriesi 2023: 445) that fall outside the EU's formal institutional framework, so it is very difficult to determine who has authority for which aspects of the border procedure (Ziebritzki 2020). The measures neither fundamentally reform CEAS nor supranationalize the EU's response to mixed migration challenges (Börzel and Risse 2018: 90–1; Schimmelfennig 2018: 981). They do not address questions such as responsibility sharing among states, safe migration routes, or legal aid for asylum seekers. In other words, while the hotspot approach can be described as an institutional innovation, it is a "soft and vague framework" (Loschi and Slominski 2022: 779) that only provides a minimal policy response to the crisis and leaves considerable room for maneuver for those working at the border.

3.3.2 In the Hotspots: International Organizations at the Border

The EU has established four hotspots in Italy—one in Apulia (Taranto) and three in Sicily (Lampedusa, Pozzallo, and Messina)—and five in Greece—on the islands of Lesvos, Chios, Samos, Leros, and Kos. The Chios hotspot is the empirical focus of my two-level case study (see Chapter 1 and Annex I on case selection and data sources). Before I reconstruct how field staff on Chios made sense of the crisis and managed mixed migration in the absence of an international regime (see Chapter 4), let me briefly introduce Chios's basic organizational infrastructure.

Chios is a Greek island in the Aegean Sea located 7 kilometers from the Turkish coast. It constitutes one of the main border crossing points along the EU external border on the Eastern Mediterranean route (see Figure 3.4).

[23] Other measures focused on disrupting smuggling networks and fighting root causes. To combat smuggling and human trafficking, the European Commission launched a military naval operation ("Operation Sophia," formerly "EUNAVFOR MED"). The EU also tripled the budget for Frontex operations in the Central and Eastern Mediterranean (Operation Triton off the Italian coast and Operation Poseidon close to the Greek coast). In contrast to the earlier Mare Nostrum Operation, the new ones did not have explicit SAR mandates. To externalize migration control and prevent people from going to Europe, the EU set up two trust funds, including the Emergency Trust Fund for Africa, which is supposed to help develop the continent's main regions that produce migrants. See Niemann and Zaun (2018: 11–2).

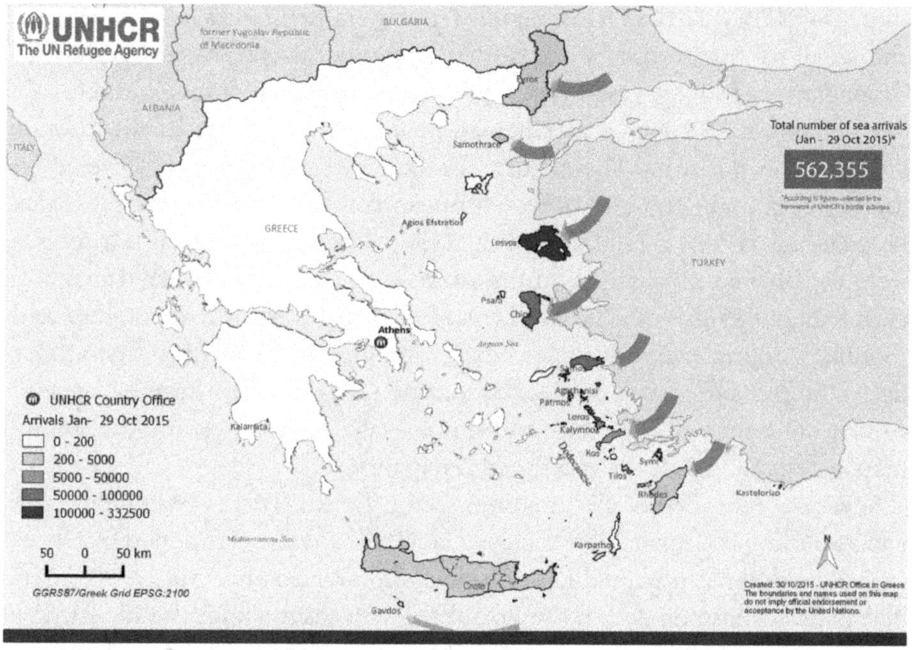

Fig. 3.4 Map of the Eastern Mediterranean route

Note: This map, titled "Number of Arrivals to Greek Islands—As of 29 October 2015," is copyrighted by the UNHCR, and available on its Operational Data Portal: <https://data.unhcr.org/en/documents/details/46405>, accessed January 24, 2024. It is licensed under a Creative Commons Attribution 4.0 International Public License: <https://creativecommons.org/licenses/by/4.0/legalcode#s6a> (for disclaimer of warranties).
Source: UNHCR Global Data Service.

The Chios hotspot is called "Vial."[24] A former aluminum factory and waste-processing plant, Vial is located near the village Halkios, 8 kilometers from the city center. The main building, a large Y-shaped hall, is surrounded by accommodation containers (see also Antonakaki et al. 2016; Pollozek and Passoth 2019). Opened in February 2016, it replaced the previous registration site, "Tabakika," which in late 2015 had been set up in a dismantled tobacco factory for the preliminary processing of the large number of arrivals.[25] From January 2015 to mid-March 2016, 152,597 people arrived by boat on Chios's

[24] The Greek hotspots are legally "First Reception Centers" but have been officially renamed "Reception and Identification Centers" (RICs). After Moria, the Lesvos hotspot, burned down on September 8, 2020, the European Commission's Directorate General for Migration and Home Affairs (DG HOME) set up a task force to construct new reception centers. The new facilities in Greece called "Closed Controlled Access Centres" (CCACs) have been built on Leros, Samos, and Kos. On Lesvos and Chios, they face significant legal obstacles and opposition from much of the local community. See Refugee Support Aegean and Pro Asyl (2023). Nonetheless, the existing facilities on the islands have also been converted to CCACs; the one on Chios is now called "CCAC Chalkios."

[25] Several actors suspended their operations in Tabakika in December 2015 because asbestos was found in the roof. In mid-2016, it was reopened as a preliminary shelter for people to be returned to Turkey.

shores (UNHCR 2016a). Most people landed on the island's eastern beaches and small fishing harbors such as Agia Ermioni. Several were brought into Chios Port by Frontex vessels who intercepted the small dinghies and towed them to shore. SAR NGOs also helped people land safely on the beaches or disembark in the ports. The majority of the new arrivals quickly traveled on to the Greek mainland and other European countries via the ferry at Chios Port. Because Chios was largely a transit site, only temporary camp structures were established in addition to the make-shift reception center, Tabakika: an informal campsite in the public garden next to Chios town square and "Souda" camp in the parking lot next to one of Chios's main tourist attractions, the ruins of a 10th-century Byzantine fort. Souda consisted of several rows of containers, Rubb Halls, and simple washing facilities, and was jointly managed by the UNHCR and the municipality.

Several weeks after Vial's opening, when the EU-Turkey Statement took effect, the hotspot turned into a closed facility that was surrounded by fences and barbed wire. In principle, everyone who arrived after March 20, 2016, had to be accommodated in the hotspot. The weekend after the EU-Turkey Statement was signed, the islands had been evacuated (with only a few people staying voluntarily) and the open camps were officially closed to prepare for new arrivals who would be subjected to the fast-track border procedure and no longer allowed to leave the island autonomously. Given the hotspot's limited reception capacity of 1,100 (EC 2017: 2), Vial became overcrowded within a week. Just one day after the EU-Turkey Statement went into effect, the UNHCR estimated that the island had a population of 1,050 (UNHCR 2016b). In response to the overcrowding, two open campsites were reestablished in Chios town: Souda and "Dipethe" (see Box 3.1).

Box 3.1 The re-opening of Souda and Dipethe

In the first few days after the hotspot was turned into a closed facility, tensions and aggressive behavior increased due to overcrowding and the lack of basic assistance. For instance, due to an internet breakdown, new arrivals could not be registered and due to water shortages there was no drinking water after 7 p.m. Following a violent altercation in Vial a hole was cut in the fence as a way to escape the unsafe conditions in the hotspot center. After standing outside Vial's gates, not knowing what to do or where to go, some 300 people, mostly families with small children, started walking toward the city center. They were unhindered by the Greek police. Reportedly, Frontex staff pointed out the location of Camp Souda in Chios town (a "dropped pin" on Google Maps). But the migrants and asylum seekers took a wrong turn and ended up at the port and squatted there for a couple of days, disrupting the schedule of the Athens ferry. Members of the local population became increasingly hostile toward them. Some of the squatters decided to move to Souda, which the municipality had reopened to shelter the people squatting at the port, others preferred to stay put, fearing that Souda would also turn into a closed camp. Meanwhile, other people walked from Vial to Souda, which also reached full capacity—five days after being reopened. However, as local protests toward the squatters at the port grew and members of the ultra-nationalist "Golden Dawn" party attacked them and a nearby café with a Molotov cocktail, the municipality allowed people on the move to camp in Dipethe, a deserted communal theater and garden in Chios town.

Source: Author's field notes, Chios, March 28 and April 1–8, 2016.

In practice, two weeks after the hotspot approach and the readmission procedure were introduced, Chios again had two open camps: Souda and Dipethe.[26]

Several IGOs, NGOs, and regional agencies operated from within those central sites on Chios (see Table 3.1). With the hotspot's closing, its management was transferred to a new Greek agency called the First Reception Service (FRS), which has since been renamed the Reception and Identification Service (RIS) (4375/2016). At the hotspot, Frontex, EASO, and Europol staff helped the Greek police and asylum services register, fingerprint, debrief, and screen incoming migrants—and also conduct admissibility interviews. Additional Frontex teams patrolled the sea border and conducted return operations. In Vial, the UNHCR and several NGOs provided information about the procedures along with legal advice and translation services. Food, shelter, non-food items (NFIs) such as clothes, sleeping bags, and hygiene kits, basic health services, and water, sanitation, and hygiene (WASH) facilities were provided by the Hellenic Red Cross (HRC), the International Federation of the Red Cross (IFRC), several large international humanitarian NGOs, and smaller transnational volunteer networks. The IOM ran voluntary return and reintegration programs.

At the open campsites, the UNHCR and humanitarian NGOs offered similar services. Several organizations only did that at the open camps, ending their work at Vial when it became a detention center. SAR NGOs patrolled the shore and organized what they called a "first reception" on the beaches: the provision of basic medical support, emergency blankets, dry clothes,

[26] Both camp sites were closed again in late 2017.

Table 3.1 Sites and actors on Chios

Sites/ Sectors	Vial hotspot	Souda site	Dipethe site	Tabakika	Port transit site	Beach landing sites
Education						
Food	HRC/ NGOs	NGOs	NGOs			NGOs
Health	HRC/IFRC, NGOs	HRC/IFRC				NGOs
Shelter & NFIs	NGOs	HRC/IFRC, NGOs		NGO		NGOs
Protection	EASO, Frontex, IOM, UNHCR, NGOs	UNHCR, NGOs				NGO
Site management	FRS, NGOS	Municipality, UNHCR, NGOs	NGOs		NGO	
WASH	NGOs	NGO	NGO	NGO	NGO	NGOs

Source: Based on UNHCR (2016c).

and food. The way transnational professionals working within that organizational ecology at the border negotiated performance of those practices, thereby effectively governing mixed migration on the ground, is the topic of Chapter 4.

3.4 Conclusion: Navigating the "Missing Regime"

Mixed migration governance is characterized by several policy dilemmas. Because it is located at the intersection of development, human rights, humanitarianism, and security, it is unclear whether regulation should protect people on the move and foster safe routes to facilitate global migration—or more tightly control cross-border movements to curb mobility, which some people perceive as a threat to public order and safety. These policy objectives are fundamentally at odds. Absent political consensus on how to address matters of international migration means mixed migration "lacks formal multilateral governance" (Kainz and Betts 2021: 65). Without a global governance framework, large movements of migrants and asylum seekers quickly deteriorate into emergencies like the European migration crisis of 2015 and 2016, which "drew attention to serious gaps in the UN architecture for responding to migration, particularly operationally" (Bradley et al. 2022: 11). It also "uncovered persistent dysfunctionalities and shortcomings" in CEAS (Niemann and Zaun 2018: 3). However, attempts to develop institutional solutions to these deficiencies have continued the previous political strategy of creating non-binding, decentralized, ad hoc bodies and mechanisms. The governance of mixed migration continues to oscillate between preliminary institutionalization and crises.

Political hesitancy to create a dedicated agency with a comprehensive and coherent legal-political framework for mixed migration governance at the regional and international levels leaves IO staff at the frontlines of this global challenge with only vague mandates, unclear policy prescriptions, and regulatory gaps. Frontex former Executive Director Ilkka Laitinen said the "central problem [...] is that Europe's leaders have still not resolved the overarching dichotomy of freedom and security. At policy level, however, more clarity is needed from Brussels. Frontex is an operational agency [...] but there is no comprehensive EU policy on migration to implement" (Frontex 2014a: 120). As a result, frontline staff in their everyday work have to carefully navigate a "missing regime" (Hollifield 2000). How do they make sense of conflicting policy goals? What effect do their actions have, including beyond specific local contexts? Chapters 4 and 5 empirically analyze how IO personnel govern migration and asylum on the ground in view of epistemic and political uncertainty and organizational complexity.

4

Situated Learning

Creating Practical Knowledge in the Field

"Then, once you are here, you see things in a different way: You cannot avoid the responsibility to attend to these people" (I-8, Annex II). This search-and-rescue (SAR) team leader's comment indicates how, finding themselves in the midst of the European migration and refugee crisis of 2015–16, international organization (IO) fieldworkers felt obliged to organize collective action on migration and asylum. Faced with large, unauthorized movement, they made spontaneous decisions and developed pragmatic solutions that consolidated into frontline practices for governing mixed migration. In performing those practices, they considerably influenced the life choices of people on the move.

This chapter investigates the mechanisms behind creating and carrying out such practices. It analyzes which practices were tested, challenged, and routinized in the field in order to reconstruct how, in the absence of comprehensive formal regulations and mandates, IO actors defined what mixed migration means as a policy concern.

The chapter is based on participatory observations on the Aegean island of Chios in spring 2016, interviews with practitioners, and internal documents such as meeting minutes, WhatsApp group chats, and emails, as well as secondary sources (see Section 1.4). Its three main parts match the first three steps of the loop model (described in Section 2.2). The first part of this chapter (Section 4.1) retraces how fieldworkers improvised during the crisis at the European external border, using their professional skills to respond to the emergency. Professional logic took over and organizational affiliation became secondary: Through interorganizational cooperation, competition, and conflict, frontline staff developed provisional solutions for dealing with mixed migration. Section 4.2 explores how competence was negotiated throughout these processes, with frontline workers making and evaluating claims to competent practice. Section 4.3 examines how improvised ways of knowing and doing that have been accepted as competent became routinized through local protocols, training, and shadowing. It provides an overview of the practices that grew out of situated learning at the border—ranging

Global Governance on the Ground. Nele Kortendiek, Oxford University Press. © Nele Kortendiek (2024).
DOI: 10.1093/oso/9780198889120.003.0004

from land patrols to SAR, camp management, asylum interviews, and returns. The chapter concludes by showing that these practices substantively regulate how IOs govern mixed migration at the border. In view of the fragmented institutional migration and asylum architecture discussed in Chapter 3, they represent a major share of IOs' overall activities governing migration and displacement.

4.1 Improvising on the Ground

IO field staff described the situation at the border as "messy," "chaotic," "confusing," "strange," and "absurd" (I-3, I-8, I-11, Annex II). Their situation was characterized by an authority dilemma: Working on a sovereign state's territory, they were bound by the directions of Greek officials. Yet the Greek authorities were reluctant to assume the responsibility that comes with their position—and hindered IO staff doing so in their stead. As a humanitarian worker stationed on Chios put it:

> It's a bizarre situation because the reason that the NGOs are here is because the European Union [EU] and the Greek government are overwhelmed. They can't deal with the influx of people on their own. Otherwise, there would be no need for us to be here and they would delegate us different tasks—maybe on the mainland. But at the same time, all of the organizations have to fairly humbly ask permission to do anything. So it's kind of this bizarre situation: I think that the authorities acknowledge that they need us here but at the same time, they don't want to be seen to be condescended to by the humanitarian machine. (I-11, Annex II)

Greek authorities were officially in charge but shirked responsibility, while at the same time they hesitated to transfer formal competencies to IO actors (see also Painter et al. 2018, who describe similar dynamics on Lesvos). Fieldworkers were thus left with extremely vague organizational responsibilities and had to carefully navigate a confused competence structure: "Decisions are made in Brussels; decisions are made in Athens. But at the moment there is a lot of gray area where we don't know who is actually responsible for what" (I-9, Annex II; see also I-1, I-3, I-11, I-15, Annex II).

This authority dilemma was associated with pronounced short-termism, in which policy-making is reactive and ad hoc (see Tazzioli and Garelli 2018: 5; Papada et al. 2020). IO frontline workers deplored the "lack of management, planning, and foreseeing" (I-9, Annex II). They not only criticized how "The authorities [were] almost completely absent" at the border

(I-3, Annex II) but also their failure to anticipate migration dynamics and the related governance challenges. When asked for policy guidance and strategies, decision-makers at headquarters responded, "Yeah, it can take several months" (I-9, Annex II) and "Nobody thought of that!" as well as "We'll see!" and "We'll cross that bridge when we come to it" (I-1, Annex II). Overall, field staff had to contend with organizational complexity, the evasion of formal responsibility, and policy gaps (on the legal gaps in the EU hotspot systems, see The Greek Ombudsman for Human Rights 2017; Ziebritzki and Nestler 2017).

At the same time, the lack of a clear institutional framework provided fieldworkers with ample room for maneuver. The observational data reveals that they were keenly aware that state inaction and the absence of a central coordinating entity opened lots of space for creativity. On the ground, they held broad discretionary powers—albeit involuntarily (I-9, I-11, Annex II).

In addition, frontline staff faced time constraints and the acute need to act because they were dealing with people who often required immediate protection and were demanding answers: "People expect us to be responsible and to respond to their needs" (I-3, Annex II). Unlike official policy-makers in the European Commission and headquarters staff at the European Border and Coast Guard Agency (Frontex), the European Asylum Support Office (EASO), the International Organization for Migration (IOM), the United Nations (UN) High Commissioner for Refugees (UNHCR), and humanitarian non-governmental organizations' (NGOs) global offices, their direct contact and social interaction with migrants and refugees made it impossible for them to dodge decision-making.

In that setting, they improvised. To remain capable of acting, they moved outside their mandates and tested new ways of handling things. "[We] work in an environment where everything changes a lot and you have to make decisions and you have to improvise a lot" (I-1). Without clear instructions, they experimented and assumed public functions. One example was SAR, the spotting of boats in distress at sea and safe disembarkation of all passengers: "That was all self-organized: Trial and error. At the end of the day, we were taking on a role that the coastguard should have been doing" (I-7, Annex II). Professional skills and personal networks were key to improvisation, as I show below.[1]

[1] It is important to note that people on the move improvise a lot, too. Not only during their journeys but also at the border and in the camps, they seek out possibilities and exploit their limited opportunities. They are autonomous human beings who make decisions, demand things from IOs, and challenge official

4.1.1 Using Professional Skills

To cope with complexity, uncertainty, and urgency, frontline workers relied on their knowledge as border guards, lifesavers, camp managers, doctors, psychologists, social workers, migration lawyers, asylum caseworkers, and escort officers. Quite often, their specific skill sets provided them with agency: "We have means, we have resources, we have the knowledge to do the things" (I-8, Annex II). The mandates of their deploying organizations provided them with only a limited base for responding to situational challenges and local expectations. Previous work experience, however, equipped fieldworkers with broad action repertoires. An EASO staff member, for example, stressed that when they first started working in the EU hotspot on Chios, which is called Vial,[2] they drew a lot on their experiential knowledge:

> When I started out with the asylum service, I worked at a reception center at the airport, which is also like a fast-track procedure center. And I've seen a lot of things and I've experienced a lot of things there [...]. But I cannot imagine [how difficult it must be to work here] if you're just [used to working] in an office building and you are not used to these daily, ad hoc situations. (I-1, Annex II)

When confronted by the fact that the First Reception Service (FRS)—the Greek authority responsible for identifying vulnerable people who are exempt from the fast-track border procedure—did not carry out vulnerability screenings when registering new arrivals, he drew on his experiential knowledge to devise a practical solution:

> There was another problem (of course, everything was a problem!): FRS was in charge of screening vulnerability cases during the registration phase. But that was something they didn't do, which was completely unfair in my view because there were so many vulnerable cases in Vial. And then they said, "Well, if we could register them first, we could send them off to Athens. But we have the order now to assist EASO with [registering people for] the [admissibility] interviews first. And we are only [...] two people and we can only register like maybe four people max each day. So what to do?" So then I came up with an invention actually: "Well, if you register the people in our name as EASO, we [will] pick out the people we want for the interview." So I picked out the most vulnerable ones in the beginning and then we

practices, see also Turner (2006); Mainwaring (2019: 2); and Pincock et al. (2020). While I do not focus on their agency, I acknowledge that it often triggers the governing dynamics I am analyzing in this book.

[2] See Chapter 3 for an overview of the institutional mechanisms that were introduced to manage the crisis, like the "Hotspot Approach," introduced by the European Agenda on Migration or the "Fast-Track Border Procedure," introduced by the EU-Turkey Statement.

> lined them up for the interview [with] us and then after just a couple of hours inside the interview, we could already say, "This is a vulnerable case that can be screened out, which will never be sent back to Turkey." Of course, the [FRS] were not happy about it in the beginning. But of course this idea went through because there were mothers alone with small children, handicapped children, tortured people, and others—and they were in your face every day! (I-1, Annex II)

Struggling with undefined responsibilities and confronted by the hardships of people on the move, the EASO fieldworker exploited the leeway resulting from the unclear authority structure and utilized their professional experience to organize the admissibility interviews. By doing that, they enabled some asylum seekers to travel on to the Greek mainland, enter the asylum process, and eventually access international protection in Europe. This, in turn, meant, that for example the many children arriving at the border could resume their education, which is very likely to substantially affect the course of their lives in the long run.

Camp managers affiliated with UNHCR and humanitarian NGOs similarly used their professional competencies to develop a system to effectively register people who had just crossed the sea from Turkey. Since arrivals must be registered before they can claim asylum, field staff from several IOs organized a simple but effective bracelet system in Tabakika, a former tobacco factory that served as the registration site on Chios before the Vial hotspot was opened in mid-February 2016.

> Eventually, we, UNHCR, and the [humanitarian NGOs] managed to develop some kind of system to manage the flow of people through the registration process because the police was never involved in managing the crowds. So we kind of stepped in into something that should have been the state's responsibility, which was the famous bracelet system. People would arrive in Tabakika, where the whole process took place: So people would be brought there straight from the beach, they would be given a group number for each group of about 50 people [all provided with bracelets in a particular color] and then that group number was used to make sure people went through the process in roughly [the order in which they'd arrived]. And people would go straight through the process: They would be photographed, fingerprinted, screened, and get their document in one go. Tabakika was where everything, the whole registration process, was taking place on a 24-hour basis. (I-4, Annex II; see also I-10, Annex II)

With formal mandates and regulations often vague or not well thought out, putting them into practice required frontline staff to draw on their professional skills to fill the gaps between directives and policies, as exemplified here by humanitarian workers and protection officers improvising to get asylum seekers into and physically through the registration process (see also Pollozek and Passoth 2019: 612, who describe this for the hotspot Moria on Lesvos). Before they managed to organize the registration lane on the ground, the majority of people arriving at the border did not get identified and registered at all: Despite the existence of the European Dactyloscopy (EURODAC) Regulation (European Parliament and the Council 2013), which is legally binding and clearly stipulates the requirement to record every entry at the EU's external border, in 2015, fingerprints were only taken from 8% of the migrants arriving in Greece (EC 2016). By making registration a reality, they created the basis for migrants and refugees to apply for asylum, thereby opening up new avenues for future action to them. At the same time, they considerably restricted their freedom of movement because once registered in the EURODAC database, people on the move could not legally travel to other European countries and apply for asylum outside of Greece.

In some instances, professional perspectives trumped organizational tasks: "Our main work [was] [...] AVRR [assisted voluntary return and reintegration]. However, it was clear to me that I want to do *my work, the thing I know*" (I-2, Annex II; emphasis added). A psychologist employed by IOM to implement AVRR programs viewed psychosocial counseling in the camps as the new arrivals' most pressing need. The overcrowded and makeshift camps, slow registration and asylum processes, lack of information, and separation from family members—as well as trauma from past experiences of war, violence, and torture in home countries and during migration journeys—caused a dramatic increase in anxieties, sleeping disorders, and general mental stress among the migrants and refugees on Chios. With other medical professionals from on-site NGOs, the psychologist began stress-management focus groups and individual counseling, especially for camp residents who'd survived attempts at suicide or self-immolation. Although not in their job description, they considered those to be urgent needs and used their knowledge and contacts with people in other organizations to offer psychosocial support. By foregrounding mental health, they treated mixed migration as a humanitarian issue (rather than a matter of mobility or security) and very immediately "affect[ed] the daily lives and fortunes of people" (Ruggie 2004: 499).

These three cases show how frontline workers improvised ways to address mixed migration at the border. They not only perceived the issues at hand through professional lenses but also used their competencies to devise solutions. Of course, not all fieldworkers were equally proactive and resourceful. In the words of a camp manager, "Some people, they just follow what is in the book as well, you know?" (I-9, Annex II; see also I-2, Annex II). Yet overall, field staff tried "to adjust as much as possible and be creative"

(I-9, Annex II). They used their know-how and experience to make sense of what was going on at the border and reconcile that with organizational tasks and international policies. In so doing, they were effectively "coordinating and constraining individual behavior" (Abbott and Snidal 2001: 345), which is usually defined as the essential outcome of global governance (see Chapter 2).

4.1.2 Interorganizational Cooperation, Competition, and Conflict

Frontline staff did not just rely on their own professional skills and that of coworkers to cope with the everyday challenges of managing migration and asylum at the border, but also worked closely with people employed by other IOs. This can be attributed to three main factors: First, most organizations have a small field presence with teams of two to forty people. Second, field positions are often entry-level jobs with short-term contracts. In the case of EASO and Frontex, operational staff were mostly seconded by EU member states, not directly employed by the agencies.[3] Third, field staff have greater geographical proximity to people from other IOs working in the same place than to their colleagues at headquarters. Thus frontline staff have often not been strongly socialized into their institution's organizational culture and easily develop close working relations with people affiliated with other IOs (see also Sondarjee 2021, who describes this for staff in World Bank country offices).

That said, organizational boundaries do not dissolve. In fact, frontline workers experience strong constraints stemming from legal mandates, commitments to donors, operating plans, and host country agreements—as well as bureaucratic procedures such as reporting requirements (I-8, I-11, I-12, Annex II). Frontex screeners and debriefers, for example, have a very narrow field of duty: determining the nationalities of people arriving at the border and gathering intelligence on migration routes and smuggling networks. On Chios that meant that even when they had less to do and were "eager to do other stuff [...], they had no mandate whatsoever" (I-1, Annex II; see I-7, I-11, Annex II).

However, personal networks allowed field staff to work around organizational constraints. For instance, Frontex coastguards, like their screening and

[3] The crisis has changed this, with EASO being able to hire their own "interim" staff due to a shortage of asylum caseworkers as early as 2016. Under their new mandates, Frontex and EASO will respectively employ 10,000 and 500 operational staff (see Chapter 5).

debriefing colleagues, were bound by quite strict lines of command and rules of procedure. In contrast, NGO lifesavers had more flexibility as to how they could obtain information and act on it:

> We work with Frontex but we cannot forget that they are police and they have limited actions: They must follow orders from, you know, Brussels or whatever. [The] Red Cross is an official institution; they are also [closely associated to] the state. And of course, we follow the law, too, of course, but we have a more open space to move and [we can do things a little differently maybe]. Maybe [...] we can work a little bit in the shadow [of the law]. We have some information and ok, [we can use that when we are] trying to do our job. Maybe this, some organizations, they cannot go this step. But anyway, we work [in a trusting relation] with everybody. So Frontex knows that we are doing ..., we have information from somewhere that they couldn't ... [laughs]. (I-8, Annex II)

Because lifesavers are in direct contact with people on the move during their journeys, they can obtain information that Frontex coastguards, in their official capacity, cannot. However, they can use informal lines of communication to inform Frontex coastguards of the specific locations of refugee boats at sea or direct them to landing sites to make sure that Frontex can assist them in safely disembarking.

This also works the other way around. A humanitarian volunteer often received information from UNHCR protection officers whose legal mandates prevented them from acting on it:

> I found that the UNHCR has been held back because they are essentially hired by the government. But they have given us information which we can use effectively to challenge certain things. And [...] we can respond a lot quicker than any of the [bigger IOs] can because the only ones we are accountable to is to ourselves which means we're not tied down by these rules and regulations. (I-6, Annex II)[4]

In another case, humanitarian professionals were constrained in terms of manpower and relied on Frontex officers in the hotspot Vial for updates:

> They are very helpful in the Hotspot—to monitor the situation and to address issues—so that we can react quickly because we do not have a 24-hour presence. Again, I think it's based as well on personal relations that we can be quickly updated on a situation, which is very good. (I-9, Annex II)

[4] Chapter 6 discusses the normative concerns that result from fieldworkers' leeway. It problematizes their discretionary powers and makes suggestions as to how to render governing on the ground more accountable.

These are just three examples of the many instances in which frontline workers from different IOs circumvented organizational constraints by sharing their knowledge. They quickly passed along new information and tried to determine who has the capacity to respond to the issue at hand.

These informal interorganizational dynamics go beyond information sharing, as the following example shows: When the Vial hotspot became a closed registration facility (after the EU-Turkey Statement took effect), the Greek military took over the catering service. At that time, it was unclear if the Greek Ministry of Defense would extend the food contract to the open camp sites on Chios, which meant that food would not be provided to people in the Souda and Dipethe camps.[5] UNHCR protection officers were among the first to hear about that but had to go through one of the humanitarian NGOs and volunteer kitchens because of their strict mandates:

> [The humanitarian NGOs] was able to fund the volunteer kitchens and for UNHCR, this was not possible. We had instructions that we could not get involved with food provision. Now this is changing but we have different mandates and we play different roles—with [them] being an NGO, and so non-governmental, and with us being an international organization supporting the authorities basically. (I-3, Annex II)

While the international NGO staff members did not prepare any meals—that was left to a small Spanish organization and a team of local Greek volunteers—minutes from the General Coordination Meeting reveal that they included a food component in their proposal when applying for funding from the Directorate-General for European Civil Protection and Humanitarian Aid Operations (DG ECHO), which eventually allowed the volunteer kitchens on Chios to provide food to the Souda and Dipethe camps. These scenes show how different organizational types, different mandates, and access to different funding sources constrain the IO field staff's possible lines of action in different ways. They also illustrate how interorganizational relations help make sense of constraints and open up new paths of action sought by frontline staff—not only to fill gaps but also in defiance of superiors' directions they consider locally inappropriate. In the words of a senior Frontex officer: "We have to consider our mandate but we also have to see the context we are operating in" (Field notes, April 23, 2016; see also da Costa and Karlsrud 2013, Kalkman and Groenewegen 2018: 5).

[5] Souda and Dipethe were the names of the informal camps on Chios island, which were run by several IOs with permission from the municipality. In contrast to the hotspot Vial, the official EU registration and accommodation site, which became a closed facility after the EU-Turkey Statement was signed, they remained open sites. For an overview of the policy framework that was designed to address the crisis in Greece and the *de facto* infrastructure that developed on site, see Chapter 3.

In fact, acting as private persons, fieldworkers often deviate from existing policy and organizational scripts and work outside the boundaries of their IOs. As individuals, they approach people in other IOs to sort out an issue they consider important—issues they perceive to be in the public interest. A rescue professional recounts how a Frontex officer approached her because his organization would not allow him to address short- and medium-term humanitarian concerns in Vial:

> I think I met Carl[6] at a landing, yes. So, Carl is a Finnish Frontex worker who had seen the situation inside Vial, in the detention center, and was really concerned about the children inside not having any education. And he [had] met a Syrian lady, who was a primary school teacher, inside Vial and she had requested to him that he could maybe try and find her supplies so she could start up a small school. So he couldn't access that through his own organization (through Frontex), so he, when he saw us at one of the landings handing things out to the refugees and helping without any strings attached [laughs], he approached us and said, "[Could you] provide materials for a small primary school session?"—I suppose [for] lessons inside Vial. So we were able to meet up with him later and give him some books, paper, pens, pencils, which was all paid out of CESRT [Chios Eastern Shore Response Team] funds, and we gave that to him and he was able to take it into Vial (which we couldn't do at that stage because we weren't allowed in) and gave it to the lady who was very, very grateful. The second time that we interacted with Carl, he was very upset because they (basically Frontex) have a container inside Vial and he [...] had a family with small children who had arrived on that day's boat coming up—it was a very cold night—saying that they didn't have any blankets for themselves or the children, and he didn't have anything to give them. So he actually called us and came all the way back down from Vial to meet up with us to pick up blankets to then take them all the way back again to give to this family. So he was quite an angel! [laughs] After that incident, Frontex received a shipment of their own blankets so that they could give them out. But, at that time, if he hadn't done that, they would have been without [any protection from the cold]. (I-7, Annex II)

This instance shows that, out of a felt responsibility, fieldworkers engage in "bad behavior," deviating from their original tasks and mandates (see Campbell 2018: 50). It also reveals that these informal initiatives often precede formal organizational responses.

In sum, frontline staff create interorganizational communities of practice to cope with acute, everyday challenges in the field. Personal networks allow

[6] All names have been changed.

them to circumvent organizational constraints and remain flexible in an ever-changing and ambiguous work setting. Ultimately, this flexibility not only allows them to respond to local pressures but also to cater to project managers and donor demands—which can be a delicate balance to strike, as this humanitarian professional explained:

> In an environment where it's fluid like it is right now, to have a fixed program at this point in the game, when everybody is kind of wondering what's going to happen ... There are more questions than there are answers ... It's ... It does more service to be able to have a flexible model. [...] But we have been granted a certain level of funding, quite a lot of funding actually, to be able to do something concrete. So, while it is important to be fluid—or just as adaptable, like water is, to shape around a particular structure or whatever—we have targets that we have set from the appeals that we have made to certain donors. But yeah, I mean, we have targets that we have to meet, but those targets are ... can be adaptable, too. (I-12, Annex II; see also I-11, Annex II)

As this quote indicates, personal networks are central to maintaining agency and integrating local and organizational expectations.

Importantly, stating that frontline workers create communities of practice and that organizational membership becomes secondary at the border does not imply that interorganizational interactions are *per se* collaborative. On many occasions, these relations are indeed characterized by coordination and collaboration, as the cases above demonstrate. There are also mechanisms for institutional cooperation, for example, in the form of a memorandum of understanding signed between two IOs to jointly implement certain services like that signed by the Norwegian Refugee Council (NRC) and the volunteer kitchens to deliver food to the open camps. In addition, there were mandated cooperation forums such as the weekly General Coordination Meeting held in Chios Townhall that was co-chaired by a representative of the municipality and UNHCR's field-unit head. Other examples of formalized cooperation included the thematic working groups like "Child Protection" and "Communicating with Communities" that were also co-chaired by representatives of two different IOs. The WhatsApp smartphone application was another, slightly less formalized, coordinating tool that made it possible to share information quickly and reach many local actors: "*Everybody* uses it. It's the main way of sharing information about what is going on on the island" (I-4, Annex II; see also I-6, Annex II and Micinski 2019 who confirms the importance of WhatsApp for NGOs in organizing a response to the crisis). These coordination and cooperation mechanisms were complemented by the numerous informal encounters, personal phone chains, and direct collaborations already discussed.

However, interorganizational relations in the field are also characterized by competition and conflict (see also Egger 2017 on NGO-NGO relations in various humanitarian emergencies and Cusumano 2021, who observed similar dynamics in SAR NGO relations during operations in the Mediterranean). Since a lot of work at the border is project-based, humanitarian NGOs in particular are often competing for the same funds. This may make "people get protective of the niches that they carve out for themselves" (I-11, Annex II; see also I-2, Annex II). Field staff are generally eager to identify the outcomes ascribable to their organization to justify their work to superiors and donors. Their clothing clearly identifies them as members of a particular organization, and they run social media campaigns highlighting their specific contributions (sometimes explicitly distinguishing them from other IOs) and keep lists of exactly what they have delivered. In addition to these rather bureaucratic forms of competition that are often oriented at external audiences—mostly donors—they also compete over the professional practice most appropriate for addressing migration and asylum, as I describe in greater detail in Section 4.2.

Competition sometimes leads to open confrontation and conflict, both among field staff engaged in similar practices and those performing different ones. Frontline staff fight over how to do patrols and provide food and how to organize collective action on migration and asylum more generally. For instance, after the EU-Turkey Statement was signed in March 2016 and the Vial hotspot became a closed center, many humanitarian professionals fought over whether to assist the authorities, for example, by providing non-food items (NFIs) such as clothes, sleeping bags, and hygiene products. Some took the position that this supports an institution that detains people on the move. They "felt pretty horrible and complicit in a very unjust system" (I-6, Annex II) and decided to stop working at the hotspot. Others "decided that the people that are in there still need help, more than before" (I-11, Annex II) and continued assisting in Vial (see Section 4.2 for an extensive discussion how such conflicts played out).

In general, however, there is sustained interaction between all fieldworkers that is rooted in trust for each other's professionalism. Despite competitive and conflictual dynamics and the general perception that coordination could be considerably improved, no deep cleavages emerged on Chios between public and private or between humanitarian and security actors. At the border, the public/private distinction that the global governance literature often uses as an analytical category to explain relations between intergovernmental organizations (IGOs) and NGOs (for example Avant et al. 2010a; Jönsson and Tallberg 2010; Abbott 2012; Steffek 2013) was not obvious. Because field teams were roughly the same size and the division of labor mainly reflected professions rather than organizations, funding sources and formal mandates were not the main drivers behind interorganizational interactions. Frontline workers generally took on *public functions* whether or not they were affiliated with an IGO (formally identified as "public") or an international NGO (legally a "private" organization). A humanitarian worker expressed this as follows when trying to describe who was doing what on Chios:

> The volunteer organizations are responsible for greeting the boats or the rafts when they come in [...]. Other actors are responsible for—and "responsible" really isn't the right word because it's a strange situation in that the Greek government and the European Union should be responsible for all this. So, when I say responsible, I mean *they've chosen to take on these tasks*. Other things that people are responsible for, or have decided to take on, are WASH [water, sanitation, and hygiene] in Vial. That's one thing. Others have taken on distribution of food: This is a big one. And then aside from actual services, there's information and [a] kind of protection monitoring. And then health provision, as well. (I-11, Annex II; emphasis added)

The same held true for security professionals, mostly Frontex officers (from border guards to escort officers) and human rights and humanitarian professionals (such as logisticians, medical professionals, social workers, and asylum lawyers). Although they often disagreed about what mixed migration is and requires, they regularly worked together. Despite having fundamentally different roles and views, they overcame their initial doubts and developed trusting relationships through repeated interaction. As a humanitarian worker involved in shore patrol described it:

> I mean Frontex are a border police. So we have to first say what they are, which is, they are to patrol the borders, which doesn't necessarily align to a lot of [our] beliefs. [...] So I think we work together as we're two [teams operating on the shore]. They have informed us when there are boats arriving so that we can provide clothes, which is great. But we weren't ever kind of patrolling together or operating as such together: It was more [like] two different parties operating on the ground and a mutual respect, I guess, for each other's work. (I-6, Annex II; see also I-4, I-8, I-11, Annex II)

A UNHCR staff member confirmed this when they recounted that conflicts over specific decisions and procedures did not damage relations because field staff worked well together personally:

> So we did have some disagreements over specific cases: how they [Frontex field staff] handled specific cases, mostly in the screening process. I would say that's the only point—I mean we didn't ... But again, I think it was mainly down to the personalities of the Frontex officers involved. We were usually able to discuss cases and sometimes we disagreed. And in some cases, they were willing to ... for example, that someone goes through the screening process again, when we thought they had made a mistake. (I-4, Annex II)

However, there was a noticeable rift between the transnational professionals working at the border and local Greek authorities. Because officials from the FRS, the Greek police, port authorities, and the Hellenic Coast Guard were often unavailable and generally avoided joint improvisation, IO fieldworkers had difficulty working with them. In the words of a UNHCR officer:

> Because FRS, so far, I think there have been four different coordinators in this time. So there has been no continuity in their work, in their activities. So it wasn't always easy to talk to them, to agree on certain things [...], which caused a lot of delays and lack of coordination and resulted in [...] chaos for everyone. (I-3, Annex II)

An IOM colleague agreed: "FRS doesn't have clear instructions; they are so afraid to take decisions. Every time they say, 'We will have to ask Athens and the Ministry'—and every decision is so delayed. So this cooperation I think is the most dysfunctional" (I-2, Annex II). Furthermore, local police demonstrably shared false information with international actors at the border:

> Yeah, instructions sometimes are unclear or contradictory and what is even worse, we have to help with the ... they call it the "decongestion of the island" so we [had] to somehow support the police in informing people [on the move] that there was an option for them to be transferred to another island [Leros or Kos]. And this happened on three different occasions. And of course, we would have to inform people about the conditions they would find on this other island and the information we received from the police was that the conditions would be pretty much the same as in Chios—so people would be basically free to move. And this was not the case. And of course, people found [that] out once they were there. So, I mean there is no trust, basically, in the words of the authorities because of this. (I-3, Annex II)

The resulting breakdown in trust was difficult to repair because Greek officials usually did not attend the General Coordination Meeting:

> And we know that they [the Greek police] are feeding us false information as well. [...] And it feels like they don't really know what to do in some places. I'm not even sure ... Like port police and Frontex don't always talk to each other. The FRS, I'm not even sure if they even talk to the police. I don't know. FRS has stopped coming to the meetings. I would say that the cooperation between the authorities and the [IOs] is not very good at the moment because at the meetings that we used to have together, they [weren't] present. (I-5, Annex II)

Because Greek authorities also often shut down other lines of communication, they did not become an integral part of the local community of practice. A rescue professional described the situation as follows:

> For the last four nights, I think, we [called] every morning to ... not to request permission but to inform them [the Greek coastguard, HCG] that we are leaving [going out to sea with the rescue boat] and their phone has never been answered in that time. We got the record that we tried to call them on our phones if they want to complain but they are very hard to reach, so how can we inform them if they don't answer their phone? [...] But the relationship with Frontex improved—alongside the relationship with the coastguard or with the Greek police, I should say, deteriorating. And similarly, the relationship between Frontex and the Greek police appears not to be fantastic. (I-7, Annex II)

In short, transnational professionals formed close-knit networks—in distinction from the Greek authorities. But IO frontline staff also expressed sympathy for their Greek counterparts. They acknowledged that local Greek civil servants were not equipped to deal with a major humanitarian emergency and that it was not Greece's responsibility to address large mixed movements, which is *qua* its nature an international issue:

> Same with the asylum office: They are really understaffed so this is delaying the asylum procedures and it's kind of difficult for them to plan in advance their calendar for the interviews. And also, there are security issues which further delay the process because sometimes they just have to stop the interviews and evacuate, for example, Vial. I mean it's ... [sighs] ... It's in general a lack of human resources, lack of clear guidance, and procedures in place. And I mean this whole situation is still quite new. OK, it's been almost three months since the agreement [the EU-Turkey Statement], but in order for the authorities, and a whole country basically,

> to readjust to the new scenario, three months is maybe not as long as one would imagine. So, they are still trying to cope, I think. (I-3, Annex II; see also I-6, I-10, Annex II)

In sum, the main cleavage to emerge during improvisation processes was that between local and global actors (see also Autesserre 2014, who observes similar dynamics in the area of peacekeeping). Those working at the border experienced a deep disconnect between policy-making in the European and international arena and realities on the ground:

> I think the EU has [agreed on] a policy in their sort of ivory tower. [...] And they've largely stepped back from dealing with the day-to-day issues and are rather dealing with it at such a high level that they really are ... I think there's such a disconnection between policy and reality. (I-6, Annex II; see also Perkowski 2019, who confirms this disconnect between policymakers and operational staff in her study of Frontex)

Border workers unequivocally described policy design and implementation as out of sync and criticized the "lack of ownership" by European and international decision-makers (I-15, Annex II). The perception of having been thrown in at the deep end and having had to "take up the slack" created strong cohesion among international fieldworkers (I-10, I-14, Annex II): "So, it's been everybody—*but here on the ground in Chios*: It's not been something that has been directed from a central level. [...] Everybody is playing a role; everybody is [filling] some kind of gap" (I-4, Annex II). Despite not always wanting to collaborate with other organizations, fieldworkers felt that "in order for this whole migrant thing to work, everybody has to work together—unfortunately" (I-12, Annex II). Because frontline staff needed to be able to respond and "[Y]ou can't be a jack of all trades and people are very much skilled in certain areas, [...] a big ecosystem of actors" developed (I-6, Annex II). In that ecosystem, they drew on their different professional skill sets to improvise, thereby managing mixed migration in the everyday.

In conclusion, this section has shown that IO field staff improvise in view of the complexity, uncertainty, and urgency that characterizes the issue area of migration and asylum. They rely on their professional skills and personal contacts with people in other IOs to respond to everyday requirements at the border. They interpret situational challenges through professional lenses and use their experiential knowledge to devise impromptu solutions. In so doing, they not only address local problems but translate policies into practice—which would otherwise remain policies on paper only and not affect change among the target population. Throughout these processes, they bend, modify, and adapt the meaning of these policies and complement them with activities they deem urgently required, even if not envisaged by official decision-makers. The following section provides further insight into these processes of pulling and hauling over how mixed migration can—and should—be governed in practice before the final sections turn to their effects.

4.2 Negotiating Competence

Improvising on the ground goes hand in hand with negotiating competence. Frontline workers on Chios not only tested ways of coping with large mixed migration movements but also reflected on the tests and argued about which were acceptable. The following two sub-sections analyze how they quarreled over which kind of professional action is needed to handle migration and displacement. The sub-sections analytically divide competence negotiations into two dimensions—making and evaluating claims to competent practice—and show that these dynamics, like improvisation, cut across organizational boundaries and involved different professional groups.

4.2.1 Making Claims to "Knowing Well"

Interestingly, the unclear authority structure that characterizes migration and asylum (see Chapter 3 and above) did not lead IO actors to seek authority: "People seem reluctant to want authority—because it's an impossible situation for almost everybody right now. So whoever takes authority has to fix a problem—and it's a problem that's unfixable" (I-11, Annex II). While it seems intuitive to assume that IO actors would seek to enlarge their influence by exploiting the opportunities that arose from the ill-defined competence distribution and the ongoing emergency (see for example Sending 2015; Kreuder-Sonnen 2019), the observational and interview data show instead that "people keep bouncing the ball" (I-3, Annex II; see also I-4, I-6, I-9, I-12, Annex II). Given the issue's extreme politicization and deep uncertainty regarding the public good that is at stake, fieldworkers, too, were hesitant to claim authority.

However, I did observe staff on Chios competing over how to do things *well*:

> There can be a competitiveness between agencies. And there can also be a lot of … People get protective of the niches that they carve out for themselves. And they're hesitant to kind of let that go or invite other actors in, which in some ways is great, like, if someone is protective of their niche *because they think that they're doing better work than anyone else would*, then [they'd worry that others] would pollute their efforts if [they] came in. And that's good: You should be protective of it. (I-11, Annex II; emphasis added)

As this quote shows, frontline workers often asserted that they were doing good work, even better than others. In other words, while testing how to effectively address mixed movements at the border, they made implicit and explicit claims to "know well." To respond to situational challenges, they used the skills that had helped them complete similar tasks in other (also non-migration-related) contexts (see above). They did so, convinced that they were acting professionally, and confronted those they considered were *not*: "I usually ask, 'This is a professional service?!' Because this is not a professional service because it is bad—because *it is not well done*" (I-8, Annex II). Importantly, in this understanding, "professional" is not about being remunerated for a particular service but rather acting competently: Professionals are "trained people, people who know what [they are] doing" (I-8, Annex II).

Making claims to competence has important implications for the ways of handling migration and asylum that become stabilized over time. By asserting that they know how to do something well, field staff indirectly or openly maintain that their approaches are the most appropriate for dealing with mixed migration. However, for these approaches to become routine, other IO actors at the border have to accept them as competent practice. I now turn to this second aspect of competence negotiations.

4.2.2 Assessing Feasibility and Appropriateness

Frontline workers on Chios agreed that "The Greek government we've seen, they're completely incompetent to handle this situation. They lack the resources, the knowledge, and skill set" (I-6, Annex II). Which skills are required for organizing migration and asylum at the border was, however, contested. Field staff argued about which kind of professional know-how was needed, on the one hand, and what counts as competent behavior, on the other. Put differently, they not only improvised on the ground but also reflected on and quarreled over what worked and what didn't

(I-1, I-9, I-10, I-15, Annex II). Situated learning at the border is based on trial and error—fieldworkers sometimes make mistakes:

> [We] have gained a huge amount of experience [because we] have taken on massive responsibilities and [were free not only to make our] own decisions but also to make mistakes and to learn from them and to actually become very astute in [our] ability to recognize what needs to be done. (I-7, Annex II)

As this quote by a rescue professional shows, to determine what works frontline staff collectively assessed their spontaneous decisions and argued about which ways of doing are appropriate for addressing mixed movements: Improvisation can fail and whether and which pragmatic solutions were considered suitable and legitimate resulted from social negotiations among professionals with different sets of skills. Importantly, these processes of negotiating competence largely unfolded without much interference from decision-makers in formal policy-making arenas, meaning that they were subject to only a few external checks and balances: *mutual accountability* within the local community of practice was the main mechanism for evaluating the feasibility and appropriateness of field-based governing activities.

Such negotiations may be driven by cooperation and joint problem-solving efforts. This is shown by the way admissibility interviews were organized under the fast-track border procedure introduced by the EU-Turkey Statement, for example: The interviews were supposed to establish if a claim to asylum was admissible in Europe or had to be lodged in the country where the person had transited before reaching European territory because it could be considered a "safe third country" or a "first country of asylum" (Greek Law 2016: 4375/2016, Art. 60, 4). For people arriving on Chios, that country is usually Turkey. EASO asylum experts were tasked with conducting the interviews and drafting opinions on the outcomes, which then had to be approved by officers from the Greek Asylum Service who, however, rarely disagreed with EASO experts (see Antonakaki et al. 2016: 8). Unaccompanied minors, other vulnerable people, and "Dublin" cases (people who are eligible for family reunification under the Dublin III Regulation because a core family member residing in another European country has been granted asylum) were formally exempt from these interviews and allowed to travel to the mainland. That said, *how* to conduct the interviews and decide whether someone could be returned to Turkey was left for hotspot experts to figure out in several rounds of learning-by-doing:

> They set up the standard frame for the interview and in the beginning, in my opinion, they thought of it a little bit too easy. "Just ask some questions: "How did you get here? Do you have any family in Europe?' And yeah, 'Why can you not go back to Turkey?'" That [was] basically the outset for this. But then in the course of time, after the first interviews were done and from the experience and also the comments from the Asylum Service, it became clear that we had to ask many more things during the interview. (I-1, Annex II)

Using their knowledge as asylum experts and caseworkers, they gradually determined what an admissibility interview actually could look like—also by addressing issues such as whether Turkey can be considered safe for Kurdish people and whether Palestinians who had been granted asylum in Syria under the 1951 Geneva Refugee Convention and who, with the outbreak of civil war, were forced to flee again, had to reapply for international protection. What was most difficult throughout these processes was determining whether someone counted as "vulnerable" (I-15, I-16, Annex II). Although the Greek law that translates the EU-Turkey Statement into domestic law lists several categories of vulnerability,[7] caseworkers struggled to establish who falls into these categories:

> And that's always tricky: What are you talking about: [a] "vulnerable" case? If you see somebody in a wheelchair, you know it's a vulnerable case. Or a mother alone with kids, it's also a vulnerable case. But if you talk about torture, for example, or people who have been in prison or have been traumatized ... How far are they traumatized, you know, so that you can say it's a vulnerable case? Those were the tricky ones in that respect. [...] So that's why a lot of times we had to discuss among the interviewers, you know, "How far do we go? And do we have enough [information] to know whether or not they are vulnerable?" So, yeah, that took a long time. And the [...] time for the interviews was also getting longer by the day. (I-1, Annex II)

This quote illustrates how caseworkers collectively reflected on how to determine vulnerability and which additional opinions were needed. At that point, legal and medical professionals entered the process of slowly deciding how to establish vulnerability. Legal experts were eager to make sure that those who potentially qualified as vulnerable could assert their rights and not only

[7] These are: "a) Unaccompanied minors, b) Persons who have a disability or [are] suffering from an incurable or serious illness, c) The elderly, d) Women in pregnancy or having recently given birth, e) Single parents with minor children, f) Victims of torture, rape or other serious forms of psychological, physical or sexual violence or exploitation, persons with a post-traumatic disorder, in particular survivors and relatives of victims of ship-wrecks, g) Victims of trafficking in human beings" (Greek Law 2016: 4375/2016, Art. 14, 8).

be exempted from being returned to Turkey but also travel onwards from the border (I-16, Annex II). The fast-track border procedure did, however, not envisage any legal counseling before or during the admissibility interview (nor the asylum interviews that would follow if someone's claim was found to be admissible in Greece). While EASO's field coordinator stressed that "Things should be as legal as possible!" during one of the protection working group's meetings (Field notes, Chios, April 28, 2016), neither EASO nor any other European agency provided legal support during the procedures. Because migration lawyers working in the open campsites considered this to be crucial in addressing mixed migration, they organized legal assistance from the bottom up:

> So a few of us went to Chios to provide legal information on the new procedures—at that point, we thought it would only be a short-term project, eight weeks maybe. But it quickly became clear that it should turn into a long-term project because there was clearly a need for legal advice beyond the eight weeks. So four of us decided to turn it into a long-term project and to create coordinating structures to ensure a certain degree of continuity because, otherwise, every time new legal volunteers would come, we would lose all the knowledge and all the contacts and it was clear to us that we could not network well and not provide good and up-to-date information and we would also waste resources. So we formally founded a non-profit organization and applied for funding in Germany and that took us almost a year. So we could start working again on Chios in May 2017. [...] So when we started working again, the Greek Refugee Council, Refugee Support Aegean and also Metadrasi [a Greek NGO funded by UNHCR] was already there as well as Praksis who are responsible for unaccompanied minors and also have lawyers—I think two at the moment; that always depends on the funding situation. And among these organizations responsibilities are pretty clear: Metadrasi is doing all the appeal, RSA does single cases—strategic litigation in particular—and sometimes appeals, too, and we do Dublin family reunifications and interview preparation and GRC also does appeals and sometimes interview preparations. [...] We do interview preparations for both types of interviews; that depends mostly on the nationality of the person—depending on the nationality, the proceeding is different. So we do both, admissibility interviews and normal asylum interviews. (I-16, Annex II; translated from German)

Usually, however, only medical experts were permitted to attest vulnerability, and they had limited capacity. During one of the General Coordination Meetings, an exhausted doctor from a humanitarian NGO complained, "Doctors should only do *doctory* things!" (Field notes, Chios, April 26, 2016).

He was overwhelmed by the number of asylum seekers requesting he provide medical assessments certifying their vulnerability—in addition to his regular activities running a small clinic in Souda camp. He did not consider it his task to help with the asylum procedure. These quarrels about deciding how to determine *who* could claim asylum *where* ultimately resulted in the establishing of specific "vulnerability interviews," conducted by so-called vulnerability experts in the hotspot (I-15, Annex II) and, parallel to that, legal aid for asylum seekers.

Another example of how frontline workers collaborated on Chios to develop a practice they deemed both necessary and professionally organized concerned distributing food in the open camps. Staff from different professional backgrounds and different IOs struggled to devise a system that would provide everyone with food but not create a black market among camp residents. The initial system of having people line up in front of two tables was ineffective because some returned for seconds so there wasn't enough food to go around: Many people went without food or water for days. Various systems were tested by different teams, including one in which each family wrote down all the meals they received in a notebook. While they initially competed and even fought over how to handle distributions, they eventually agreed to acknowledge the competence of a camp manager who had organized food distribution in other refugee camps. She proposed a token system, giving each person a card to record all the meals they consumed in a week. Her approach went through several test runs, was discussed in the weekly food-group meeting, and tweaked. Frontline workers worked closely to ensure that the most basic needs of migrants, asylum seekers, and refugees were met. They considered it a humanitarian imperative because undernourishment and malnutrition had become a major problem on Chios, especially among children. Staff also considered proper food distribution to be political, particularly after a visiting European Commission representative implied that she could understand why the Greek government might not be keen on improving camp conditions, preferring to maintain them as being as transitory as possible to discourage migrants from crossing to Europe (Field notes, Chios, April 28, 2016).

The organization of food distribution shows that, like the mechanisms underlying improvisation, competence negotiations may be driven not only by cooperation but also by competition and confrontation. Shore patrol clearly illustrates the competitive dimension of competence negotiations. When the crisis began, shore patrol was conducted by different teams with different operating procedures—who intensely competed over how to spot migrant boats and help them land safely. They often accused others of acting unprofessionally and argued over the best shoreline route, the best lookout spots, the safest landing sites, and who should be informed first when a boat was spotted. Eventually they reached an understanding about which professional skills were needed to address the large number of migrant boats: Lifesavers and other rescue professionals know how to systematically scan the shoreline for boats, intercept and tow boats to ensure that they do not capsize, and perform lifesaving and man-overboard procedures. Based on the recognition of these skills, they gradually determined how to competently perform shore patrol and established fairly defined procedures (see I-6, I-7, I-8, Annex II).

This process also included determining what *not* to do during shore patrol or related SAR practices: For example, the registration of new arrivals (see Box 4.1).

Box 4.1 Knowing and doing shore patrol

It is 6 in the morning; we receive a message from "useful Tim" (a Frontex intelligence officer) on WhatsApp: A refugee boat has been spotted and is being brought into the port by Frontex. Ben, one of the coordinators of our team of international volunteers, is on the Alpha phone duty. I sleep in my clothes on the couch of a small holiday flat that we share among five volunteers. Ben wakes me; we are the on-call shift tonight. We throw on our high visibility vests and drive down to the port in our car, stocked with clothes, water and snacks. The boat has not yet arrived but Joris and one of his Dutch colleagues from the Frontex Border Security Team are there. Joris tells me that about 60 people are on the boat. The Romanians are pulling them in right now but he is not sure where they will land: "Maybe in front of Goodys"—a café on the other side of the port. We wait in front of the office of the port police for the boat to arrive while the sun is slowly rising.

After the boat docks, the Romanian coast guards quietly and in a much-practiced manner disembark the people. Then, we do a headcount: 21 men, 28 women and 23 kids. Ben posts the number of the new arrivals in the Refugee Partners Group on WhatsApp—this is important for the UNHCR people on the island, who compile "daily data snapshots" of the people arriving, but are never at the landings themselves. While we wait for the port authorities, people, tired from the crossing, sit down along the dock, many of them with nothing more than the change of clothes on their backs or small backpacks. We provide them with water, juice boxes and cakes.

Eventually, two officers from the port police arrive on the scene; a woman in uniform and a male officer in plain clothes. "Do you have these bracelets?," the man asks me in order for me do a first registration of the new arrivals. I am a bit astonished by this question: I know that people who have been brought into the port by Frontex yesterday got pink paper bracelets with a hand-written number on them while they were still on their vessel in order to count them but am very surprised that the Hellenic Coast Guard asks me to do the first registration of the new arrivals. Knowing that a proper registration with the police is important for people to register their intent to claim asylum and access international protection, I politely decline: "I am sorry; I think I cannot do the registration" and insist "This is really not my job." He walks off, mumbling that he will try to find some bracelets himself. The other officer reluctantly allows us to walk people over into the parking lot across the street as the ferry from Athens is about to come in and they want the new arrivals out of the port area so that usual port business can resume.

In the meantime, I try to find out whether people can be walked over to Souda to be accommodated there. Usually, new arrivals must first be transported to the hotspot Vial to get registered, screened and debriefed. Today, however, the bus is not coming. Since new arrivals refused or simply have not been able to pay the fee for the bus, the driver stopped coming to landings. Stuck in the parking lot of the port with 72 new arrivals, a third of them children, we try to find a solution to provide them with shelter and get them registered. I walk into the building of the port authorities to see whether they agree that we take people to Souda. "People can go to Souda now but will have to go up to Vial at a later point." If they are not going to Vial directly, we shall write down their names and inform the port police as soon as they go to the registration site in order for them to be able to inform the local police up there. Ben, however, just found out that Souda management refuses to take any more people. The camp is at a breaking point, tensions and aggressions have risen over the past couple of days and more and more people are already dwelling under tarps and blankets on the small beach by the sea side, just outside the camp.

As we are trying to come up with a solution, Chris, from Red Cross, shows up in the port. He has a small bus and volunteers to take some of the people up to Vial straight away. Our volunteers with cars can also take a couple of people up there now, at least the pregnant women and the boy who cannot walk and his family. I ask the officer from the port police, whom I talked to earlier and who followed me outside, if she can call a few taxis so that we can transport some more of the people to the hotspot, 8 kilometres away from the port, in the hinterland of Chios. "There is a taxi stand, just down the road," she snaps at me. Whereas she will not help by calling a taxi, she wants to know the number of people that will go to Vial now so that she can inform

continued

Box 4.1 *continued*

her colleagues in the hotspot. She wants me to call and confirm the number once the people have left and leaves herself. We organise and pay for a few taxis to take people up to Vial. I call the women from the port police and confirm the number of people that are now on their way. I feel angry that she does not assume any of her responsibilities towards the people who have just landed on Chios and, officially, are under her care, not ours.

Source: Author's field notes, Chios, April 2016.

As the extract in Box 4.1 from my field notes exemplifies, on several occasions, Greek port authorities requested that lifesavers and humanitarian workers record the identities of people who had just crossed the maritime border into Europe: "We had that on Leros as well [...]: 'Oh, can you count everyone and write down all of their names and passport details?' ... 'No, *what?!*' [laughs]" (I-7, Annex II). They agreed that this was the domain of professionals who were also authorized to record the new arrivals' intentions to claim asylum in Europe.

Cooperation and competition were complemented by conflictual negotiations. Conflicts sometimes erupted regarding a practice's proper performance. Once, as a migrant boat was landing at Chios Town port, there was a confrontation between a Frontex officer and a humanitarian volunteer. While distributing water, dry clothes, and diapers to the new arrivals, the volunteer observed a Frontex officer he'd never met, who was probably on a new rotation, verbally abusing the people disembarking. When challenged about that, the officer responded that they had only come to Europe "to rape our women" (Field notes, Chios, April 27, 2016). During another landing that day, the volunteer informed Frontex officers who had been on Chios for a while of the incident. They agreed that such behavior was unacceptable and promised to discuss it with the new officer, who subsequently acknowledged his error to the humanitarian worker. After the humanitarian worker and the coastguards had taken issue with the border guard's abusive behavior, judging his actions as incompetent border guarding, they called on their colleague to have it stopped (Field notes, Chios, April 27, 2016).

Another example of such conflicts over a practice's correct performance relates to registration. As briefly discussed above, registration was not easily organized at the border. Not only was crowd management a problem, the lacking technical infrastructure also hindered the effective registering of new arrivals (see also Pollozek and Passoth 2019). Because there was no internet connection at the hotspot Vial, registration was done by pen and paper (see Figure 4.1).

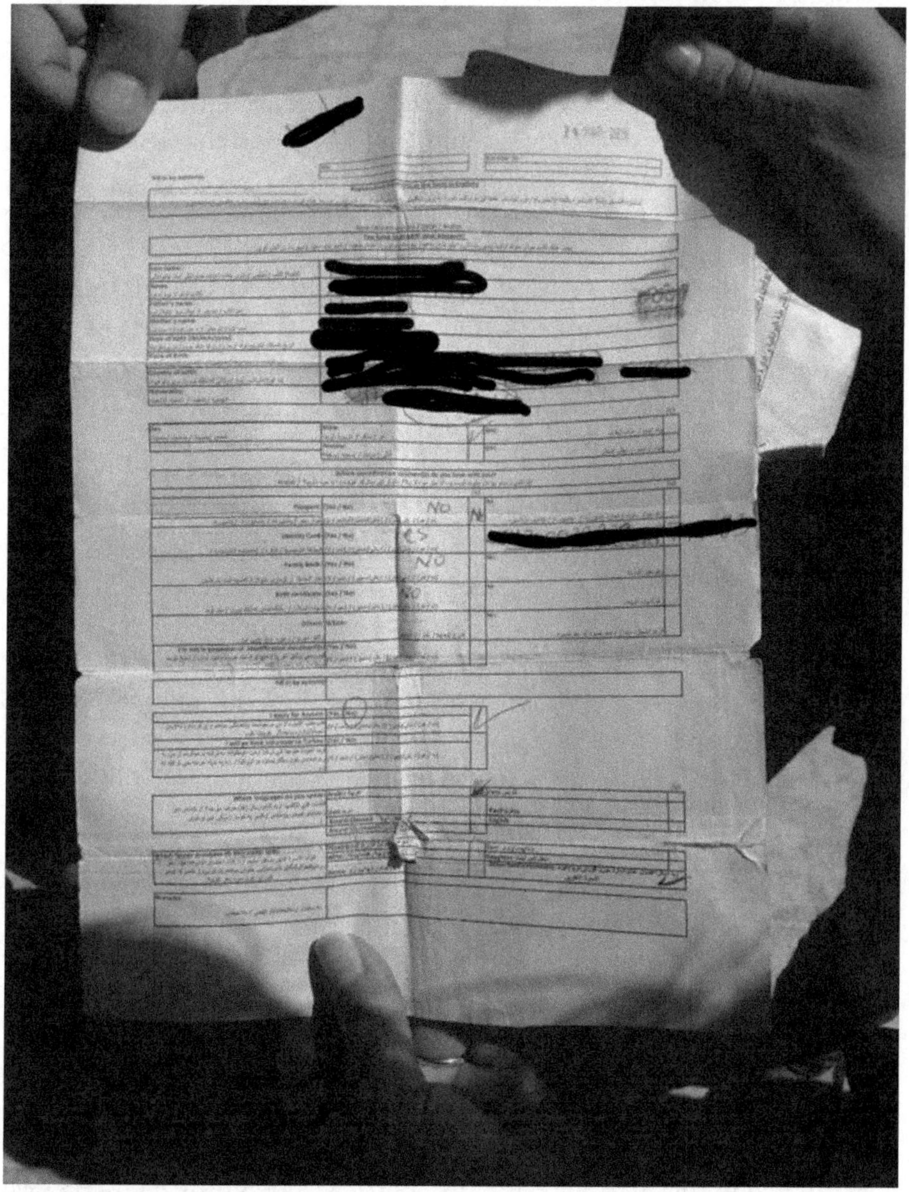

Fig. 4.1 Registration paper

Source: Photo taken by the author, Chios, March 2016.

The Greek police, who registered new arrivals before Frontex would take fingerprints and upload them in the EURODAC database, screen for nationalities, and debrief incoming migrants, also had the task to register intents to claim asylum during this first registration. On Chios, they simply did not do so until protection officers confronted them. When the police started lodging asylum claims they did not ask, however, *if* people wanted to claim asylum but *where*. Creating the impression that asylum seekers had a choice, many unknowingly named Germany, Sweden, and other Northern European countries. In reaction, the police would circle "no" on the papers because people on the move did not explicitly express their wish to apply for asylum *in Greece* (see Figure 4.1). As soon as humanitarian workers, protection officers, and legal experts found out about this practice, they challenged the police and provided bus shuttles to the registration site, making sure that every asylum seeker on the island had a chance to lodge her intent to do so (Field notes, Chios, April 21, 2016). In brief, border workers improvised to get a practice off the ground and fought over how to carry it out properly.

In that sense, the field became a site for contestation where IO field staff not only tried to cope with the reality of large mixed movements but also resisted particular ways of addressing them. When some frontline workers sought to make border and coastguarding only about deterring people on the move and curbing mobility—as described above—others confronted them. In most cases, these instances of contestation and confrontation led to a compromise in the different professional visions of how to organize a collective response to migration and asylum (see below). In some cases, however, they also created practices that were considered harmful by many on the ground: push-backs are exemplary of this. On several occasions, it was observed that (mainly Turkish) coastguards, instead of assisting refugee boats, quickly drove around them in circles to create high waves that would make the boats capsize and prevent asylum seekers from reaching Greek waters (see also Aegean Boat Report 2022). Such activities were seen as detrimental to the governance of mixed migration, against basic human rights, and in breach of international law by many humanitarians and migration lawyers on Chios. Despite their criticism of it, however, this practice has continued. This illustrates that the professions do not always come to an agreement about how to perform practices in a competent way and that creativity and the adaptation of international norms to local realities is not *per se* a progressive process (see Chapter 6 for a discussion of the normative concerns related to governance on the ground as well as the question of whether it is effective in solving global issues).

In addition, conflicts sometimes took the form of disputes about the kind of professional action a situation requires. During a landing on a beach near the Agia Ermioni port, a small fishing harbor on Chios's eastern shore, for example, I observed that humanitarian workers, lifesavers, and medical professionals considered that getting everyone ashore safely had priority. They helped navigate the boat to the rocky beach and the passengers to land, conducted medical check-ups, and distributed water and sweet snacks, space blankets, and dry clothes. During all that, a border guard, in contrast, was trying to arrest someone he had identified as the boat's pilot because he thought the most important thing in that situation was to arrest smugglers. Some of the new arrivals gathered around the guard, agitatedly explaining that the person he was detaining had only helped steer the boat and that the smugglers had stayed in Turkey. When the border guard realized he would not find enough people willing to testify that the man had been the pilot, he released him (Field notes, Chios, April 2, 2016). This case was not about a clash in views of how to competently perform a particular practice but rather different understandings of the right practice to apply.

Competence negotiations involve struggles over both which practices should be used to address mixed movement and how to carry them out appropriately—issues that are linked, as the following example illustrates. Despite generally opposing returns of any kind, a humanitarian worker considered that Frontex escort officers were competently conducting readmissions to Turkey:

> My personal relationship with them [Frontex] has been up and down. But they're starting to come out as the good guys [laughing] [...]. Like with the deportation [the first forced returns to Turkey]: I was quite confident that some level of respect was [maintained] because Frontex was there. And that's just sad. (I-5, Annex II)

Because readmissions were carried out professionally, the frontline worker could accept them as one practice governing mixed migration. This illustrates how, on Chios, the cooperative, competitive, and confrontational negotiations over competent behavior described above led to specific practices for governing mixed migration becoming socially accepted. Frontline workers collectively evaluated (a) which practices were suitable for governing mixed migration on the ground and (b) how to properly perform them. Against the background of their professional knowledge, they assessed competing ways of knowing and doing and (often) reached agreement about which tentative practical solutions were feasible and appropriate based on whether or not they perceived them to be performed professionally.

Such understandings were contingent upon being continually renegotiated. Newcomers, bringing in new professional skills and understandings of particular situations, sometimes disagreed with specific procedures and challenged what counts as competent practice. In addition, local conditions changed as the political situation evolved and migration dynamics shifted. Yet as I show in the following section, these agreements over competent practices became stabilized on the ground through routinization, producing frontline practices that now largely determine how IOs govern mixed migration at the border (on the organization-wide consolidation and diffusion of these practice, see Chapter 5).

Having said that, improvisation and competence negotiations are not always followed by routinizing practice. Situated learning is not a deterministic process whereby governance gaps are progressively filled. The observational data reveals that, in several cases, attempts at finding local solutions to govern migration and displacement were considered insufficient but fieldworkers did not manage to come up with more adequate ways of doing things. For example, given the lack of appropriate accommodation facilities and guardians, unaccompanied minors were often taken into police custody. Many agreed that this is not a good solution but failed to improvise and agree on a different practice. The initial solutions that are routinized, however, have been tested, contested, tweaked, and accepted by the professionals who work in the interorganizational community of practice at the border.

In sum, this section has demonstrated that frontline staff not only experiment to cope with local pressures and implement organizational mandates. They also reflect on their spontaneous decisions and quarrel over which ones are suitable and appropriate. They thereby further spell out what particular mandates and policies actually mean when implemented on the ground, adapting and complementing them as they go about their daily work. Through defining which practices are required and how to carry them out correctly, they substantially shape how migration and asylum is to be handled at the border.

4.3 Routinizing Practice

Creating the practical knowledge necessary for organizing collective action on migration and asylum in the field "was an uphill struggle all the way" (I-7, Annex II). To integrate lessons learned and reduce the burden of having to test and negotiate responses to migration and displacement, fieldworkers established local protocols and organized training sessions. This section demonstrates that by routinizing their decisions and procedures, they established specific frontline practices for governing large movements and discusses how these practices fix the meaning of mixed migration and its public regulation.

4.3.1 Protocols, Shadowing, and On-the-Job Training

Through improvising and negotiating competence, frontline staff on Chios generated practical knowledge: "We now have the knowledge to handle the situation here, so yes, it's OK, we continue working and adapting to the situation" (I-8, Annex II). To stabilize that knowledge and convey it to new practitioners, they wrote protocols, checklists, and other documents laying out standard operating procedures (SoPs) and referral mechanisms. For instance, a SAR team leader created a handover report sheet to standardize the transfer of medical cases from landing sites to the hospital (I-8, Annex II). Similarly, frontline workers doing shore patrol created detailed maps of the island that recorded the key lookout spots, landing sites, and patrol routes. They developed an elaborate phone chain and a detailed checklist for boat landings that consolidated their procedures which had evolved through improvisation and competence negotiation. In a third case, several members of humanitarian NGOs created a spreadsheet on distributing NFIs in the camps. These documents were frequently updated in light of new experiences. As the EASO field coordinator for Chios said, "We are all learning by doing. [On] Lesvos, the SoPs have been revised five times" (I-15, Annex II). They were living documents geared toward consolidating local experiments and the experiential knowledge they produced (see also Bueger and Edmunds 2021: 186–8, who analyze how informal, experimental practices for maritime governance become consolidated through capacity-building).

To further stabilize and transmit that knowledge and the practices that it sustains, field staff organized training opportunities that included newcomers shadowing more experienced frontline workers (I-1, I-7, I-11, Annex II). They also facilitated exchange through workshops: "Many organizations have done seminars for their staff but also invited local people and volunteers or people from other organizations" (I-10, Annex II). And they ran practical exercises and simulations:

> So the exercise was that the [...] rescue boat with, I think, three of the team members on it was pretending to be a refugee boat. So they went to one of the most common landing areas, turned the engine off and just floated whilst two people or three people got in the water and swam about, i.e., they were refugees who had fallen off the boat. So the whole thing was kind of a simulation of what could

> happen. So then a volunteer on the land saw them—saw the incident—called the rescue team, and the local rescue team then came to help out. So they took the people onto their own boat, who had fallen into the water, took them to land, made sure that they were received by a rescue team and an ambulance, and then they went back in their boats and they towed the fake refugee boat into the harbor, which is exactly what would be done if it was a real refugee boat: [They] got the people off safely at the harbor—and that was the whole exercise really. (I-7, Annex II)

Because practical knowledge is easily lost if not constantly practiced, they sought to routinize it through protocols and training, as this rescue professional explained:

> The problem that I see right now is that because there is no massive coming of refugees, maybe we are losing some kind of knowledge [about] handling the situation and this is why I try to make some practices, some exercises, just to retrain [...] that. Because in wintertime, we had arrivals—five, ten boats per day—and everybody knows perfectly what do to. Everybody knows all the points, arrival points, where the clothes are, how to go there and to handle the groups, and because now there are new volunteers, all this knowledge [is getting lost]—and this is one of my main concerns: not to forget that! (I-8, Annex II)

The outcome of these routinizing activities, which stabilize the ways of handling migration and asylum that have been found competent, are practices: patterned actions that are based on professional background knowledge and performed to achieve specific goals. IO field staff carry out these practices to handle mixed migration at the frontlines. They express their specific understanding of what mixed migration means as a policy concern and how it needs to be addressed to bring some degree of order to spontaneous, irregular movement and the turmoil it causes in the absence of an international regime. In the remainder of this chapter, I discuss the different definitions of mixed migration as a public challenge that these practices embody and act out and why their performance largely determines "who gets what, when, and how" (Lasswell 1936) at the border, therefore qualifying as a form of governing.

4.3.2 Frontline Practices in the Making

At the beginning, many IOs were overwhelmed by the crisis. As UNHCR and IOM (2016: 8) put it: "The international community was caught unprepared for such large numbers of people [and] the overall response has remained unstructured." A Frontex spokeswoman said, "It was new, you know [...]. We've never had situations like that" (I-19, Annex II). Policy guidelines were scarce and formal mandates fragmentary—with a large number of organizations involved. To respond to the ensuing complexity, uncertainty, and urgency, IO frontline staff learned on the ground. This chapter has reconstructed *how* their everyday experiments created practical knowledge and routines for addressing mixed movements.

The practices that ultimately resulted from situated learning at the border range from patrol, SAR, registration, screening, and debriefing, through camp management, asylum interviews, legal aid and protection, to relocation and returns. Mirroring the complexity of mixed migration and covering a broad range of aspects, they essentially define mixed migration and how to deal with it (see Table 4.1).

The table lists the various practices and who performed them (see columns one and two). It provides an overview of how, in the field, IOs determined what mixed migration means as a policy concern and how to address the public challenges it raises (see column three).

Table 4.1 Frontline practices for governing mixed migration

Practices	Actors		Public goods at stake	
	Profession	**Organization**	**Problem definition**	**Proposed answer**
Search and rescue	Coastguards Lifesavers Firefighters Rescue professionals	Greek coastguard Frontex SAR NGOs Volunteers	Lack of safe migration routes	Spotting of migrant boats, rescue procedures, safe disembarkation
Land and sea patrol / border guarding	Coastguards Border guards	Greek coastguard Frontex	Irregular border crossings	Surveillance, apprehension
First reception and transportation	Humanitarian workers Paramedics Social workers	Volunteers SAR NGOs	Basic short-term needs of people on the move	Medical check-ups, provision of basic goods (clothes, food, water), and referral to registration and accommodation sites

Continued

Table 4.1 *Continued*

Practices	Actors		Public goods at stake	
	Profession	Organization	Problem definition	Proposed answer
Screening, registration, and debriefing	Police Border guards	Greek police Frontex	Potential security threat / not knowing who enters a country	Identification of nationalities, personal details, and Migration routes
Protection and monitoring • Child protection • Protection from sexual-based violence	Lawyers Social workers	UNHCR NGOs	Access to international protection (under the UN Refugee Convention and other human rights treaties)	Observing compliance with international law as well as identification of vulnerable groups and organizing access to specific procedures
Camp management • Food • Shelter • NFIs • WASH • Medical care • Psychosocial support • Educational activities	Humanitarian workers Logisticians Doctors Psychologists Social workers	UNHCR NGOs IOM Volunteers	Basic short-, medium-, and long-term needs of people on the move	Provision of basic goods to all people on the move (food, shelter, health, education)
Interviews • Admissibility interviews (fast-track border procedure) • Eligibility interviews (asylum procedure)	Caseworkers / asylum experts Vulnerability experts	EASO Greek Asylum Service	Distinction between people in need of protection and those who can return / have access to asylum	Collecting information on migration journey and reasons to leave home country
Legal aid	Lawyers	NGOs	Access to human rights, adherence to legal procedures	Information provision, legal counseling, strategic litigation

Relocation • To the Greek mainland • To other EU countries		Volunteers UNHCR EASO	Overcrowding of hotspots, overstraining national reception capacities	Finding alternative accommodation sites, redistributing asylum seekers
Return • Detention and forced readmissions • Voluntary returns • AVRR	Escorts Social workers Psychologists	Frontex IOM	Abuse of asylum and welfare systems, lack of reception capacities	Physically removing people on the move from border sites (either voluntarily or involuntarily)

For example, SAR establishes that mixed migration is primarily about safe migration routes, which it seeks to provide through the resources available to lifesavers and rescue professionals: land, sea, and air patrol, man-overboard procedures, and safe disembarkation (see also Cuttitta 2017). Asylum interviews, in turn, define mixed migration as providing people who were forced to flee their home countries with access to safe states, while readmissions and returns frame the phenomenon as primarily being about distinguishing those in need of protection from those who can stay in their countries of origin—and physically returning the latter. Camp management characterizes mixed migration as a humanitarian emergency that requires satisfying the most basic needs of people on the move—irrespective of their legal status. Border guarding makes clear that mixed migration's key problem is the unauthorized crossing by migrants and the potential security threat that results from not knowing who enters a country. The public good at stake when it comes to mixed migration is hence public order and security, which is provided by the containment of irregular movement, mostly in the form of surveillance and apprehension. In brief, by proposing very different practical solutions, these practices very differently define the problem that large mixed movements pose (see also Obendiek 2021).

In performing these practices, IO actors restrict or enable how people on the move can go about their lives. They not only make decisions about their resident status and assist them in making use of their rights—such as the right to family reunification or the right not to be returned to a country where they face persecution—but, by ensuring their safe passage, apprehending them at the border, or guaranteeing their physical and mental health, they actively shape their life choices. They determine, at the micro level of international migration and asylum policy-making, "who gets what, when, and how." They do not do so to assist them in private matters but because they believe this to be an important public task. In other words, by organizing collective action to reduce the disorder and confusion that prevailed at the border, frontline staff directly influenced the possibilities for action of people on the move—effectively governing mixed migration on the ground (see Section 2.3 for a conceptual discussion of governance).

Sometimes the different frontline practices coexist; sometimes they compete or clash (see above). Together they map what mixed migration is and how to govern it in the field. Chapter 5 explores the content of these practices in greater detail and shows how they anchor a certain understanding of how to regulate the migration-asylum nexus within the IOs, beyond the local context of Chios and the European external border. It analyzes the skills and routines that IOs consolidate and diffuse to demonstrate how, in the absence of a comprehensive and coherent international regime, they manage migration and asylum through practice on the ground.

4.4 Conclusion: Governing at the Border

IO staff working at the EU's external border during the migration and refugee crisis of 2015–16 were directly confronted with a high number of people irregularly crossing the border. The lack of comprehensive mandates and clear policy guidance on mixed migration notwithstanding, they felt obliged to organize collective action: "[W]e had to do something. We couldn't just sit around and do nothing" (I-1, Annex II). To do so, they *improvised*, using their professional skills and personal networks. Improvisation overlapped with *competence negotiations*. Frontline workers quarreled over which ways of dealing with mixed movements were suitable and appropriate and how to carry them out in a professional manner. They ultimately *routinized* their impromptu actions to stabilize and transfer their new practical knowledge. These three mechanisms produced a series of practices for addressing migration and asylum at the border.

In creating and performing these practices, IOs in the field *de facto* governed mixed migration: Not only did their everyday decisions directly affect the life choices of people on the move, but the practices they produced through situated learning at the border have also largely come to define how IOs regulate migration and asylum in view of scanty regulations. Because formal policy-making at headquarters level is usually blocked due to the deep political contestation of migration matters (see Chapter 3), IOs govern at the frontlines—through practice on the ground.

Let me illustrate this twofold governing function of frontline practices one more time by taking the admissibility interviews as an example once again: The way field staff conducted them directly impacted on where asylum seekers were allowed to go. The interviews are of course based on formal policy—mainly the EU Asylum Procedures Directive and the EASO Special Operating Plan to Greece (EASO 2016) and the Greek law implementing the EU-Turkey Deal—but "the legislative provisions are not directly usable to carry out decision-making" at the street level (Infantino 2021: 1029). EASO hotspot staff needed to interpret, bend, and transform them substantially to adapt them to local realities and put them into practice. The way fieldworkers process frontal, horizontal, and vertical pressures (from people on the move, colleagues in the local interorganizational community of practice, and superiors at headquarters) thus determines how these polices actually come to bear on the lives of displaced people. It is *their practice* which directly enables or constrains asylum seekers' possible actions.

Their practice has also largely shaped the form and content of admissibility interviews, thereby substantially determining how EASO addresses migration and displacement at the border.[8] This is even more consequential given the absence of an integrated international regime for mixed migration with clearly stipulated organizational responsibilities.[9] In light of formal authority and policy gaps, IO actions on the ground represent an important share of their overall activities governing large mixed movements.

That said, it is important to note that such governing on the ground is often involuntary and arduous. Fieldworkers experience deep frustration because they can only change things slowly and incrementally (I-1, I-3, I-6, I-9, I-11, I-12, Annex II). They acknowledge that they are not in a position to make

[8] Federica Infantino (2021) observes the same dynamics with respect to putting EU visa policies into practice: Consular staff from different national embassies form local communities of practice in their operational work environments and by learning to implement the policies, change them from below. Kalkman and Groenewegen (2018: 2) characterize frontline workers in interorganizational settings as "active policy-making agents." Katerina Glynidaki also finds these interorganizational, street-level policy-making dynamics in urban refugee and migration governance in Athens and Berlin (2021), while Daniela DeBono (2019) analyzes them among "borderworkers" in hotspot sites in Malta and Italy. Shoshana Fine (2017) studies the community of practice of "bordercrats" in Turkey and shows how they created Turkey's first asylum law.

[9] The European Center for Constitutional and Human Rights (ECCHR), a human rights NGO, filed a complaint with the European Ombudsman because they thought "EASO's influence on inadmissibility decisions exceeds the agency's competence." They observed that "EASO officers exercise *de facto* power on decisions in relation to applications for international protection" that exceeds the agency's formal mandate (ECCHR 2017: 2).

fundamental decisions and that their muddling through is less effective and far-reaching than formal and coordinated policy-level responses. In addition, given the limited institutional checks, it is prone to failure and arbitrariness (see Chapter 6 for a more general discussion of effectiveness and legitimacy concerns related to governing through practice).

A final caveat of governing on the ground is that staff in the field work in the shadow of state sovereignty and formal authority: Their on-site governing is not disconnected from decision-making at headquarters. For example, their judgment may be suddenly and drastically restricted after formal policymakers agree on a joint framework—often ignoring what frontline workers have learned and developed. This happened when the EU-Turkey Statement was signed in March 2016, as a humanitarian volunteer describes:

> One of the biggest disappointments for me was we worked so hard—all the [organizations] and the volunteer community—to get to a really effective system, and it was working! [...] Everyone knew their role, we were talking a lot, going to all these meetings, the volunteer community and the others were holding each other accountable: The IOs, when they needed something, they would call the volunteer community and we could take it there. And the lines of communication were really opening up, and they really relied on us—with unaccompanied children, for example. And we were working effectively like that. And then, within the week the deal was signed and implemented, everything fell to pieces. NGOs withdrew [from Vial], all the systems broke apart. And everything we worked on for the sake of the refugees was just completely destroyed. (I-6, Annex II)

The recent criminalization of SAR NGOs is another example of curtailing the discretionary powers and practices of (particular) frontline workers (Cusumano and Bell 2021). In short, this shows that IO staff in the field and at headquarters often work according to different logics and timeframes—but not in completely separate spheres. The following chapter (Chapter 5) turns to the links between the different organizational sites. It analyzes how governing on the ground is connected to decision-making at headquarters. It investigates stabilization processes to shed light on how headquarters staff influence governing on the ground on the one hand, and the consolidation of the specific content of different frontline practices on the other. It continues the case study to reconstruct how IOs govern mixed migration through practice on the ground before Chapter 6 discusses the theoretical, normative, and institutional implications of this governance mode.

5
Stabilization
Consolidating and Diffusing Frontline Practices

What happens in the field does not go unnoticed at headquarters. Secretariat staff in the training and operations units of the international organizations (IOs) that work at the border closely observe what their colleagues do on the ground and use their experiential knowledge to develop and update training tools, thereby codifying operational practices. While field staff often engage in boundary blurring, closely working with people from other organizations, headquarters staff more actively try to demarcate their organization's turf by consolidating practical knowledge and claiming competence for it. In doing so, they exert considerable influence over which knowledge from the field travels—and which is ignored.

This chapter analyzes how training and operations officers at headquarters consolidate and diffuse practices from and to the field, reconstructing their attempts to stabilize what has been learned at the border and to standardize on-site practice. It examines headquarters staff's role in governing on the ground and sheds further light on the skills and routines that define how mixed migration is governed in practice.

The chapter is based on interviews with IO staff members at the headquarters of the European Asylum Support Office (EASO), the European Border and Coast Guard Agency (Frontex), the United Nations (UN) High Commissioner for Refugees (UNHCR), the International Organization for Migration (IOM), the Norwegian Refugee Council (NRC), and the humanitarian umbrella organizations and interagency initiatives Sphere, the Protection Standby Capacity Project (ProCap), the International Association of Professionals in Humanitarian Assistance and Protection (PHAP), and the Humanitarian Leadership Academy (HLA). The chapter relies on my analysis of their training materials and operational documents (see Chapter 1 and Annex II). Its two main parts correspond to the last two steps of the loop model (see Section 2.3). Section 5.1 traces how IO staff members who conceptualize learning programs influence the consolidation of on-the-ground policy solutions. It also details the frontline practices that the different IOs

Global Governance on the Ground. Nele Kortendiek, Oxford University Press. © Nele Kortendiek (2024).
DOI: 10.1093/oso/9780198889120.003.0005

use for dealing with mixed migration. Section 5.2 then explores the way they are diffused through training. This underlines the iterative nature of governing on the ground. The chapter concludes by reflecting on the feedback effects on formal policy-making, and demonstrates that governing on the ground not only regulates mixed migration through practice at the frontlines but also informs official policies and mandates.

5.1 Consolidation: Designing Learning Materials

Chapter 4 shows that at the border, the "capacity or experience of people who have competencies in their relevant area of work" is key (I-9, Annex II). Professional competencies provide frontline workers with the agency to improvise and negotiate acceptable practice within and across organizational boundaries as they gradually routinize what they have learned during the crisis. Albeit context-specific, some of these skills and routines do not stay put: they are consolidated at headquarters through operational training programs. The following two sub-sections reconstruct *who* is involved in this process at headquarters and *what* substantive know-how and patterns of action are stabilized through training.

5.1.1 In the Control Room: Training and Operations Officers in IOs

While the field-based governing processes described in Chapter 4 occur with little interference from headquarters decision-makers, some of the secretariat staff members who primarily work in operations and training units act as "bridges" and channel "information from the headquarters to the field and vice versa" (I-35, Annex II). Because they provide field staff with practical guidance for applying international norms to concrete situations, they work at the interface between field and headquarters.

Their primary function is to operationalize existing policies: it is their job "to find a way to translate them to make them practical" (I-35). They develop training materials and run workshops to give fieldworkers a general understanding of the relevant legal conventions. For example, UNHCR operational staff are familiarized with questions such as, "What's protection at sea?" "What are the Palermo protocols?" "What are some of the substantive areas of law that intersect in particular with mixed migration?" and are trained to apply them using "differentiated case management strategies" and best practices for protection in mixed migration scenarios (I-33).

However, interviews revealed that headquarters staff not only translate policies and legal regulations "downwards" but they also create training tools from the bottom up. Across organizations, interview partners confirm that the field signals new training needs. A UNHCR staff member explains that "the conceptualization of the [mixed migration] learning program was a result of the genuine interest that had been expressed from the field in the first place, essentially from various different operations in the Middle East and North Africa" (I-34). When frontline staff are confronted with new problems, they request support from headquarters. In response and to create new training tools, headquarters staff then "try to capitalize on as much information as possible that we can gather from informed sources that are or could be our target audience" (I-34). They debrief field staff, organize consultation processes, and run stocktaking exercises to consolidate experiential knowledge produced on the ground in different locations around the world that could be useful to field staff in similar contexts (I-19, I-22, I-29, I-30, I-35). Despite different training mandates and capacities,[1] in all the organizations studied, training officers filter information from the field "upwards."

This is also demonstrated by statements in training documents. All the handbooks analyzed express the authors' thankfulness for input from practitioners worldwide. For example, the foreword to the "UNHCR Tool for Participatory Assessment in Operations" clarifies:

> This Tool is the product of collaborative efforts, resulting from consultations and contributions from UNHCR staff and partners in the field and at headquarters in Geneva; it was piloted in 14 countries and has been applied in 40 UNHCR field operations. UNHCR would like to thank all those who contributed to the development of this Tool. (UNHCR 2006b: 2)

[1] IOs organize training differently. EASO and Frontex have an explicit training mandate. Training thus makes up a large proportion of their operational activities. While a highly integrated institutional infrastructure goes with it, other IOs do not have separate training units. IOM is a highly decentralized organization and learning takes place in the different thematic units in the different departments or in interagency committees. UNHCR, in turn, created its own Global Learning Center, located in Budapest, to streamline the developing and delivering of training within the organization. Humanitarian non-governmental organizations (NGOs) either pooled their learning resources by creating umbrella organizations or collaborate in informal networks to create and implement learning activities. Organizational structures and resources for training are hence situated along a broad spectrum of institutional options and vary in terms of the degree of coherence and centralization. Importantly, however, the different organizations that are involved in governing mixed migration on the ground all deliver some type of learning activity in their respective areas of competence and develop handbooks, best practice guides, and other learning tools to train fieldworkers. See Annex II for a brief description of the different IOs' respective learning programs.

In a similar vein, a newsletter announcing publication of the revised "Sphere Standards" and accompanying training package reports:

> This year started off with our final revision workshop to finalize the fourth edition of the Sphere Handbook. That workshop capped a far-reaching and inclusive global consultation process, with feedback from practitioners in more than 65 countries. As the consolidation of those consultations, the new Sphere standards are built on local knowledge and established practice. (Sphere email correspondence with the author, December 19, 2018)

It is important to reiterate that information gathered in the field is not merely feedback on how to implement pre-existing rules expediently. IO training and operations staff run pilot projects on the ground "to learn from the operations and see what works in practice and what doesn't" (I-32). Surprisingly, though, the field is not just the site for testing policy implementation: training also consolidates new experiences with unforeseen—thus, not yet regulated—issues. For instance, Frontex's "Common Core Curriculum" for border guards had to be continually updated as the context changed along the Mediterranean Sea routes—emphasizing new operational requirements such as contingency planning, international cooperation, and protection-oriented border guarding:

> The Europe refugee situation, which began unfolding in 2015, brought the nexus between border management and international protection to the spotlight once again. The arrival of around a million persons that year, with the EU Member States in the Mediterranean shouldering the bulk of responsibility for the rescue and reception of the refugees and migrants, underlined the need for protection-sensitive and rights-based border management, contingency planning and cross-border cooperation. (Frontex 2017a: 16)

That is, people in the field report changes in the problem structure and request guidance—while also providing a key resource for developing such guidance: frontline knowledge and practices.

Hence, when IO headquarters staff create new training programs, they try to consolidate what the field staff already know and do: they seek to stabilize frontline practices generated through improvisation on the ground. The head of EASO's Department of Operations put it in a nutshell:

> So, there was a lot of this [improvisation during the crisis], which was good, which was a good learning experience, and now, obviously, the next *challenge will be*

> *to make all of this much more stable* because the reality is, it [mixed migration to Europe] is not going to go away. We'll probably maintain a level of support in Greece; the nature will change [...] a bit but they're still going to need support because they're still one of the hotspots. So, the challenge is going to be to make sure that next time it comes around, it's a lot better planned and we have systems in place. (I-24; emphasis added)

As this short interview extract indicates, operations and training officers try to capitalize on practical knowledge generated in the field to prepare their organizations for similar scenarios. A UNHCR staff member confirms this with respect to the mixed migration learning program:

> So, it's quite new. It was only piloted in December last year [2016]. It's been in the works for quite a while but it was established sort of in view of the fact that there is not necessarily a deep level of knowledge in UNHCR—both in headquarters and more broadly—about how we interact with other partners in responding to mixed migration flows, such as we are seeing in many parts of the world at the moment. [...] *The idea is that we skill up the organization in terms of mixed migration.* (I-33; emphasis added)

This quote shows that headquarters staff engage with fieldworkers and devise teaching materials "to skill up" organizations by benefiting from their colleagues' experiential knowledge.

At the same time, the headquarters staff acknowledged that frontline practices are often provisional (e.g. I-22). This is expressed in many training documents. One of IOM's psychosocial support tools explains that handbooks and practical guidelines collect pragmatic, improvised solutions:

> The tools do not aim at academic consistency, but are tailored to suit the operational aim, emergency timing, and limited quantitative and qualitative capacity of IOM assessments teams in emergency. As such they are not the best tools in general, but proved to be the best possible ones in order to grasp the complexity of the situation in the given time and operational capacity. (IOM 2009b: 15)

The UNHCR Guide of Good Practices for operational protection in camps and settlements also makes clear that these practices are "not perfect":

> More than forty "good practices" are included in this Guide, drawn from some twenty-three different country operations. The good practices included are not exhaustive and certainly not perfect. They may address a part of the problem but

> not be comprehensive in scope. They likely present the best achievable solution to an issue in a difficult working environment. (UNHCR 2006a: 11)

Staff in operations and training units codify practical knowledge created on the ground—although they may well be just make-shift solutions. Working with what they have, they draw on operational knowledge and experience to create training materials.

The frontline practices stabilized in training tools often substitute for formal policies. As the EASO former head of training said, "Normally, the training is about something [e.g. a policy] which already exists. But indirectly and quite often, the training content becomes guidance because in many situations, there is not really a pre-existing guideline and so the training material becomes guidance as such" (I-22). When official regulations are lacking, fieldworkers have to use learning materials and best practice guidelines to make decisions. In other words, headquarters staff consolidate frontline practices that complement—or even substitute for—official rules and policies. This emphasizes the governance function of creating teaching materials: consolidated frontline practices become a form of policy in their own right.

Interestingly, the design of learning materials reveals an interorganizational dimension. While IO field staff frequently engage in boundary blurring—working closely with people from other organizations (see Chapter 4)—headquarters staff demarcate the boundaries around their IO's jurisdiction by codifying particular practices. They engage in boundary work by specifying *which* practical knowledge *their* organization controls (see also Kranke 2022). Of course, they interact with learning experts in other IOs, consulting them "in order to take advantage of their expertise" (Frontex 2017a: 19). The EASO training team, for example, works with "different external partners. [...] [They] guide the content group by giving advice, by reviewing what has been developed and to make comments" (I-22). However, exchange and cooperation not only help clarify the meaning of particular practices but also serve to define an organization's turf. One of UNHCR's liaison officers with EASO who worked in the UNHCR Global Learning Center before going to work in Valletta, explained how each organization uses its own jargon to demarcate its activities:

> There is lot of jargon and there [are a] lot of in-house ways of addressing issues and channeling information and because it is so particular, it feels almost like there needs to be a *translation* unit: [...] some people who are capable of processing all of this information that comes from within the organization and putting it into other

> words and then channeling it to the outside world—and in this case, channeling it to EASO which has its own jargon, which has its own structure, its own modus operandi. (I-25)

This quote illustrates that each IO has its own way of doing things. And by putting local experience into the language of *their* organization, headquarters staff show that they are responsible for particular practices. A UNHCR colleague confirmed that, during consultations on learning materials and operational guidelines, staff from different IOs compete for "Deutungshoheit" (interpretational sovereignty) (I-31). They defend their jurisdiction and, at the same time, are careful to not press too far into new issue areas. In short, they become knowledge brokers who translate knowledge from the field and assert their competence *vis-à-vis* other organizations—also to signal control to their superiors in their home organization or external principals such as donors (I-27, I-30, I-31).

This also means that some knowledge from the ground does *not* travel. For example, the Sphere Standards, negotiated by over 400 humanitarian non-governmental organizations (NGOs), does not include some local experiences. One trainer who was closely involved in writing and updating the handbook said, "A lot of things are simply not covered in Sphere. They are not covered because they couldn't be agreed—not that they are not important" (I-30). He illustrated his point by discussing the competition between the Sphere Standards and UNHCR's emergency handbook:

> I, for example, work a lot with UNHCR and historically, they were extremely protective of their mandate, of their guidance. They had the UNHCR emergency handbook, they had their own set of standards and indicators, which in the end were quite close to Sphere. Their UNHCR emergency handbook predates the Sphere by two decades, so they've been doing that for a long time. And so, when Sphere came along, initially they were very resistant: "This has nothing to do with us, we have our own standards." As of today, they have abandoned the hard-copy emergency handbook and they now have an online emergency resource which replaces their handbook. And if you look at the entries in that online emergency handbook, many of them simply refer you to Sphere. So today UNHCR and Sphere—I have actually done the comparison: they are like 95 percent identical guidance in terms of the sectoral indicators. You know, how long you wait at a water tap to get water, how far away should a water tap be from someone's home? How close or how far is a latrine? How big is the site for a camp site? All of these things ... There, they are virtually the same and right now, there is no distance, there is no fighting

> between Sphere and UNHCR. [...] I think Sphere is a good vehicle for people to come together. (I-30)

This comment shows that when headquarters staff devise handbooks and practical guidelines, they try to prevent other IOs from encroaching on what they view as their area of expertise. An IOM staff member confirms: "With some topics, collaboration is more difficult. For example: 'Do the guidelines only refer to migrants or to migrants and refugees?' It has been quite difficult to agree with UNHCR on a definition—it is always quite difficult to find a common denominator on that [laughs]" (I-27). Inevitably some field knowledge *does* get lost in translation: learning materials do not fully depict what happens on the ground.

Whether it is normatively or politically desirable for some local practices to not be consolidated depends on one's *substantive* standpoint.[2] Some observers might deplore that extensively construing "vulnerability"—as some asylum experts in the EU hotspots did to permit the greatest number of people on the move access to international protection—was not normalized by headquarters. But those same observers will be happy that pushbacks are not in the training syllabus.[3] Analyzing *the mechanics* of the stabilization process linking IO field and headquarters does not allow us to decide whether knowledge traveling is good or bad. But it does demonstrate that to create learning tools, bureaucrats from different organizations come together to clarify their understandings of how (not) to organize migration and asylum at the border.

Overall, interview and document analysis shows that operations and training units are the central control room where IOs make sense of field practice, and stabilize and claim competence for it. Creating training materials is not a mere technical exercise but a *political* site where the content of specific practices is negotiated (see also Holmes 2019). It is where mixed migration experts from different IOs negotiate jurisdictions and compete over practical knowledge, while consolidating and streamlining it. This knowledge, and the patterns of action it informs, fills formal policy gaps and defines how to treat mixed migration in practice across the world.

[2] See Chapter 3 for a discussion of the competing understandings about which public good is at stake in governing mixed migration. The main conflict lines are marked by security and border protection versus the rights of migrants and refugees. See Chapter 6 for a discussion of how to normatively assess the process and outcome of governing on the ground.

[3] Not that this knowledge stays put. Frontex board members try to hide their involvement in pushbacks (Glouftsios 2023) but national border guards in particular continue to push back people on the move. In fact, it is so common that some observers refer to pushbacks as a "shadow" or "de facto" migration policy (Deutsche Welle 2023).

5.1.2 Frontline Practices for Governing Mixed Migration

How does frontline practice define mixed migration? Has the definition changed in view of the crisis in Europe and similar on-the-ground operations at other borders worldwide? To answer these questions and move from mechanics to substance, I zoom in on three key practices identified in the previous chapter: border guarding, search and rescue (SAR), and asylum interviews (see Chapter 4, Section 4.3.2). These practices largely cover the spectrum of organizations and professions involved in governing mixed movements in practice and well-illustrate how they define the migration-asylum nexus as a policy issue that intersects security, humanitarianism, and human rights.

Border Guarding

Border guarding is inherently linked to the right to enforce a country's border control laws. Therefore, it is performed and developed by Frontex, which is mandated to protect the Schengen border (see Section 3.2.1). As a practice, it includes several routines, such as checking travel documents and detecting forged or falsified papers, patrolling land and sea borders, as well as registering, fingerprinting, debriefing, and screening people on the move who have irregularly crossed borders.

Border guards primarily use law enforcement skills to perform these routines. They learn how to "examine and assess the validity and usage of travel-related documentation" (Frontex 2017a: 67) and to communicate "effectively during border control activities taking into account the presence of factors making individuals and groups nervous, irritated or angry" (Frontex 2017a: 54). This includes recognizing "risks and threats to safety, security and well-being of self and others during border control activities according to abnormal behavioural indicators" and behaving "assertively with persons showing nervous, aggressive or deceptive behavior" (Frontex 2017a: 54). Further, generic border guard training teaches "competencies like taking responsibility for the decision to grant permission to travellers to cross the borders of a state" (Frontex 2017a: 29). In contexts of "mass migration flows," controlling borders also means "apply[ing] methods and techniques for maintaining crowd calm and comfort" (Frontex 2017a: 58). When conducting border controls, guards must also be able to "identify persons in need of international protection in order to facilitate their access to the asylum procedure and take responsibility for referring persons in need of international protection to the competent authorities" (Frontex 2017b: 74). And they must be able to profile "persons crossing the border in accordance with risk indicators" (Frontex 2017a: 12) to recognize "potential terrorists/foreign fighters" (Frontex 2017a: 106).

Border guards also learn surveillance techniques, how to use specific electronic data bases, and how to identify and arrest human traffickers and smugglers (Frontex 2017a: 297). To monitor the "green border"—irregular border crossing points—and "prevent irregular cross border activity including illegal border crossing" (Frontex 2017a: 123), they learn how to conduct "surveillance patrols" along "observation and control posts" and to "ambush" people on the move using "thermo-vision cameras; night-vision goggles; binoculars; photo and video equipment; UAVs [unpiloted aerial vehicles]; portable document-examination devices; compass and GPS" (Frontex 2017a: 132). In other words, border guards are taught to use technological tools for detecting cross-border crimes, interpret the results, and report incidents "as potential intelligence to aid the prevention and detection of such activities" (Frontex 2017b: 107). In addition, all border guards receive "law enforcement basic training" to "be able to use physical force safely and coercive measures efficiently and proportionally" (Frontex 2017a: 144). This includes skills such as "basic movement, stances, distance and falling techniques; blocking and releasing techniques; takedown techniques; transportation techniques; arrest techniques; basic strikes and kicks; protection of the service weapon" (Frontex 2017a: 148).

More tailored routines such as debriefing involve interviewing migrants "in a way which enables the systematic extraction of information for intelligence purposes" (Frontex 2015: 14). It aims at collecting tactical information that "might point at safe houses, meeting points or suppliers of forged documents" as well as strategic information that "will teach more about modus operandi, trends, [and] routes" used by migrants who irregularly cross borders and their facilitators—or "push and pull factors" (Frontex 2013a: 114). It includes carrying out "voluntary, anonymous, informal and confidential debriefing interviews" and profiling "irregular migrants from target countries," as well as recognizing "possible suspects involved in people smuggling and other cross-border crime" (Frontex 2018b: 27). People on the move are seen as sources of information about migration routes and networks that is processed and conveyed to border and surveillance officers (Frontex 2017b: 6–10).[4] In terms of competencies, debriefing requires social and psychological skills, as the Frontex course catalogue explains:

[4] Human rights groups reported their concerns to the European Ombudsman that debriefing interviews at the Frontex-Spain Joint Operation Indalo at the Spanish-Moroccan sea border must be voluntary and maintain legal safeguards, see <https://www.ombudsman.europa.eu/en/decision/en/171951>, accessed September 4, 2023).

> How does this course prepare you for the job? You will learn how to prepare yourself for a debriefing interview, how to select the interviewee, gain his/her trust and collect information for intelligence purposes by means of understanding and applying cognitive interviewing techniques and psychological insight. You will also be shown how to draft a debriefing report after each interview. (Frontex 2018b: 26)

In sum, these examples of how Frontex teaches and performs border guarding practices demonstrate that mixed movements are primarily regarded as one of several "irregular cross-border activities" (Frontex 2017a: 29). Because border guarding uses law enforcement competencies and routines, such as gathering intelligence and apprehending people, its practical prescriptions *vis-à-vis* mixed migration view people on the move as *threats*. For border guards, the primary object of reference is not the *people* crossing borders but the borders themselves. Of course, asylum seekers must be identified at borders but it is the *borders* that are "vulnerable" and "at risk" (e.g. Frontex 2016a). Border guarding frames the migration-asylum nexus as a problem of organized crime and, echoing discursive securitization practices, views mixed migration as a threat to international security. Migration and displacement must be governed to prevent illegal acts from destabilizing public order (see also Léonard 2010).

Frontex's pragmatic definition of what mixed migration means as a policy concern has not fundamentally changed since the crisis of 2015–16. Negotiations with migration lawyers, protection officers, humanitarian professionals, and asylum caseworkers in the field and during the creation of learning materials raised awareness that border control procedures are critical junctures when people are allowed or prohibited from accessing international protection (e.g. I-20, I-21). But border guarding generally continues to treat mixed migration as an issue of order and security.

Yet within that framework, the crisis consolidated and enlarged this concept of border guarding by increasingly including returns. In the course of the crisis and especially following the decision to institute the fast-track border procedure in the hotspots (see Chapter 3 on the official policy response to the crisis), Frontex had to learn to deploy return escorts to repatriate migrants who voluntarily wanted to leave or whose claims to asylum in Europe had not been found admissible. A senior Frontex official describes how the organization adjusted its operational plans:

> When the EU-Turkey Statement was signed, it was estimated that there [would] be 500 migrants being sent back to Turkey a week. That was the estimate. So we were requested to have hundreds of escort officers on the islands. Because nobody had done that before, there were certain assumptions that turned out to be wrong.

> [...] So, we've learned. So now we have a system, we now know how the system works. We sort of reached the level of deployment of escort officers that works: We know *this* is a realistic number of people needed for the ferries and for the planes flying to Adana. And also we adjusted: So, the officers, when they are not working as escorts—because it doesn't depend only on us, it doesn't even depend on the Greeks fully, it also depends on the Turks because they have to accept the lists of the returnees ... So, you know, there are lot of dependencies and a lot of people that have nothing to do with us have to say "yes" for us to actually do our work. So you can image how that—in terms of budget, in terms of efficiency [laughs]—that doesn't work very well. So now these officers can do other things: We've adjusted the operational plans. But, you know, as a European agency who deploys people in operations, you can't just say, "Ok, and now you fingerprint." No, because you've deployed people to do a specific job; you told their employer this is what they are being deployed for. You cannot just say halfway through the week: "Well, by the way, there are not many returns, so go do something else." So we've now created a system and adjusted and agreed with the member states that there might be a sort of "double profile." So this person, who is deployed as an escort, also has a profile as fingerprinting officer. (I-19)

As the informant explains, returning (rejected) asylum seekers is becoming an integral part of border guarding. Guards who know how to return people to their countries of origin or "safe third countries" are now also working as screeners, debriefers, and registration officers. In other words, due to changed operational requirements at the border, regular border guards increasingly have professional backgrounds as return escorts. They are trained in "body search and escort procedures" (Frontex 2018b: 40) as well as "control and restraint techniques" (Frontex 2016b: 13). They learn how to apply coercive measures (Frontex 2018a: 12), including how to handcuff a person without creating "discomfort to the person concerned and the risk of injury in case of accident" (Frontex 2016b: 16) or causing positional asphyxia. This strengthens border guarding's focus on maintaining order and averting potential security threats: It puts additional emphasis on managing flows and controlling mobility.

Interestingly, IOM staff members have criticized the stronger connection between border controls and returns, which they fear will blur the boundary between voluntary and forced returns:

> Frontex until recently had a mandate to do only forced returns. However, the new mandate of Frontex allows the agency to do also voluntary returns [...] Our opinion is, however, that voluntary return should be kept separate from forced return to

> the largest extent possible because it is important to have different actors doing different things to keep the integrity of the voluntary return process and to avoid the confusion that you [...] have one actor that does returns and another actor that does another kind of returns and it is very easy to blur the line between voluntary and forced returns, especially if the same actor does the two things at the same time. Whether this will be the case in a few years' time, I cannot put my hand in the fire but it [would] be good if this difference was kept. (I-26)

IOM officers, who, before the crisis, were the main actors to implement voluntary returns in mixed migration contexts, are concerned that by increasingly integrating return activities in regular border guarding, border guarding will also rub off on returns as a practice. They underline that voluntary returns have usually been done by psychologists and communication experts (I-2, I-26) and, in defending their IO's turf, they reject a law enforcement approach to readmissions. This exemplifies how the content of specific mixed migration governance practices is negotiated and contested by different IO staff members with different professional worldviews—not only during operations but also during the consolidation phase at headquarters.

Search and Rescue

SAR is a long-established seafaring practice that is codified in international law. The International Convention for the Safety of Life at Sea (SOLAS) and the International Convention on Maritime Search and Rescue (SAR Convention) are the two central treaties that stipulate the duty to assist all persons in distress at sea. Although the European Union (EU) is not currently running a SAR mission, SAR is part of the EU integrated border management strategy that is carried out by Frontex. Accordingly, SAR belongs to all patrol and border control activities implemented by Frontex, and their coastguards are trained to recognize "the components of 'distress messages' received in emergency situations," to "communicate effectively with individuals and groups in the context of SAR activities at the sea borders," and "operate a specific range of search and rescue technology and equipment" (Frontex 2017a: 313, 310). They learn how to identify and communicate information on "objects in distress (vessels, aircraft, persons); position of distressed object (geographical coordinates); nature of distress or casualty and kind of assistance required; weather in immediate vicinity, wind direction, sea and swell, visibility" (Frontex 2017a: 312).

These skills and procedures are not unique to Frontex. They are also taught and practiced by national SAR and coastguard agencies, as well as voluntary organizations such as the German Maritime Search and Rescue Service and the United Kingdom (UK)'s Royal National Lifeboat Institution, which have joined forces in the transnational network International Maritime Rescue Foundation (IMRF) that runs training programs for its members. A third group of organizations engaged in SAR are humanitarian NGOs founded to save migrant lives at sea, such as the Migrant Offshore Aid Station (MOAS), SOS Méditerranée, and Sea-Watch. Médecins sans Frontières (MSF) and Save the Children have started to include SAR missions in their work (see Cuttitta 2017; Cusumano 2021: 553–7). Humanitarian NGOs also belong to the IMRF. Like Frontex, these organizations train their staff to employ "search and rescue tactics and techniques to ensure the safety of all persons" (Frontex 2017a: 314), including maneuvering, emergency steering and rigging, mooring and towing, and crowd control, as well as "swimming whilst wearing a lifejacket and protective clothing" and "taking on board survivors from any lifesaving appliances or other floating objects and from the water" (IMRF 2011: 25, 11). This involves watchkeeping, radar navigation, man-overboard procedures, and avoiding mass panics (IMRF 2011: 7–14; SOS Méditerranée 2019). SAR also includes "maintaining a continuous state of vigilance by sight and as far as practicable by hearing as well as by all other available means, with regard to any significant changes in the operating environment" (IMRF 2011: 29). Hence, there is broad consensus about how to practice SAR across humanitarian and coast- and border guard agencies.[5] It is anchored in training tools and, since 2015–16, new SAR NGOs have consolidated their procedures in new learning programs:

> SOS MEDITERRANEE has been active in mass rescue operations in the Central Mediterranean Sea for three years. Throughout these years, SOS MEDITERRANEE has professionalised and standardised its procedures to conduct lifesaving operations at sea. The knowledge and experience gained from rescues in the central Mediterranean has led SOS MEDITERRANEE to pilot a specialised Search and Rescue (SAR) competency-based training for its search and rescue team members. (SOS Méditerranée 2019)

In addition, they have agreed on shared codes of conduct, such as the *Voluntary Code of Conduct for Search and Rescue Operations Undertaken by Civil Society Non-Government Organisations in the Mediterranean Sea*, which outlines an "agreement on baseline operational principles between

[5] The consensus has been institutionalized in the "International Aeronautical and Maritime Search and Rescue (IAMSAR) Manual" developed by UN agencies to help governments meet their obligations under the SAR and SOLAS conventions.

on-scene responders [...] with the aim of 'minimising organisational divides in terms of individual concepts of operation and SOPs [standard operating procedures]'" (Human Rights at Sea et al. 2017: 2, 7). Thus, despite competition between humanitarian SAR NGOs (see Cusumano 2021), the crisis helped adapt and stabilize the centuries-old practice of SAR to the context of migratory movements (see also IMO et al. 2015).

The practical instructions for approaching people on the move traveling along sea routes, which SAR addresses, frames mixed migration as a humanitarian issue. First and foremost, it addresses people's most basic need to survive and as such does not differentiate between groups of people. The official definition in the SAR Convention (§2.1.10) reads: "Parties shall ensure that assistance be provided to any person in distress at sea. They shall do so regardless of the nationality or status of such a person or the circumstances in which that person is found." It underlines our shared humanity and emphasizes the intrinsic worth of every life by providing the necessary competencies and routines for rescuing. The underlying problem, then, is the absence of safe migration routes.

Has this definition of mixed migration changed during the crisis? On one hand, we observe that the notion of who is in "distress at sea", has been enlarged to encompass more people. The conventions leave the term quite open but SAR professionals have come to treat *every* migrant boat as being in distress (I-7, I-8; informal group interview with a Frontex crew, Chios, April 7, 2016). This is illustrated by a report about a workshop organized by UNHCR, IOM, and the International Institute for Humanitarian Law that brought together practitioners and experts from state SAR services, naval and coastguard authorities, the shipping industry, intergovernmental organizations (IGOs), NGOs, and regional agencies. The workshop "aimed to examine evolving practices concerning search, rescue and disembarkation of refugees and migrants crossing the Mediterranean toward Europe" (UNHCR et al. 2016: 1) and clarified the meaning of "distress":

> Participants commended the widespread practice of considering vessels that are apparently unseaworthy, overcrowded, or lacking a professional crew on board, to be in "distress" from the moment they depart from the coast. For many participants, this "precautionary" approach was understood to reflect the common sense of experienced and competent seafarers, and to increase the chances of survival of those on board by allowing timely SAR responses without waiting for an evident and often inevitable risk of loss of the vessel to materialise. (UNHCR et al. 2016: 2)

This example shows that by embracing a "precautionary" understanding of "distress at sea," the crisis initially led to a "humanitarian turn" in SAR—and thus in governing mixed migration on the ground more generally. By responding to mixed movements with more rescue and solidarity measures, SAR came to be defined as a matter of providing safety and protection.

But after the crisis had peaked, new strategies of avoidance and hindrance emerged in reaction to the humanitarian framing: "Some participants also indicated that, while seafarers on the whole take their SAR responsibilities very seriously, there have been occasional reports of vessels which fail to respond to the distress signals or switch off their Automatic Identification System (AIS) tracking to avoid being requested to assist with SAR operations" (UNHCR et al. 2016: 3). While some actors, especially merchant vessels, began to refuse to perform SAR by switching off their tracking systems, as this quote indicates, new actors stepped into the gap, notably humanitarian SAR NGOs.[6] However, as their numbers grew, national authorities increasingly interfered with their activities. National Maritime Rescue Coordination Centers (MRCC), which are responsible for indicating ports of disembarkation for rescue ships, started to withhold permission to dock or designated ports several hundred sea miles away—instead of assigning the nearest port per standard routine (see Stierl 2023). This delay tactic has been accompanied by criminalizing SAR missions. For instance, since 2017, the Italian government has imposed restrictions on NGO activities, resulting in the confiscation of several ships and the captains' arrests (Tazzioli 2018; Cusumano and Bell 2021). In brief, the "humanitarian turn" in SAR has been met with strategies of containment to deter people on the move by making the migration journey even more dangerous.[7] The main problem is no longer the absence of safe routes but the number of people migrating. This is another example of how the struggles over how to conduct SAR not only determine its content but also what mixed migration governance is supposed to achieve—revealing the political nature of disputes about "competent" practice (see also Cuttitta 2017).

Asylum Interviews

Migrants who claim asylum have the right to tell their stories and have their cases assessed individually. The interview with the person who has

[6] This was also in response to EU and national governments terminating official SAR missions such as Mare Nostrum (see Chapter 3).

[7] In 2017, members of the right-wing Identitarian movement chartered a ship, and under the slogan "Defend Europe," tried to disrupt and block humanitarian rescue missions. The ship's engine failed after just a few weeks, effectively ending the action, but this is another example of operational spaces becoming political arenas.

applied for international protection is a crucial step in the asylum procedure because "information acquired through the personal interview would in most cases play a principal role in the examination of the application" (EASO 2017b: 14). Interviewing is thus a central practice between patrol, rescue, reception, and accommodation, on the one hand, and return or relocation, on the other. EASO trains asylum caseworkers across Europe to use "the appropriate interviewing method to gather sufficient, detailed, and reliable information that is necessary to assess the application" (EASO 2018b: 15). Interview training "promotes the use of a structured dialogic communication method of interviewing and guides the participant through its stages, from appropriate preparation to the activities that may be necessary following the interview" (EASO 2017b: 14). EASO trainers promote the use of a specific interview method and protocol (EASO 2018b: 14). The program divides an interview into different sequences, trains interviewing skills, and provides "guidance regarding the substance of the application which needs to be explored during the interview" (EASO 2014: 1, n.d.a). Asylum experts and caseworkers also learn to assess evidence provided during an interview and to draft decisions about the application. This includes "establishing the material facts of an individual case through gathering, examining and comparing available pieces of evidence" (EASO 2017b: 13–14; cp. EASO 2018a) and interpreting information gained during an interview with respect to the 1951 Refugee Convention. It resembles the UNHCR refugee status determination procedure carried out on behalf of governments when a state is not a party to the 1951 Refugee Convention or has no fair and efficient national asylum procedure (UNHCR 2019, 2020a, 2020b): the main purpose is to "analyse an applicant's case to determine which protection status should be given" (EASO 2018b: 18).

Asylum interviews thus define access to international protection as the key problem in mixed migration. For an asylum caseworker, the "mixed" nature of migration movements is the main challenge, and the principal concern is to distinguish the people who have well-founded claims to asylum from those who do not. The public good concerns correctly identifying those who deserve protection and helping them realize their rights under international refugee law—while singling out those who would overstretch reception capacities and overburden asylum systems (see van der Klaauw 2010).

The crisis at the European external border had an important impact on the conduct of asylum interviews. EASO used to train national asylum experts but its staff was not directly involved in the asylum procedure. This changed during the crisis, which staff at EASO headquarters described as "revolutionary."

> The most interesting developments at this moment for EASO and for [European] asylum policy really is what's happening in Greece and the involvement of EASO in Greece, which is much more than what we do, for instance, in Italy. Because in Italy, in fact, we are involved in relocation but relocation is really an administrative [job] and I don't see that as something revolutionary. But what we do in Greece is of a really different nature because—and for the first time really—so from the EU-Turkey Deal of 18 March 2016, we are really involved, together with the Greek administration, we are directly involved in the processing of the asylum cases, individual cases. (I-22)

The fast-track border procedure introduced after the EU-Turkey Statement (see Chapter 3) led to EASO experts starting to conduct admissibility interviews to determine whether a claim to asylum could be lodged in Greece or had to be filed in a country through which a person had traveled. With the new procedure, EASO caseworkers had to learn how to determine "vulnerability" because vulnerable people were exempted from the border procedure (see Chapter 4). Learning how to do that in specific cases was consolidated through EASO's training tools, post-crisis. Asylum experts now learn how to identify "vulnerabilities, mental and physical impairments, medical conditions, and traumatic experiences" (EASO 2018b: 18, EASO n.d.b; see also UNHCR-IDC 2016). Experience has shown that such people often cannot coherently recount their stories or provide valid evidence. Interviewing vulnerable people requires specific skills:

> Medical conditions and traumatic experiences, which occurred in the country of origin, during the flight or even in the host country, can all influence the amount and quality of information the applicant is able to provide during the personal interview. It is crucial for case officers to be equipped with the knowledge, skills and attitudes needed to identify and address the special procedural needs of such applicants. (EASO 2017b: 15)

EASO training tools also provide detailed interview templates with indicators for the vulnerability screenings created during the crisis and updated at the hotspots (I-15). Since "the operational definition of vulnerability [remains] largely undefined" in policy documents (Welfens and Bekyol 2021: 1), these practical guides clarify how to identify vulnerable people who cannot be returned from Europe. Vulnerability assessments determine which nation-state is legally in charge of leading the asylum procedure (EASO 2018b: 56–7) and thus directly affect the life choices of people on the move (see Chapter 4). What is important here is that they also offer a counter-reading of vulnerability.[8] In contrast to vulnerability in border guarding—which is shaped by factors such as "border permeability (terrain, infrastructure, capabilities, flows), operational activities (staff, training, interoperability); effectiveness of countermeasures; pull factors" (Frontex 2017a: 159)—it focuses attention on *people* who need protection and re-emphasizes the importance of human rights in mixed migration governance. However, it runs counter to the humanitarian framing of SAR and other humanitarian practices that stress the worth and dignity of every human life, irrespective of legal status (e.g. NRC 2016). This again shows how different understandings of what is at stake compete with, challenge, and shape each other and mixed migration governance as a whole.

Similar dynamics of consolidating, contesting, and changing frontline practices in light of experiences in the field can be observed with regard to other border practices, including psychosocial support, legal aid, camp management, and protection. For example, the latter, which in the migration-displacement context mostly refers to the legal practice of upholding refugee rights by informing asylum seekers about their rights and monitoring registration procedures, as well as flagging misconduct and abuse during border control procedures (UNHCR 2014, 2015: 67, 2017: 10–11; see also I-3, I-4, and I-24), now increasingly also means identifying victims of trafficking. A UNHCR officer described this when she explained how she and her colleagues discuss with their IOM counterparts about how to institutionalize burden-sharing:

> For example, we are working with IOM to agree SOPs for victims of trafficking. So this would be … I mean, if UNHCR comes across a victim of trafficking who is not a refugee, we don't sort of say [laughing], "Off you go, see you later!" We already work on the ground on this [how to identify and refer victims of trafficking]. But the idea is to institutionalize a system whereby … if either UNHCR or IOM have a trafficking victim in front of them, they refer to the agency who has a mandate for that person, whether they are a refugee or a migrant, and if the other agency is not operational, look after that person and ensure that they get the support they need. I mean that's the basic concept. And I think that that sort of summarizes UNHCR's policy position on protection in mixed movements more broadly. It's not "refugees

[8] The extensive focus on vulnerability brings its own problem because it creates "vulnerability contests" among people on the move and cements the legal-discursive distinction between "deserving" and "undeserving" people on the move (see Welfens and Bekyol 2021; Welfens 2023). The terms stratify different groups of people on the move and create inequalities and exclusion.

> = good, migrants = bad." That's absolutely *not* the idea. It's noting that agencies have respective mandates but also that there are persons in need. So what can we do to put some predictability around this and what can we do to ensure that there are clear lines of cooperation and communication with other relevant partners to ensure that the persons in need are given the support they need. (I-33)

This quote shows how headquarters staff discuss how to consolidate on-the-ground practices in formal SoPs, thereby clarifying and codifying what protection means in mixed migration contexts—and global mixed migration governance more generally.

In sum, analysis shows that the frontline practices performed and developed on Chios are practices taught by the IOs: the skills and routines reconstructed in Greece are part of a larger system of practices carried out at borders around the world. Previous or preliminary versions of these practices already existed within the organizations before the crisis of 2015–16. New experiences, including those gained during the crisis at the European external border, at least partially fed back into those documents and programs or revealed gaps in existing practical repertoires and stimulated the creation of new handbooks and guidelines. Creating and updating these teaching tools is a *political* process during which the content and adequacy of substantive professional practices is negotiated and contested: IO staff members define and change how mixed migration is understood as a global policy concern through situated learning on the ground and the consolidation of ad hoc policy solutions at headquarters. Of course, it is not the only international arena in which different actors fight over how to define and treat migration and asylum, but the field is a policy-making arena in its own right.

5.2 Diffusion: Training Field Staff

Governing on the ground is not a unidirectional process. The empirical analysis in this and the previous chapter has thus far reconstructed the first four steps of the loop model (improvisation, competence negotiation, routinization, and consolidation) to trace how frontline practices are created and changed in IOs from the bottom up. The remainder of my analysis focuses on how these skills and routines are transmitted "back down." It looks at how practical knowledge is diffused across operations, depicts how IO headquarters staff aim to harmonize street-level decision-making, and shows the iterative nature of governing through practice in the field.

5.2.1 Transmitting Practical Knowledge across Operations

The headquarters staff analyzed in this chapter, the "translators," do not just create handbooks, best practice guides, and other learning resources to codify what their organization has learned on the ground. They also train field staff to diffuse this knowledge within the organization (see also Campbell 2008: 22). According to an IOM staff member: "[We try] to make sure that what we do in one region is known to the other regions: what the practice is in one, is then replicated into the other so that there is coherence and there is knowledge-sharing beyond just sharing reports" (I-26). This is a challenging task because practical knowledge cannot simply be "uprooted and repackaged for circulation" (Seely-Brown and Duguid 1991: 54).

To respond to this challenge, secretariat staff at the UNHCR, IOM, Frontex, EASO, and the humanitarian NGOs studied here try to foster active learning: instead of lectures and other methods for transmitting abstract knowledge, they usually make use of practical exercises, simulations, scenario building, case studies, and role-play. They rely on learning-by-doing. A humanitarian professional working on Chios explains how his NGO trains people on the job:

> So there's a lot of on-the-job training. At least my organization will have people spend like a month or two on the ground to see how things actually work and then they'll pull them out to go to training events. So the training is kind of framed within the context of the environment in which I actually work in. (I-11)

An EASO staff member described a similar experience:

> There were quite a number of EASO experts already working there, on Lesvos. Well, not *working* ... It was in the middle of setting up the whole procedure and everything was ... I don't know, maybe 50 or 60 people who came from all different countries: a lot from Germany, also from Finland, Norway, Sweden, you name it. All these experts were put together and they went on a training first from EASO, for a couple of days in Athens, and from there, they went to Lesvos and they were doing like a trial run. (I-1)

Before being deployed to the field, newcomers go through induction training and a pre-deployment briefing (I-19, I-24, I-30, I-35). In their deployments, they usually first shadow more experienced colleagues (EASO 2017a: 81). Fieldworkers generally learn from each other as they rotate across missions:

> During the operation itself, there isn't that much time for training. You learn by doing, you learn from your colleagues, you learn and you adjust because, you know, this is a situation that is not constant. It changes and changes and the challenges change, too. And the teams change. I mean, you have people being replaced by [others]—so that's rough. [But] there is always an overlap. There is always a debriefing with those who are leaving, followed by a briefing with the new ones. (I-19)

A similar mechanism for fostering knowledge exchange among field staff is to connect them via online platforms and virtual "communities of practice" (e.g. CCCM 2015a: 3). Many IOs stress that their training documents and toolkits are "iterative" and "living documents" (CCCM 2015b: 7; Human Rights at Sea et al. 2017: 8). Most of the handbooks and operational guidelines included in the document analysis also emphasize that those currently working on the ground should seek direct contact with those who have worked in the field offices and operations that provided input:

> NGOs and UNHCR field offices looking to replicate such practices, in ways appropriate to their local context, are encouraged to contact the UNHCR field office or NGO listed in the good practice [section] for further information, including updates and lessons learned that have emerged since publication. (UNHCR 2006a: 3)

Operations and training officers know that practical knowledge can never be fully codified: it must be continuously relayed in and through practice. They use active-learning tools to create institutional memory and diffuse the practical knowledge that their organization has generated at the front lines of global challenges.

5.2.2 Standardizing On-Site Practice?

By diffusing practical knowledge, trainers and operations officers seek to standardize on-site practice. They not only want to foster knowledge-sharing but also try to control decision-making in the field, as this example of Frontex border guarding shows:

> An EU border guard has on average just 12 seconds to decide whether the traveler in front of them is legitimate or not, or to assess if their documents are genuine. For tens of thousands of people each year, refusal at the border post can change a life. [...] The border guard's decision, in other words, can have the profoundest consequences for the individual standing before them—*and it has never been more important to get this process right*. (Frontex 2014a: 15; emphasis added)

The two interrelated reasons behind the efforts to harmonize on-site practice are (1) guaranteeing a minimal level of performance and (2) consistency. Analysis reveals that secretariat staff first try to prevent grave mistakes by preparing field staff and ensuring that they work together well in the field (I-17, I-26, I-33). In his foreword to the *Voluntary Code of Conduct for Search and Rescue Operations by NGOs in the Mediterranean Sea*, the former chief executive officer of the IMRF, Bruce Reid, states:

> We have seen, in other contexts, the effects of uncoordinated responses, which can compromise safety, can leave gaps (and people die in those gaps), and can lead to unhelpful competition—and at the IMRF we say that our only competitor is the sea ... So we very much welcome this Code of Conduct as a useful aid to better strategic coordination. The IMRF congratulates Human Rights at Sea and partner NGOs for developing it, and we align ourselves with its aims. Working together in this way makes all involved stronger—and saves lives. It's as simple, and as important, as that. (Human Rights at Sea et al. 2017: 3)

The authors of the UNHCR training catalogue similarly maintain that their workshops and peer-to-peer sessions provide space for discussing how to improve emergency responses:

> The workshop has been designed to improve response to emergencies by exploring problems, standards and best practices in key areas of emergency and disaster management. Areas explored in detail included protection of the rights of affected people, emergency assessment, food and nutrition, emergency shelter, water and sanitation and coordination in emergencies. (UNHCR 2015: 199)

Perhaps unsurprisingly, IO trainers seek to professionalize field staff, enhance coordination, and improve performance through training.

The second, and related, motivation to streamline practice through training is what Frontex staff call "interoperability" (I-17): the capability of field staff to work together to deliver the same kind of service, no matter where they come from or the mission they are deployed to. EASO's former head of training explains:

> We realized that it was very important that we had all those tools—like the training as well as the guidance for the caseworkers ready for the context of operations in emergency situations. Because if we hadn't had that before, then we would do a bit (in French I would say "*n'importe quoi*" [nonsense]) because the idea is not only to send people to the field, and people coming from different member states, and you send them to Greece or to Italy or wherever and you say [clicks tongue]: "*Do* it!" But then: "Do *what?*" So that's why, in fact, it was very important that we had this in place. (I-22)

He describes field staff from different professional backgrounds and organizations or, in the case of Frontex and EASO, seconded from different national government agencies, who often respond very differently to similar situations. Headquarters staff try to minimize incoherence through training. The UNHCR Guidelines on determining the best interests of the child also reflect this endeavor to ensure a uniform level of practice:

> In the almost ten years since the publication of the 2008 [...] Guidelines, UNHCR operations have continued to identify areas of work that require additional elaboration and clarification. Many operations have developed their own or used other guidance documents, training materials and tools to fill these identified gaps. These field-level initiatives include many excellent pieces of work, but also contribute to a *wide variation in the application* of best interest procedures from operation to operation. [...] As a result, in 2017, UNHCR undertook a process of revising the Guidelines to ensure that they continue to be relevant [...]. In addition, UNHCR and IRC [International Rescue Committee] have developed a training package for caseworkers implementing UNHCR's Best Interests Procedure, responding to a gap identified by UNHCR and partner staff. (UNHCR 2018: 15–16; emphasis added)

Coherent performance, in turn, is again linked to solving problems effectively in the field. In one of its best practice reports, Frontex quotes a return officer who says that returnees' behavior has noticeably changed in the past five years:

> Eighty percent of return operations these days are peaceful, and there is much less resistance. I think it is because we are consistent in the way we treat returnees, so they know better what to expect. (Frontex 2014a: 103)

In brief, all the IOs studied know the consequentiality of street-level decision-making and seek to standardize on-the-ground practice.

They do that by providing sample tables, interview guidelines, and similar tools with highly detailed instructions on how to perform a particular practice. For example, EASO's practical guides on doing asylum interviews and interpreting the evidence contain checklists and flow charts for each step (see Figure 5.1).

In addition to providing such templates, the headquarters staff who compile learning materials usually select the trainers that instruct field staff how to act in certain situations. A PHAP coordinator says:

> We have our expert pool. We have the people we know are excellent trainers, [...] we put really high demands on the quality of our trainers and try to make sure we have a good mix of different perspectives. That being said, [...] we simply try them out in practice. I mean, they basically come in through recommendations by others. (I-40)

This indicates that training and operations officers are central nodes in the expert networks that shape training content and control *who* gets to teach (see also I-33, I-36, I-37). They also certify staff (I-18, I-40). One certification program for transnational professionals working on mixed migration

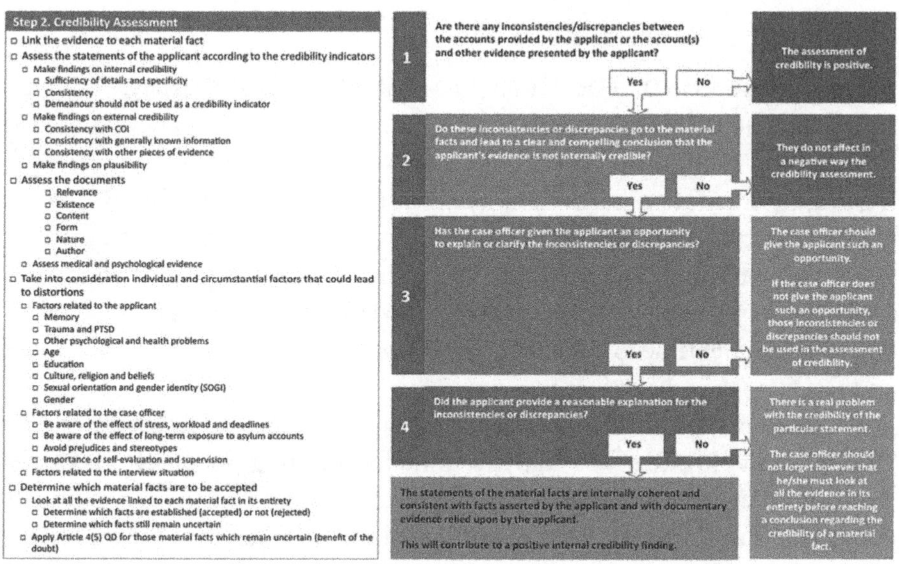

Fig. 5.1 EASO "Credibility Assessment" guides for determining refugee status
Source: EASO (2015: 3 and 11).

is the "Humanitarian Passport Initiative." Run by the HLA, located at the headquarters of Save the Children, it aims to standardize the skills of humanitarian and protection workers across organizations. HLA's global learning director explains:

> We are trying to cut across organizations by introducing this concept of a humanitarian passport, which tries to align with a more globally accepted competency framework, and [are looking to use] things like ISO certifications and open badges as a way to recognize learning, skills, and experience across the sector. [...] So [we're] going to try to aim for some standardization and professionalization of skills. We rolled out a few initial micro certifications and we are working on an open badge system which will allow anyone to have a digital passport, which will then allow them to collect skills as they go across the different organizations. (I-38)

This example demonstrates how staff in global offices establish recognition schemes that turn particular skills into accredited capabilities. The schemes codify specific competencies that fieldworkers are incentivized to acquire because they promise to enhance their chances of being employed across organizations. In short, through certification programs, as well as by controlling the network of trainers and providing detailed templates for decision-making in the field, IO secretariat staff seek to streamline what operational staff do in the field.

5.2.3 In the Loop: The Iterative Nature of Governing on the Ground

Despite the attempts to harmonize frontline practice described here, IOs cannot fully control what happens in the field. In fact, in many cases, fieldworkers only receive minimal training and have never heard of the handbooks and learning tools (see also Infantino 2021: 1031; Weaver 2008: 4). Quite often, they also have no time to consult any organizational resources but must think on their feet (see Chapter 4).

The headquarters staff interviewed for this book are highly aware of this: "When we deploy, there's usually no time for learning [laughs]!" (I-19; see also I-22). They know that it is impossible to completely standardize on-site practice and acknowledge that the organization is better served by a certain degree of flexibility: a Frontex officer commented that the main lesson from the crisis at the Schengen border was that "we need to be flexible" (I-19). Because headquarters staff cannot predict situational challenges, they cannot anticipate the actions their colleagues in the field will need to take and must rely on fieldworkers' professional judgment (see also Honig 2018).

Therefore, many of the handbooks and guides studied here are broad enough to be applied to different operational circumstances. IOM staff notes, for example, that their tools for psychosocial needs assessment have been used in very different contexts in Kenya, Iraq, Jordan, and Lebanon:

> This set of tools proved to be very flexible and adaptable to different contexts. IOM staff together with its local partners employed it in 2005 to assess the psychosocial condition of IDP communities in Iraq; in 2006 to respond to the displacement of Lebanese populations due to the July war and in late 2007 to research the psychosocial needs of Iraqis displaced in Jordan and Lebanon. At the beginning of 2008, a simplified version of the tools was used in Kenya to assess the psychosocial well-being of the Kenyan communities affected by displacement. (IOM 2009b: 14)

Instead of presenting rigid rules, this type of learning material mainly describes how people have handled comparable situations. Similarly, *The Field Handbook on Unaccompanied and Separated Children (UASC)* developed by an interagency working group including the UNHCR, the United Nations Children Fund (UNICEF), the International Committee of the Red Cross (ICRC), and Save the Children reads:

> In 2014, West and Central Africa regional offices of the IOM and UNICEF developed joint regional guidelines on assistance and protection to non-refugee (such as internally displaced, migrant, returnee or third-country national) UASC in humanitarian emergencies. The guidelines, which are complementary to country-level standard operating procedures, set out possible joint and coordinated actions. These actions include joint assessments; data-collection/sharing; pre-identification/rapid registration of UASC for identification, documentation, tracing and reunification; transfer/transport of UASC; temporary care arrangements; psychosocial support; prevention of family separation and awareness-raising; coordination processes; advocacy and fundraising. The guidelines stem from good practices in the Malian crisis in 2012 (involving internally displaced persons) and in Chad (returnees) due to the Central African Republic crisis in 2013. (IASC 2017: 92)

This extract illustrates how many handbooks make ways of doing and knowing that have worked in particular geographical locations known to other mixed migration sites—and thereby serve as anchor points for communities of practice at other borders. Although they cannot resolve the contingency and unpredictability of concrete field operations, they do reify practical knowledge (Wenger 1998: 58) and provide points of reference for decision-making in other operations. That fieldworkers can lean on practice from other missions is illustrated by the following counterfactual:

> Jan Karl Hoilund, a police detective on a four-year secondment from Denmark, is particularly frustrated by the EU's approach to minors at the border. "The legislation is inadequate, and there is a remarkable absence of guidelines and best practices in it, leading to a myriad of interpretations among border guards. [...] There is a severe lack of 'best practice' to lean on." (Frontex 2014a: 89–91)

The border guard describes how the absence of best practice guides creates confusion at the border, especially when fieldworkers also lack formal policy guidance. Practical guidelines can help fieldworkers make sense of local challenges. In the words of an EASO trainer: "I am not saying that [they] always want to spend extra time reading everything but [practical guidance] [exists] and normally, they are quite well-equipped that way" (I-22).

"*However*, these guidelines should not be used as a cookbook" (IASC 2007: 9; emphasis added). Although they suggest actions, fieldworkers must make sense of local realities and make decisions that cannot be foreseen and controlled by staff at headquarters. While the document analysis reveals that practical knowledge does travel from one operation to another, no two operations are the same and, in the field, people always have to improvise. In fact, some headquarters staff stressed that they primarily aim to equip fieldworkers with the skills and professional judgment to do just that, with a UNHCR officer commenting that their learning program on mixed migration is about

> increasing understanding, for example, of how non-refoulement works in a protection at sea context. I mean there is clear—well, perhaps not *clear*—but there are *some* existing legal standards in relation to that; so it's about increasing the level of understanding in the field and *empowering people to go into those situations*. (I-33)

Despite the attempts to standardize practice, many trainers acknowledge that the best they can do is to encourage their colleagues on the ground to go into particular situations and to provide them with the background knowledge that they think will be needed for making meaningful decisions. While headquarters staff do not *determine* actions on the ground, with their consolidation and diffusion activities, they participate in the professional struggles over how to govern mixed migration at the frontlines.

Experiences in addressing new situations on the ground are sometimes integrated into IO operational knowledge repertoires: "With what we learn in the field, we feed that back into the upgrades, updates or the ongoing [training] modules that are being developed" (I-23). For example, EASO's training curriculum states that it needs to constantly adjust its operational training as field conditions change:

> Initially implemented as a form of support in the framework of the EU hotspot approach and of the EU relocation scheme under the European Agenda on Migration, the EASO Operational Training is under constant development and adjustment, depending on the needs on the ground and on the changeable operational contexts. (EASO 2017b: 52)

Some fieldworkers interviewed were doubtful that their experiences would find any resonance in their IO:

> Sometimes I tend to be a bit cynical and I don't know if they *want* to learn this lesson—to be honest. [...] But hopefully, I don't know, the efforts of all the organizations working here [at the border] will make it and achieve some improvements on the ground. That's what we need to hope for and believe in to keep doing what we are doing. (I-3)

Others are more optimistic that the way they organize collective action on the ground will be reproduced in other places:

> For me, it's always learning-by-doing and you pilot a situation where maybe we will have another crisis that will be handled this way ... I'm not sure ... in another country. But what I want to emphasize: we are still at the beginning of it. Like, for me, it's like baby step after baby step. (I-9)

Whether practical knowledge is effectively stabilized and reapplied remains an open question. But the case study does show that experimentation in the field and normalization at headquarters are linked through nested feedback loops. Headquarters staff train fieldworkers, who then deviate from scripts when confronted with unforeseen situational challenges—thereby creating new experiential knowledge that is at least partially consolidated in training tools and diffused to the field: "It's a never-ending circle" (I-23). Even if this practice-based form of governing remains provisional, it directly affects the lives of people on the move (see Chapter 4), and by defining the content of the professional practices used at the border, establishes mixed migration as a policy issue (see Section 5.1.2).

5.3 Conclusion: Feedback Effects on Formal Policies and Mandates

In this chapter, I have analyzed how frontline practices created and transformed through situated learning in the field are stabilized by training and operations officers at IO headquarters. By developing learning materials and training operational staff, they consolidate and diffuse know-how and routines, embedding experiential knowledge within their organizations—that is subsequently applied, adjusted, reinvented, or ignored. Reconstructing how IOs create practical knowledge on migration and asylum through training adds to our understanding of how IO knowledge production influences migration and asylum policy. It contributes to scholarship about the role expertise plays in shaping migration policies (Boswell 2008), for example, by focusing on the creation of benchmarks and indicators (Robinson 2018) or providing country-of-origin information used to determine refugee status (van der Kist et al. 2019). It demonstrates that practical knowledge remains precarious—it is difficult to make explicit and institutionalize—but impacts on how IOs deal with migration and displacement. In brief, the case study in this and in Chapter 4 shows that IOs govern mixed movements by creating, applying, transforming, and transmitting professional know-how and routines. This distinct mode of governance operates in the gray zone between formal rules and mandates.

Initial evidence also indicates that governing on the ground affects official policy and precipitates institutional change. After the crisis, EASO, which "had already been operating at the very limits of its mandate" was redesigned and became a "fully-fledged asylum agency" (renamed the European Union Agency for Asylum, or EUAA) with a permanent asylum reserve pool of 500 operational staff members and the right to not only more comprehensively assist EU member states during the asylum procedure but also to directly cooperate with non-European third countries (EUAA 2022). During the crisis, EASO had already begun to slowly expand its remit: with a view to operational gaps, it negotiated the right to hire so-called interim caseworkers. The person responsible for asylum expert training explains how EASO, along with the European Council and EU member states, pragmatically decided on the institutional innovation, which became codified *ex post facto*:

> Now, concretely about the training: there were in fact three different situations. We started immediately with the first group of experts [who were experienced caseworkers from the member states]. But there was always an important gap [in terms of the asylum experts requested from the member states and the ones actually

> seconded]. [...] And we would put out call after call after call and everybody was annoyed: we were annoyed, the member states were annoyed ... but nothing changed [...]. So, we needed additional measures to get more [asylum] experts. And so there was a first attempt [to change the system] following a decision of the EU Council in October. The EU Council told us—and that was after some member states had told us: "Well, you have too high requests in terms of the quality and experience of experts. You should accept to have junior experts from member states but then you train them, you use them, and then later, they can go back to us but at least, they will come back more experienced." It was a kind of win-win, which was not a bad idea except that ... when the call [to the member states] was sent, we received *four* answers [laughs]. EASO still organized specific training for them [the second groups of experts]. That was much more comprehensive training of course because they were junior experts. We wanted to show the Council and the member states that if they ask us to do that, we *do* it. But look, again member states didn't play the game because they asked us to do it and then they didn't send the [junior] experts. [...] The third group came following another decision of the Council. This time it was in December[9] because every time the topic was coming back: "Well, we lack experts: what do we do?" And so, there, they came with a new idea and the new idea was that EASO could recruit local interim staff. But really interim staff would do the same work as the deployed member state experts: [they were hired] to do the interviews, to do recommendations. (I-22)

This interview excerpt shows how the crisis created new operational demands, exposed gaps in institutional capacities, and paved the way for a temporary solution (interim caseworkers), which then became formalized in EASO's new right to employ its own operational staff.

After the crisis, Frontex, too, received a new mandate that built on its operational activities at the border (Niemann and Speyer 2018; Deleixhe and Duez 2019). In 2019, the new Frontex Regulation 2019/1986 entered into force, giving the agency new competencies, such as independently organizing and implementing return operations, as well as a standing corps of 10,000 border guards, a larger budget, and its own equipment: the agency was granted "unprecedented supervisory and executive power" (Fjørtoft 2022: 557). IOM also ventured into new operational spheres and slowly renegotiated its organizational capacities (Hall 2016; Kreuder-Sonnen and Tantow 2022) to finally become a "Related Organization to the UN" in 2016. IOM's operational role in the 2015–16 crisis accelerated the process (Bradley 2021: 5).

[9] See European Council meeting (December 15, 2016), "Conclusions, Point 5," p. 2.

Operational knowledge also informs official policy-making. IOs with experience on the ground are highly motivated to share their practical insights, especially because that expertise allows them to claim a seat at the table and consolidate their role in the global governance of migration and asylum. During negotiations over the Global Compact for Migration, for example, IOM was keenly interested in contributing its experience of implementing Assisted Voluntary Return and Reintegration (AVRR) programs:

> Our intention is to bring into the Global Compact our knowledge, the knowledge that we have been building and that we have collected—specifically on AVRR—in these nearly 40 years of implementation [...] because it will be important that what we have learned in these years of actions is properly reflected. (I-26)

The UNHCR strategy during the phase leading up to the compacts' final adoption was also to "scale up current practices"—rather than to push for more fundamental reform of the international refugee regime (Micinski 2021: 73). NGOs contributed their experiential knowledge about family reunification and alternatives to detaining people on the move to the consultation and stocktaking process that became part of the final document (Rother and Steinhilper 2019: 252). Anecdotal empirical evidence thus reveals that both public and private IOs use practical knowledge to influence negotiations of international treaties and formal policies.

At EU level, experiences with managing mixed movements during the crisis influenced the reform of the Screening Regulation, the European Dactyloscopy (EURODAC) Regulation, the Reception Conditions Directive and the Asylum Procedures Regulation.[10] The reformed Screening Regulation, for instance, envisages a mandatory preliminary screening of asylum seekers at the European external border who are then directed to different procedures based on nationality. People from countries with low recognition rates go to asylum border or return procedures (Rasche et al. 2022: 3–4). Thus, the regulation codifies a practice tested in the hotspots during the crisis.

While the conceptual link between global governance on the ground and formal policy-making lies outside the book's loop model, there are empirical indications that what happens in practice also impacts institutional and official policy developments: Sometimes governing in the field precedes formal policy-making; in other cases, it circumvents it and directly addresses global problems where they become acute.

[10] See Thym (2022) on the EU's proposed New Pact on Migration and Asylum.

6
Conclusion
Moving beyond the Border

International organizations (IOs) are important policy-makers beyond the state. They set agendas, advocate change, establish standards, make rules, negotiate treaties, and monitor compliance with international norms in issue areas ranging from peace and security, financial stability and economic development, to public health, human rights, and the environment. They make collectively binding decisions that organize expectations, formulate shared goals, and outline ways to achieve them. Through these activities, they define the issues that require an international response and also coordinate behavior, opening up or restricting opportunities to act. However, IOs govern global challenges not only through laws, policies, rules, and standards but also *through practice in the field.* The way the United Nations (UN) High Commissioner for Refugees (UNHCR), the International Organization for Migration (IOM), the European Union Agency for Asylum (EUAA), the European Border and Coast Guard Agency (Frontex), and international non-governmental organizations (NGOs), such as the Norwegian Refugee Council and Save the Children, organized collective action on migration and asylum at the European external border during the migration and refugee crisis of 2015–16 shows that IOs govern on the ground.

The IOs organized land and sea patrols, search and rescue, transportation, registration, accommodation, food provision, child protection, psychosocial support, asylum interviews, translation, legal advice, relocation, and returns. Thereby, they directly affected the life choices of people on the move who are the final governance addressees in this issue area. By improvising in the field and consolidating and diffusing practical solutions, IOs coordinated and constrained the behavior of migrants, asylum seekers, and refugees, and defined "mixed migration" as a global public challenge—a topic so deeply politicized it has remained largely unaddressed by formal policy-making. By making practical policy prescriptions, they determined what mixed migration means as a global policy concern at the intersection of humanitarianism, security, and human rights.

Global Governance on the Ground. Nele Kortendiek, Oxford University Press. © Nele Kortendiek (2024).
DOI: 10.1093/oso/9780198889120.003.0006

My book reconstructs *how* IOs govern mixed migration on the ground (Chapters 3–5). It shows that IO field staff, faced with political and epistemic uncertainty, urgency, and organizational complexity in their everyday work, made spontaneous decisions, negotiated which actions count as competent behavior, and routinized their local ways of doing things. They created and performed provisional practices for governing mixed movements. At headquarters, training and operations officers devised learning materials and trained field staff, embedding the new field practices in organizational repertoires and disseminating them across operations. In other words, IOs *de facto* governed migration and asylum at international borders. They addressed mixed migration—which was not yet formally regulated—at the frontlines of global governance, blurring the boundaries of public and private IOs and diffusing practical solutions across organizational sites via training.

The empirical study presented in this book is grounded in an *interorganizational* and *cross-level perspective* on IOs and global governance, which combines a street-level bureaucracy view of IO policy-making with insights from the sociology of the professions, work, knowledge, and organizations. Based on this shift in theoretical perspective, which moves away from a view of IOs as coherent, collective actors, I have developed a *loop model of governing on the ground* that highlights the agency of transnational professionals in IOs. It foregrounds their practice in the field to account for how IOs govern emerging, contested, or unsettled global issues, such as mixed migration. It underlines that their knowledge and personal networks enable them to reconcile organizational tasks with situational challenges and local expectations. Knowledge and networks also enable IO field staff to make sense of organizational constraints stemming from legal mandates, donor interests, national laws, and bureaucratic procedures and to deviate from policy scripts. In doing so, they fill governance gaps and put into practice vague and scanty policy frameworks, changing them from the bottom up. Their peripheral location within the organizations and moments of crisis and contention create permissive environments conducive to learning on the ground and the *post hoc* normalizing of on-site experiments by headquarters staff in training and operations units.

The loop model first zooms in on *situated learning* in the field to conceptualize how this combination of contextual factors and agential resources can create new practical knowledge and organizational routines in three steps: *improvisation*, *competence negotiation*, and *routinization*. The model then conceptualizes the *stabilization* of local practical solutions via *consolidation* and *diffusion*, pointing out that governing on the ground works iteratively and likely restarts when new field missions begin and unforeseen problems arise.

The theoretical argument I make by proposing this model suggests that practice on the ground is a distinct mode of governance that cannot be explained by conceptually equating governance with the exercise of authority. Accordingly, I develop a more minimalist definition of global governance (see Chapter 2). My reconceptualization centers on the *governing effects* of IO activities (instead of sources, such as delegation and authority negotiations) and can accommodate dynamic governing modes that operate at very low institutional thresholds, such as the one described in this book.

This approach to the way IOs govern adds to a growing body of research about how knowledge and practice function in global governance and sheds new light on informal governing dynamics in world politics. Beyond this contribution to the literature on IOs as global governors (see Chapter 1), the book also has implications for wider debates in IO studies and global governance research. In this concluding chapter, I address one central debate: *space* in international relations (IR) theory.

In the following, I revisit the insights of this book with a view to this debate to point out the key theoretical implications of this study for future research (Section 6.1). I argue that taking concrete, geographical places seriously advances our understanding of how global governance works, who has power in international decision-making, and how change can occur in international institutions. I then turn to the institutional and normative implications of the case study (Sections 6.2 and 6.3). Based on my theoretical propositions and empirical findings, I assess the effectiveness and democratic nature of governing on the ground—and discuss how IOs can counter the risks of failure and arbitrariness. I conclude by outlining still-open questions and point out the need for further research about how IOs govern on the ground (Section 6.4).

6.1 Theoretical Implications: Global Governance in Concrete Spaces

Global governance takes place beyond meeting rooms, conference halls, IO headquarters, and courtrooms in New York, Geneva, Washington, and other hubs, such as Nairobi and Brussels. While they are key sites of global policy-making (Betsill and Corell 2008; Jepsen et al. 2021; Reiners 2022; Yildiz 2023), advocacy, diplomacy, and decision-making also happen in digital arenas (Adler-Nissen and Eggeling 2022; Hall 2022), domestic settings (Slaughter 2009; Roger 2020; Stürner-Siovitz 2023) and, as I argue here, at operational sites (see also Autesserre 2014; Bartley 2018; Honig 2018). This forces us to revisit our assumptions about space in global governance.

Global governance scholarship has thus far paid little attention to geographic spaces. While *social* spaces have been researched intensively over the past decade, especially in IR studies inspired by social theory (Bicchi 2011; Furnari 2014; Goetze 2017; Lesch and Loh 2022), *geographic* places have been neglected (see also Banai et al. 2014). Only very recently have global governance scholars taken up the "spatial turn" in peace and conflict studies influenced by human geography (Brigg and George 2020). The central idea here is that "space is a geographic dimension in the context of which events unfold, and which affects how they unfold" (Björkdahl and Buckley-Zistel 2022: 660). Following this basic assumption, some IO scholars and IR theorists have argued for examining how spatial constellations influence the form and substance of global governance (Liste 2016; Gazit 2018; Lambach 2022; Kimber and Maertens 2021). Lisa Smirl (2015), for example, advocates a decidedly materialist approach to international disaster recovery work to highlight how physical infrastructures such as gated compounds shape the outcomes of humanitarian interventions. She argues that specific natural and built environments influence how decisions are made and programs carried out.

To push the boundaries of this burgeoning debate and our conceptions of global governance more generally, I contend that we need to reassess the rather abstract notions of "levels" of decision-making that are still found in theories of global governance (see also Scholte 2021: 181–2). Introduced by first-generation global governance researchers, these ideas have been very helpful for overcoming the "territorial trap" (Agnew 1994) and demonstrating that political decisions are not only made within the domestic polity but also beyond the nation-state. Theorists like James Rosenau (1992), John Gerard Ruggie (1993), and Philip Cerny (1995) made great theoretical and analytical innovations by arguing that rule and collective action are not bound by territoriality. Yet—and perhaps ironically—this way of thinking has stripped decision-making locations from their physical connotations and introduced an implicit hierarchical ordering among "global" and "local" sites: equating the latter with implementation sites, where decisions made elsewhere are merely carried out and, at times, resisted (Acharya 2004).

To counterbalance the abstractness of "the international," which is usually looked for in immaterial "domains" (Ruggie 2004) or "spheres" (Rosenau 1997: 145) and contrasted with the territorial embeddedness of the "national" or "local," I suggest conceiving of different "levels" of decision-making as concrete places. Emphasizing the material, physical side of political arenas beyond the state is not denying that places are also ideational constructs changed by social interventions (Björkdahl and Buckley-Zistel 2022). Just as nations are "imagined communities" (Anderson 1991), the "international" must be envisioned in its various tangible manifestations. A court becomes an international arena if we envisage the transnational relations and issues on trial as global concerns (see Liste 2016). By implication, the "field" is a geographic space in which global governance takes place, as well as a notion that representatives of the state and senior IO staff frequently mobilize to further their own interests (Sending 2015; Anderl 2016; Goetze 2019). Those positioned to produce knowledge about, and who claim to represent, the "field" often do so to consolidate their standing as experts. For example, politicians who travel to conflict zones usually do so to be able to make truth claims based on "having been there." They seek to legitimize themselves to their peers and the broader public but do not really engage with local ways of knowing and doing (Guevara and Kostić 2017: 3). In this sense, it is important not to turn the "field" into a "hold-all category that acts as a flat counterweight to the international" (Brigg and George 2020: 412).

On the contrary, one of this book's main theoretical implications is that actual *places of governance* should be taken seriously analytically. Places such as the European border in Greece, coastguard training centers in Warsaw, high-level meetings at the UN headquarters in New York, and multilateral conferences in large conference hotels in Marrakesh then all become sites of global governance (see Chapters 3–5). This shift in perspective draws attention to new spaces—borderlands (Côté-Boucher et al. 2014), factories (Bartley 2018), embassies (Cornut 2015; Infantino 2021), training academies (Broome and Seabrooke 2015), boardrooms (Kentikelenis and Seabrooke 2017), and universities (Hanrieder 2019)—and centers analysis on under-researched actors, including fieldworkers, trainers, labor inspectors, and consular staff. That leads to the study of new governing tools such as governing on the ground. In brief, starting from questions like "What happens in Geneva?" and "How does being in Geneva enable and constrain the behavior of people making global policies?" (see Dairon and Badache 2021), as well as "What happens in country offices in Burundi and how does being located there condition decision-making?" (see Campbell 2018), helps provide new insight into who actually influences global governance and how.

6.2 Institutional Implications: Fit for Purpose?

The book's main analytical-conceptual goal has been to theorize governing on the ground as a mode of governance that those IOs with operational branches use when confronted with new, politicized, or crisis-ridden issues—that is, issues which are underregulated. It set out to conceptualize and analyze the relevant mechanisms at play behind this way of governing to produce new insights into how IOs shape international policy-making and to reconstruct how mixed migration is being governed, including beyond formal mandates and policies. The book's ambition thus has not been to make predictions about specific long-term trajectories of governing on the ground or to identify and test the key factors of success or failure. I have also not aimed to show that governing on the ground is better at addressing global challenges than other modes of governance. Keeping these limitations in mind, I now turn to the question of how to assess the effectiveness of this mode of governance. I begin by briefly discussing institutional concerns and then outline how more leeway for fieldworkers, combined with improved staff mobility and professional training, could strengthen IO capacities to govern on the ground.

6.2.1 Inaction and Failure in Governing on the Ground

Improvising in the field and stabilizing what has been learned in practice are often second best compared to other ways of organizing collective action on global problems. The empirical analysis reveals that those who govern on the ground experience deep frustration: fieldworkers, for instance, report that their everyday solutions only change things slowly and incrementally. They underline that the results do not match the effort in governing on the ground: they would prefer more coordinated, far-reaching, and binding ways of making policy. However, such tools are usually unavailable in the policy areas studied here so that governing on the ground is the pragmatic alternative IO staff members rely on to cope with the issues at hand—and their muddling through has governing effects (see Chapters 4 and 5).

However, saying that IOs use their access to the field to improvise governing does not mean that IOs always effectively manage global challenges through practice on the ground. First, fieldworkers might lack creativity or be afraid of deviating from organizational mandates and policy scripts. My empirical study revealed that some staff members strictly follow rules, even those they consider inadequate (see also Ruffa and Rietjens 2022), and, as a result, do not improvise viable solutions. Second, there is a strong possibility that practical knowledge is not scaled up within the IOs. Limited headquarters jobs, poorly functioning rotation systems (see Benner and Rotmann 2008: 56), and few incentives for IO senior staff to take local knowledge seriously (see Autesserre 2014: 72) mean that much of the practical knowledge generated at the frontlines will likely be lost. Of the fieldworkers observed and interviewed for this book, the majority quit their organizations. Some have remained within the organizational ecology, moving, for example, from the UNHCR to the EUAA, while others left for entirely different jobs, taking their experiential knowledge with them (see also Hardt 2018: 221). Headquarters staff in training units also state that they are underfunded and have limited resources for ongoing and comprehensive fieldworker training. That means that practical knowledge is often not effectively stabilized within IOs, so fieldworkers do not know what has already been learned and start all over again.

Situated learning may also go wrong, with new routines that are harmful or detrimental to governing specific issues becoming routinized, consolidated, and diffused. Charli Carpenter (2003) has famously shown how, during the 1990s Balkan wars, UNHCR fieldworkers and delegates from the International Committee of the Red Cross (ICRC) who were confronted with the new task of protecting civilians from ethnic cleansing, decided to treat women, children, and the elderly as "particularly vulnerable" and evacuate them first. Established early on, this frontline practice resulted in the massacre of military-aged males, who were actually at greater risk.[1] In cases where failure is less drastic and clear-cut than in this case, professional and organizational standpoints determine how field-based governing practices are rated (see Schindler and Wille 2019). For example, the fact that hardly anyone is currently being returned from the EU's external border (UNHCR 2020c) might be viewed as a failure from a border guard's or Frontex's perspective but a success from a migration lawyer's or the UNHCR's point of view. Both issues—"no" and "bad" outcomes on the ground—have been explored in the peacekeeping literature. I draw on that research in the remainder of this section to discuss potential institutional solutions to inaction and failure.

6.2.2 Fieldworker Discretion, Professional Training, and Staff Mobility

To harness the productive side of governing on the ground and more effectively influence its direction, IOs should consider allowing fieldworkers more discretionary power. It is widely recognized that autonomous action by IO staff is in fact desired (Barnett and Finnemore 2004: 5; Hawkins et al. 2006b: 8). The case study shows that IOs should expand ***fieldworker***

[1] This is akin to what Barnett and Finnemore (1999: 721–2) call the "normalization of deviance"; the stabilization of exceptions to the rule that lead to policy failure.

autonomy even further. This might be a difficult choice because reducing centralized control over organizational activities can produce pathological behavior. However, diffusing authority to frontline workers can enhance organizational performance if it is accompanied by risk controls—most importantly, professional training and staff incentives such as job rotation, as for example Honig (2019) has recently shown with respect to development aid (see also Autesserre 2014: 26, 72; Campbell 2018; Froitzheim et al. 2022; Heinzel 2022). Because fieldworkers are inevitably confronted with unpredictable events in their everyday work, more leeway to make decisions allows them to better respond to situational challenges—and more leverage and flexibility can increase motivation. In other words, recognizing fieldworkers' importance as decision-makers in IOs can counterbalance inaction and failure.

The better field staff are trained, the more resources they have—in terms of skills, expertise, and professional judgment—which my findings show to be crucial for decision-making leeway to result in effective improvisation. Thus, a second factor for making governing on the ground better able to address transnational challenges is ***professional training*** in IOs (see also Hardt 2018: 216). With scarce funding, capacity building for in-house staff usually has low priority in IOs. However, priorities might be shifted if governing on the ground is recognized as effective bottom-up policy-making when other governance modes are blocked. Similarly, IOs should aim to employ *enough* well-trained field staff: the analysis shows that field officers are usually overworked, and tired and frustrated fieldworkers make more mistakes and have little time to reflect on their actions.

IO ***staff mobility*** is a third factor that helps make governing on the ground productive. Field positions are often entry-level jobs or based on consultant contracts. The prospect of being promoted to headquarters positions could provide important incentives for operational staff to work toward "robust governance solutions that are sufficiently adaptable, agile and pragmatic to uphold a particular goal or function in the face of continuous disruptions" (Ansell et al. 2021: 949; quoted after Lenz and Eckhard 2022: 1). In addition to motivating fieldworkers, staff mobility is an important institutional feature for ensuring that knowledge travels within IOs. Students of organizational learning in UN peacekeeping have demonstrated that knowledge circulation in IOs is often obstructed by the lack of regular job rotation (Howard 2008; Benner et al. 2011). By implication, increasing opportunities for field staff to work in other IO positions will help disseminate improvised governing practices and operational knowledge more easily. This should include both field staff moving up in the organization and senior personnel, whose experience is an important resource for making local decisions, being deployed to the field (see Honig 2020). Overall, increased mobility, better training, and more discretion can enhance learning on the ground and knowledge transfer in IOs (see also Dijkstra et al. 2019).

6.3 Normative Implications: Do the Governed Have a Say?

In this book, I have argued that not everyone who governs is authorized to do so. Some IO actors *de facto* govern in concrete spaces, outside the boundaries of their IO's established authority. I now discuss why this is a matter of concern from a normative perspective and explore possible institutional solutions.

6.3.1 Arbitrariness and Abuse in Governing on the Ground

In the previous section, I argued that increasing decision-making leeway for IO fieldworkers can make governing on the ground more effective. However, it is not difficult to think of cases where the discretionary power of those governing in practice led to abuse. In the field of peacekeeping, UN Blue Helmets have sexually abused people they were supposed to protect. On-site personnel in the North Atlantic Treaty Organization (NATO)-led Stabilization Force in Bosnia (SFOR) was involved in human trafficking and violated detainees' human rights (Hirschmann 2019: 20–2). With respect to migration and asylum, those who govern at the border have prevented people on the move from gaining access to safe territory, arbitrarily detained migrants and asylum seekers, and made faulty decisions regarding their applications for asylum. In one particular instance, frontline staff decided not to register their intention to claim asylum by systematically asking misleading questions, effectively keeping people on the move from claiming asylum in Europe (see Chapter 4). Yet, there are few control mechanisms and limited redress for those directly affected.

Generally, the governance addressees analyzed in this study have little say in the decision-making process—although their life choices are greatly impacted by on-the-ground governance. This contradicts the "all-affected principle," according to which the "people who are significantly affected by a policy decision should have an opportunity to influence that decision" (Koenig-Archibugi 2017: 172). When this key normative yardstick for assessing the democratic quality of global politics is violated, global governance can hardly be considered legitimate. In short, governing on the ground is a concern because it opens the door to arbitrariness and the misuse of discretionary power and generally offers limited opportunities for affected populations to influence policy. Theorizing this governance mode thus requires us to not only think about how it works (effectively) but also to discuss its possible legitimation (see also White 2022).

6.3.2 Complaint and Participation Mechanisms

Previous research has demonstrated that the "participatory pattern of legitimation," which ensures that those affected by a decision have a direct say in how it is made, is the most demanding legitimacy standard for IO governance and difficult to implement (Heupel et al. 2018: 347; see also Zaum 2013; Steffek 2015). Accountability—"a process by which individuals or institutions answer for their actions and the consequences that follow from them" (Deloffre 2016: 726)—is often considered a viable alternative (see Steffek 2010; Hirschmann 2020). However, it is also difficult to hold fieldworkers to account: many get away with poor performance or abusive behavior. Recent studies on UN peacekeeping have shown that even high-ranking field staff, such as civilian and military leaders, are rarely replaced when their missions fail to prevent armed conflict or their troops engage in sexual exploitation (Lundgren et al. 2021). In addition, because field staff often rotate across missions or are employed on short-term contracts, *post hoc* corrective action might not be the most expedient legitimation mechanism, except in cases of gross misconduct. Because formal vertical accountability chains in IOs are difficult to enforce and fieldworkers frequently change positions, I argue in the following that *horizontal accountability*—direct accountability toward the governed—is more promising for making governing on the ground responsive to the claims of affected people. This means that instead of thinking about how to improve accountability toward member states, donors, and senior bureaucrats (see for example Grant and Keohane 2005; Gent et al. 2015),[2] we should turn to mechanisms that put target populations front and center.

Importantly, horizontal accountability is distinct from the *mutual* accountability of field staff: This book's case study reveals that fieldworkers demand

[2] These "legal," "political," "managerial," and "supervisory" types of accountability focus on staffing and controls rather than input. For an overview and discussion of different classifications of accountability relations, see Hirschmann (2020: 17–28).

justifications when they argue about what constitutes competent professional action (see also Deloffre 2016; Pouliot 2021: 4–5). Competence negotiations are a normative process in which fieldworkers quarrel over what is feasible and acceptable practice. They contest other practitioners' activities and claims of knowing, and cooperate, compete, and fight over what constitutes appropriate behavior (see Chapter 2). Hence, although governing on the ground is not devoid of accountability, it lacks input and redress channels for governance addressees.

To start closing the accountability gap, IOs need to strengthen ***complaint and participation mechanisms***, for instance, by establishing review and inspection panels to monitor the situation on the ground and hear from target groups. The ICRC, for example, has a long history of visiting detention sites and speaking to prisoners to prevent torture and degrading and inhumane behavior (see Lesch 2023. Similarly, in 2016, the European Parliament's Committee on Civil Liberties, Justice and Home Affairs (the LIBE Committee) sent delegates to hotspot centers in Greece and Italy to develop recommendations for ensuring respect for fundamental rights during asylum and return procedures (European Parliament 2016). Such visits are one way to provide the governed with the opportunity to voice their opinions. They should be regularly conducted by external or independent commissions that report directly to IO governing bodies.

Governance addressees should also be given the opportunity to file complaints with an independent ombudsperson. For example, the European Ombudsman can receive complaints about administrative irregularities, unfairness, discrimination, the abuse of power, failure to reply, withholding of information, or unnecessary delay—but only from EU citizens, not migrants or asylum seekers. However, in 2012, the office of the European Ombudsman started its own inquiry into Frontex operations, and in its final report recommended that Frontex "should set up a mechanism whereby it could deal directly with complaints from people claiming to have had their fundamental rights breached by Frontex." It further explained that, "[r]egrettably, Frontex decided not to accept this recommendation" (European Ombudsman 2013). Although people on the move are therefore still not allowed to petition the European Ombudsman or an independent monitoring body, in 2011, Frontex created the position of a fundamental rights officer (FRO). The 2019 mandate gave the FRO even more competencies: it remains subordinate to Frontex's executive director but can now investigate all Frontex activities and carry out regular on-the-spot visits with a team of "fundamental rights monitors." Making use of its new powers, the FRO recently recommended that Frontex stop operations in Greece because

of serial abuses by Greek border guards, including violent pushbacks of asylum seekers to Turkey, degrading treatment of migrants, and the separation of migrant children from their parents (NT 2023). The critique by the European Ombudsman and the FRO, combined with an investigation into allegations of harassment, misconduct, and pushbacks by the European Anti-Fraud Office (OLAF) and pressure from advocacy groups led to Frontex Executive Director Fabrice Leggeri resigning in 2022. It thus appears that independent ombudspersons are an effective accountability mechanism—if they can be addressed anonymously and regardless of the complainant's nationality, have enough staff and resources to follow up on complaints, are granted access to the field, and can make recommendations to key decision-making bodies (see also Heupel et al. 2018: 344; Guild 2022).

Besides inspection committees and ombudspersons, it appears that facilitating legal appeals can also reduce accountability deficits in governing on the ground. For instance, migrants whose applications for asylum have been deemed inadmissible in the hotspots can contest being returned to Turkey: the Greek Appeals Authority overturned most of the first-instance return decisions under the fast-track border procedure (*Guardian* 2016; UNHCR 2020c). With support from migration lawyers and NGOs, people on the move can also seek redress for rights violated in regional and international courts and file complaints with the UN Human Rights Committee. Several cases challenging the treatment of migrant children, reception conditions, pushbacks, and procedural violations have been brought before the European Court of Human Rights.[3] Recent research has shown that when there is a high degree of judicial independence, courts often safeguard migrant rights (Zaun et al. 2023). For these accountability mechanisms to work, the capacities of the relevant appeals committees must be strengthened, political interference reduced, and barriers to appeals and court procedures, such as limited access to free legal aid, lowered.

Finally, to be genuinely responsive to input from those governed means that their feedback must be systematically integrated into decision-making in the field: by regularly consulting with refugee- and migrant-led organizations, conducting household surveys or establishing monitoring groups and organizing community committees in the local coordination structure (see Murtaza 2012; Campbell 2018: 51; Steinhilper 2021). Migrant and refugee representatives had a seat at the table in most of the IO working

[3] See the European Council on Refugees and Exiles (ECRE) list of legal submissions: https://ecre.org/ecre-publications/legal-submissions/, accessed April 13, 2023).

groups analyzed.[4] Humanitarian NGOs and UN agencies generally agree that accountability in humanitarian action is about making the voices of their "beneficiaries" heard. However, despite broad consensus on the need to prioritize target groups' rights and agency, especially NGOs feel pressured to report tangible—that is, measurable—results to justify their activities in the field. Thus, they continue to focus on reporting short-term successes and mainly communicate with donors (Schmitz et al. 2012; Gent et al. 2015). Yet there is some evidence that donors, too, have started to change their stance on measuring "good" behavior in the field, and are now focusing more on community participation and durable solutions (Deloffre 2016: 743–5). Continuing this trend, IOs should make it possible for governance addressees to sanction them when things go wrong and provide input on the direction and content of governing on the ground. Because that might be difficult to institutionalize, horizontal accountability could be informal, with field officers allowed to use their creativity, enterprise, and willingness to invent effective accountability mechanisms. This brings us back to the importance of fostering entrepreneurship among field staff (see Campbell 2018: 51).

In brief, if IOs directly regulate individual behavior and do not just exercise authority over states, which, at least initially, consented to the authority relationship (see Heupel et al. 2018: 346), those individuals need to have a say in IO governance decisions. If states no longer mediate between IOs and their citizens, and truly democratic participation in IO decision-making is hard to achieve, governance addressees need to be able to effectively challenge those decisions and receive justifications. Horizontal accountability is not primarily about punishing fieldworkers but rather providing target groups with the chance to change decisions and routines in a *post hoc* fashion. Target groups need opportunities to contest organizational behavior on the ground—and IO field staff need more room to admit failure and learn from their mistakes (see also Schmitz et al. 2012: 1178; Hardt 2018; Eilstrup-Sangiovanni and Hofmann 2024). Only if IOs are reflexively structured can organizational practice integrate the demands of the governed. In turn, increasing horizontal accountability can potentially make governing on the ground more effective. In her study on peacebuilding, Susanna Campbell (2018) shows that organizational performance and accountability are indeed connected: informal local accountability toward the governed is first and foremost a mechanism for effectively achieving change on the ground. Instead of facing a trade-off (Acharya 2016: 16),

[4] While this comes with its own problems of representativeness—as most fieldworkers are aware—integrating diverse local stakeholder groups can help reduce cleavages among them (Campbell 2018: 21).

different criteria for good governance on the ground thus might interlock. Promoting inclusion of those governed can improve the normative quality of governing on the ground *and* foster the underlying rationale of effectively addressing global problems because global governance is ultimately about mobilizing different groups of people to find ways of dealing with issues of public concern—which cannot be done without the participation of the most affected and their intimate knowledge of the problems at hand.

6.4 Outlook: Global Governance in Uncertain Times

> *Studying the frontlines should be an obvious starting point for those interested in international politics.*
>
> **(Cooper and Cornut 2019: 301)**

In this book, I have argued that to understand how global issues are governed, we need to closely investigate how field staff in different types of international organizations make sense of global problems and organize collective action in response.

With this argument, the book contributes to a growing body of research which shows that governing is often messy, provisional, and must continuously deal with uncertainty and complexity—without ever fully resolving it (see also Best 2012, 2014; Koinova et al. 2021; Pouliot and Thérien 2023). Instead of IOs exercising their mandates in neatly defined spheres of competence for solving global problems, governing often takes place in the in-between spaces between formal institutions and regimes (Pouliot 2021; Lesch and Reiners 2023). It is often driven by actors in IOs who elude formal accountability mechanisms, such as consultants, (Seabrooke and Sending 2019; Eckl and Hanrieder 2023), and often works in a *de facto* manner, with people in NGOs, intergovernmental organizations, and domestic institutions using direct action to change things without being tasked or authorized do so (Eilstrup-Sangiovanni and Sharman 2022; Rankin 2022). The book sheds new light on the individuals in global governance institutions who work toward achieving cooperation and collective action, especially under conditions of crisis, contestation, and gridlock.

By drawing attention to informal, practice-based governing in and across IOs, the book also recasts the question of "private action and the public good" (Powell and Clemens 1998). It shows that non-state actors and private persons effectively regulate public issues on the ground, blurring the boundaries between public and private organizations, comparable with "governance entrepreneurs" who craft public-private partnerships at the secretariat level (Green 2013; Andonova 2017). My book provides new empirical evidence for the argument that the boundaries around what counts as "public" are constantly being redrawn by a myriad actors—not only those with official positions (see Eriksen and Sending 2013; Best and Gheciu 2014: 15). It contributes to studies demonstrating that global governance often takes a "hybrid" form (Srivastava 2022: 43–6): it does not necessarily flow from authorized public institutions but is crafted by and enmeshes public and private actors in their struggle for political solutions and influence.

These findings point out the need for further research about which actors actually "make" global governance. Instead of primarily analyzing formal mandates and institutional features, we should focus our research on who in IOs is crafting public solutions beyond the public-private divide. In the words of Jan Aart Scholte, IO studies should not limit themselves to questions of how a "particular governing body operates, but how a given substantive matter is handled. After all, to examine institutions is only a means; the greater aim is to understand concrete problems" (Scholte 2021: 182–3). Especially when formal governance arrangements are challenged by politicization, stalemate, and backlash, we need to thoroughly investigate who is (claiming to be) handling global issues of public concern and with what outcomes. Only then can we know "who governs the globe" (Avant et al. 2010a) and how to hold them to account for their decisions.

Beyond these broader lines of inquiry, four open questions remain with respect to governing on the ground. The first relates to ***fieldworker traits***. In this book, I examine IO fieldworkers' professional backgrounds to understand how their knowledge and networks drive situated learning in the field and help stabilize frontline practices in headquarters. These dynamics can also be influenced by other characteristics including organizational culture, gender, national origin, and age (see Coning 2010; Bove et al. 2020; Oksamytna et al. 2021; Buitelaar 2023; Jenne 2023). Further inquiry into the personality traits that dispose people to break the rules and innovate when confronted by unforeseen challenges in the field can help us better understand how governing on the ground works and what makes for successful improvisation in practice. Scrutinizing those who govern on the ground can also expand our knowledge about when individual actors act as "arbitrators" within organizations (see Karlsrud 2013) or "boundary spanners" and "linking pins" between IOs (see Schneiker and Joachim 2021; Kranke 2022)—promoting or obstructing the circulation of practical knowledge from the field.

The second open question relates to ***structural constraints***. Grounded in social-constructivist IO studies and practice-oriented IR research, this book focuses on how individual actors make sense of situational challenges within their institutional environments. It focuses on the different logics of action and agential resources of practitioners whose peripheral positions in the organization require them to reconcile local demands with organizational tasks. Further research on how structural factors condition IO field staff behavior could complement this study (see Campbell 2018; Honig 2019). Systematically comparing how mission size, budget, reporting requirements, and mandate design influence governing on the ground would provide additional insight into what shapes governing dynamics in the field as well as their outcomes.

The third open question regards the ***local context***, in which IOs governing on the ground are embedded. Focusing on interactions in the international interorganizational community of practice at the border, this book does not systematically analyze how international staff engage with national and local actors (see Mosse 2011a; Autesserre 2014; Witt 2022). Deeper analysis of IO field staff positionality in relation to the local lifeworld in which they operate could help us better understand the factors that shape successful learning in the field. How are field staff bound by local laws and expectations? How do they locally negotiate room for international action? How much do they collaborate with—or differentiate themselves from—national and local authorities? What are the crucial points of friction and resistance?

The fourth open question pertains to the ***agency of the governed***. The book has paid particular attention to how IO personnel experiment in the field using the discretion that results from their peripheral locations within the organization as well as personal relations and professional skills, which help them remain capable of acting in an unpredictable work environment that demands quick, practical solutions. Importantly, the case study shows that people in IOs only had to act because migrants and asylum seekers started moving, challenging the international border regime, and pushing international actors to move too. Their capacity to actively challenge international norms and organizations posits the need for future research on how decision-making by those governed shapes global politics (see Triandafyllidou 2017; Mainwaring 2019; Pincock et al. 2020). More studies are needed about how the governed, rather than being conceptualized as "governance receivers," *drive* global public policy.

ANNEX I

Researching Global Governance on the Ground

In this Annex, I describe and discuss my research strategy, the empirical material, as well as the data collection and analytical process. I also provide some reflections on research ethics (on the case selection and generalizability, see Section 1.4).

Research Strategy

The open character of this book's research question requires an inductive approach. I therefore relied on an interpretive-qualitative research design that is geared toward reconstructing the meaning-making processes of the people who govern mixed migration on the ground (see Schwartz-Shea and Yanow 2012). To implement it, I conducted an organizational ethnography, which, most basically speaking, is the ethnographic study of organizations and their organizing processes (van Maanen 1988; Neyland 2008; Ybema et al. 2009: 4). Rather than beginning with concepts defined *a priori* and seeking to test them in the field, it is concerned with understanding how the members in the situation under study make sense of their surroundings. It does so by going into the organizational field and observing, at the scene, the complexity of everyday organizational settings through immersing oneself in ordinary, routine workflows. The benefit of such an approach is that it allows you to explore the tacit knowledge which organizes work practices but usually goes unnoticed (Ybema et al. 2009: 1–2; see also Acuto 2014; Solomon and Steele 2016; Adler-Nissen and Drieschova 2019).

This approach requires research strategies which go beyond an analysis of texts, speech acts, and discourses (Bueger 2014: 4). Observations and thick descriptions of in-depth case studies are the main strategy to reconstruct from the practitioners' perspectives how they perceive their role, how they go about their daily routines, and how they justify their actions (see Geertz 2000; Côté-Boucher et al. 2014: 200). In a first step, I thus went into the organizational field on Chios, one of the central border crossing points along the Eastern Mediterranean route to Europe (see Section 3.3). I began my research with fieldwork at the border in order to observe directly how transnational professionals on the ground make sense of mixed migration and respond to it. In a second step, I conducted interviews at the headquarters of the organizations that I had encountered on Chios. I did not pre-select the international organizations (IOs) but started from the transnational professionals who work in the field and sought to understand, from there, how their practices organize mixed migration governance also beyond the local setting. The book starts from local practices—practical knowledge is the central unit of analysis—and aims at bridging the micro (what people say and do), the meso (routines), and the macro (organizations, institutions, order) through showing that global governance is often the effect of interconnected practices (Pouliot 2007; Miettinen et al. 2009: 1309–12; Nicolini 2009b: 1392; van der Waal 2009: 24). In other words, while the research design is actor centered and produces detailed close-ups of interactions in practice through fieldwork on Chios, it also analyzes how local practices are embedded in global structures by turning to organizational learning at headquarters.

Data Collection

The fundamental strategy for fieldwork is "being there" or "hanging out" in order to get close to the activities and everyday experiences of insiders and to observe how they interact with each other and their surroundings (Bayard de Volo and Schatz 2004: 267; MacKay and Levin 2015; Nair 2021). The key benefit of participant observation is that it allows the researcher to access practical knowledge and study how it emerges in the everyday (Nicolini 2009b: 1400).

Participant Observation

Organizations, and IOs in particular, have a political character and can therefore be difficult to access (Lie 2013: 206; Nair 2021). Researching IOs is a form of "studying up": Of switching the analytic lens and standing of the researcher from studying down—the study of the powerless, colonized, and poor "natives"—to studying up—the study of the powerful, often at home and higher up the social hierarchy, who can restrict access and evade being researched. How did I manage to gain access to the community of practice on Chios? Through personal contacts with people in local refugee support structures in Germany, I came in touch with a small grassroots organization which had formed around the events at the Budapest Central Station. This organization coordinated volunteers across Europe and had a close-knit network of volunteer teams and local initiatives along the European external border and the Balkan route. After consulting with one of their main coordinators over email and telephone, I decided to travel to Chios and join one of the transnational volunteer groups on the island. In advance of the trip, I joined volunteer coordination groups on the social media platform Facebook to get further information on the situation on-site and, eventually, simply booked a plane ticket to Athens and a ferry ticket from Piraeus to Chios. Once arrived on the island, I sent Facebook messages to the local coordinators of the three volunteer teams I knew of and was able to set up a meeting with one of the groups in the afternoon of the same day at their warehouse. Here, I got the induction for new volunteers and was issued a simple, laminated piece of paper that showed my affiliation with the team and registered me as a volunteer with the local police.

Through the daily team meetings of the volunteer group, I was quickly able to get a first impression of who else was operating on the island and where their work intersected. I got daily updates on the activities of the team as well as encounters, conflicts, and cooperation with other organizations. We discussed events, challenges, and changes on the island, results from coordination meetings and workings groups, and planned new projects. Through my participation in all the activities of the volunteer group, I effectively became a member of the local community of practice and quickly met practitioners from other organizations operating on Chios. After three weeks, I attended my first general coordination meeting at the town-hall of Chios, where all the different organizations came together on a weekly basis to discuss and coordinate their work. I also joined several of the thematic working groups and thereby not only got to know the most important local stakeholders on a personal level but gained first-hand insight into their more formalized coordination practices. Through these personal contacts, it was also relatively easy to set up interview appointments with practitioners from different organizations and with different professional backgrounds.

Volunteering thus proved to be an effective strategy for gaining access to the community of transnational migration, asylum, and border professionals on Chios. And yet, there are some limitations to this strategy. Being a volunteer certainly influenced how I moved in the organizational field, how I perceived the interorganizational dynamics, and how I experienced the role of organizational boundaries and mandates. Not being employed by an organization with a formal mandate and structure, and not being officially accountable to a superior or dependent on a salary certainly influenced the vantage point from which I observed my and others' participation in governing mixed migration on Chios. Being a member of European Border and Coast Guard Agency (Frontex), European Asylum Support Office (EASO), United Nations (UN) High Commissioner for Refugees (UNHCR), International Organization for Migration (IOM), or one of the non-governmental organizations (NGOs) would most likely have produced a different account from the one that I present in this book. This independence, however, also allowed me to participate freely in all activities and to engage with all the different practitioners and thus to get close to many different viewpoints and experiences. Further, it turned out that volunteers played a crucial role in the organizational ecosystem on Chios. Many times, they were the crucial linking pins between different organizations, and their flexibility has been decisive in organizing a collective response to mixed movements. As such, the role of the volunteer not only allowed me to directly study interorganizational dynamics in governing migration but also is one of the chief research findings: Given overlapping mandates and authority gaps, volunteers were a resource that many transnational professionals relied on to creatively find solutions to everyday challenges in governing mixed migration on the ground.

The degree of participation during participant observation can vary. Brian Moeran (2009) argues that a fieldworker should make a subtle shift from participant observation to "observant participation," as a more active role can entail a qualitative leap in understanding. He describes this shift from being an outsider to an insider (the *rite de passage*) as a "lucky break"—the moment during fieldwork, when the researcher moves from front- to backstage, gets closer to informants, and gains insight into local knowledge (Moeran 2009: 146). During my fieldwork, this lucky break happened after the first weeks of volunteering. Patrolling on the eastern shore of Chios, taking part in the landings of migrant boats, doing needs assessments and distribution of clothes and food in the camps eventually turned me into an insider. While I felt overwhelmed and confused when I first arrived, not understanding the setting and procedures nor the personal contacts and hierarchies, I gradually became more familiar with the different tasks and activities as well as the people. I began to understand processes and routines, the geographical outline of the island, and who was doing what and how (see Lie 2013: 213). A second qualitative leap in understanding occurred when I gained access to the coordination meetings and working groups. Before, I would only hear second-hand reports from the volunteer coordinators who had attended. Through participating myself, I was able to learn more about the other people and organizations who operated on the island; I was starting to understand their "local language" and getting to know the politics behind coordinating the response.

During interviewing, the degree of participation decreases and the researcher will find herself on the observer end of the spectrum (Schwartz-Shea and Yanow 2009: 68). During the second stage of the research process, at the headquarters, I thus did not actively participate in organizational processes but largely withdrew to my position as a researcher. This shift in the degree of participation was, for instance, reflected in my clothing: While I was mostly wearing boots and functional wear in the field, I exchanged the outdoor garments for formal office attire when at headquarters.

The duration of participant observation can also vary and depends on a number of factors like research funding or the willingness of an organization to grant access. Importantly, the degree of participation and the duration of fieldwork should be determined primarily by the research question and only subordinately by research pragmatics. As a general rule, the fieldworker should exit the field when her data is sufficient for an ethnographic write-up. This point might be reached when the fieldworker does not produce any new examples of organizational activities or has gained a reasonable degree of confidence in speaking as an insider and is hence able to provide a detailed account of organizational life (Neyland 2008: 148–9). I stayed in the field for forty-three days. Importantly, the duration of "a day" in the field as well as the periodicity of observations, i.e. the regularity with which the researcher interacts with participants, have been very long and high (Schwartz-Shea and Yanow 2009: 65). While forty-three days might seem rather short compared to fieldwork that lasts up to a year, I have been exposed to many different activities, interactions, and viewpoints in a condensed amount of time since a working day on Chios lasted up to twenty-four hours. In sum, I collected 530 hours of observation and left Chios when I felt that experiences had started repeating themselves and staying longer would not produce fundamentally new insights.

No matter the degree or duration, the ability to listen and observe carefully is key to recording data during participant observation. Organizational ethnographers recommend beginning observations with spatial explorations. As the spatial is often an expression of the social, it can be a "useful heuristic tool for making sense of underlying social frameworks" (van der Waal 2009: 35). On Chios, I first familiarized myself with the different refugee camps, the ports, and other important landing spots along the shore where migrants and refugees would arrive as well as the warehouse, the accommodations, restaurants, and cafés where volunteers stayed and hung out. At a later stage, I also got to know the "UN hotel," where staff from the bigger organizations were accommodated and workshops took place, as well as IOs' local offices and the Chios townhall, where coordination meetings happened. Rodi Bar in Chios city center was another important location because many transnational professionals would meet there for a coffee or a drink. Getting to know the layout of the research site turned out to be highly instructive: It helped me to get a good first understanding of the different migration governing practices and, just by being in these places, many opportunities for participation, observation, and conversation arose.

Next to mapping the socio-spatial, following events is treated as a central strategy for participant observation. This involves going to meetings and shadowing people who are willing to take the researcher along (Czarniawska 2007; van der Waal 2009: 31). As the key sites on Chios are spread out across the island, a car was indispensable to go to meetings, attend events, and, generally, be able to participate. Since I do not know how to drive, I had to rely on others to give me a ride. Making necessity a virtue, it turned out to be very useful to share a car with the volunteer coordinators of my team as this allowed me to shadow them during their daily activities. As a general strategy, I therefore always asked the more experienced volunteers to take me along wherever they went and tried to be as present and available as possible, for instance, through signing up for as many shifts as possible (often reducing sleep to a maximum of three hours a day) and going to all events and incidents. This strategy allowed me to witness a high number of actions and interactions in a rather short amount of time.

Significantly, the different participatory and observatory activities need to be accompanied by the documentation of the researcher's observations. The writing of *field notes* serves as a fundamental means to build up the record of spaces visited, events witnessed, the people worked with and talked to, and the documents read during fieldwork (van der Waal 2009: 35). While in the field, I took preliminary notes whenever possible, combining the two general methods for writing field notes identified by Robert Emerson and his colleagues (Emerson et al. 1995): The first one, called salience hierarchy, proposes to start by writing down what strikes the fieldworker as most interesting or telling. I always carried a little notebook and a pen to write protocols during meetings and take notes after important events and interactions. The second one, called comprehensive note-taking, suggests systematically describing everything that happens, whereby notes are organized chronologically (Wolfinger 2002: 89–91). Using the calendar application in my smartphone, I recorded everything that happened chronologically. Chronological note-taking has the advantage of recording things that seem trivial or strange at first glance but will prove insightful in light of later observations. Once I had returned from Chios, I immediately typed out my preliminary research diary, ending up with ninety-nine computer written pages of field notes.

In addition to writing field notes, I started recording the decisions I took during my daily routines, which led me to meet and talk to some informants while closing off other experiences in an *audit* (Schwartz-Shea and Yanow 2009: 61). Alterations in my research strategy mainly pertained to the people I selected for more formalized interviews to complement my observations, experiences, and conversations.

Interviews

Conversational and more formalized interviews with people who are experts in a practice due to their participation in it for an extended period of time can usefully complement participant observation. The book also relies on interviews because they are another fundamental tool for reconstructing knowing in practice (Devault and McCoy 2002: 756–61; Yanow et al. 2012).

As typical for interviews in qualitative research, I aimed for diversity rather than representativeness (King and Horrocks 2010: 29). I therefore relied on two "sampling strategies": I was always open to opportunity and tried to maximize social relationships to strike up conversations with insiders during my stay in the field on as many occasions as possible (Moeran 2009: 151; van der Waal 2009: 25). Meeting Frontex officers during patrolling the shore, having a coffee with them after they pulled a migrant boat into the port, speaking to members of UNHCR during a migrant protest in the hotspot Vial, conversing with EASO staff after a coordination meeting, and chatting with NGO personnel during the distribution of water or hygiene kits in the camps presented opportunities to learn more about their experiential knowledge.

However, one cannot rely on encountering all key participants by "hanging out at the water-cooler, coffee or copy machine" (Yanow 2009: 194). I thus also used snowball and purposive "sampling": I arranged various meetings after a couple of weeks in the field, when I had gained enough local knowledge to identify the most experienced practitioners. Whom I had spoken to before influenced whom I reached out to for the next interview. Guided by the principle of diversity, I aimed at covering varied areas of know-how and multiple viewpoints. I was careful to ensure exposure to a variety of areas of expertise and lived experiences and stopped once a point of saturation was reached—when I started to hear the same kind of information or the same kind of names of who I should talk to (see Schwartz-Shea and Yanow 2009: 67). In sum, I conducted sixteen more formalized interviews in the field (which lasted between thirty and ninety minutes), trying to strike a balance between organizations and professions (see Annex II).

During the second stage of the research process, I arranged interview appointments in the operations and training units at the various organizations' headquarters. Interviews in the operations unit helped me to cross-check my field experiences and to gain contextual knowledge on the governing practices observed on Chios. These interviews allowed me to learn more about how staff members at headquarters level make sense of what their organization does in the field, adding a valuable layer of interpretation. Interviews in the training units, in turn, have been crucial for reconstructing the standing of practical knowledge within and across the organizations and to understand how much they rely on field experiences to design their learning programs.

In choosing the interview partners, I aimed for organizational balance and diversity in practical experience. Of the twenty-five interviews which I conducted at headquarters level, five have been with UNHCR staff, five with IOM staff, four with Frontex staff, three with EASO staff, one with a UNHCR-Frontex liaison officer, one with a UNHCR-EASO liaison officer, five with humanitarian NGOs, and one with a professional association for humanitarians (lasting from thirty to ninety minutes). For most interviews, I traveled to the headquarters or liaison offices in Geneva, Warsaw, Brussels, and Valletta—not only to facilitate access but also to get a first-hand impression of the work environment and to improve the quality of the interviews.

However, since headquarters and global offices are geographically spread out, I also conducted some interviews on Skype.

Again, there are some limitations to the interview material thus generated. The caveat of not pre-selecting single organizations as case studies but communities of professional practitioners with different organizational affiliations is the limit of interviews that can be conducted per organization. With a higher number of interviews per organization, more information on intra-organizational learning processes could have been produced. Expert interviews at headquarters—similar to observations, conversations, and interviews in the field—often made me aware of the breadth and depth of insights that could be gained beyond the empirical material which I collected.

For interviews in the field and at headquarters, I used topic guides which primarily aimed at meaning and experience and tried to avoid strong presuppositions. Being aware that the interviewer helps the interviewee to render her tacit knowledge explicit (King and Horrocks 2010: 134–7; Bueger 2014: 18), I tried to reduce my role to that of moderator. Acknowledging that it is important not to guide the interviewee too strongly with my questions, I still tried to make sure to ask enough questions to establish a rapport and to avoid that she digress too far from my research interests (King and Horrocks 2010: 25). For the expert interviews at headquarters, in particular, I thus used more direct knowledge question. Generally, I used probes (follow-up questions) and prompts (interventions) to clarify and extend upon the answers given to me and often repeated them back to the interviewees to make sure that my interpretation of what has been said was in line with the participants' own understanding.

Documents

I used additional text material for this study which can be sub-divided into two categories. First, I relied on intergovernmental organization (IGO) and NGO reports on the situation on the ground on Chios and the neighboring islands to contextualize and cross-check my interpretations of what was happening here. I also read press releases and statements from European Union (EU) institutions on EU migration policy at the external border.

Second, I analyzed the organizations' curricula, handbooks, and training material for frontline workers. Handbooks and manuals can give clues about organizational practices and the tacit knowledge that informs them (Bueger 2014: 19; Beerli 2018: 76). To compile the document corpus, I systematically searched the homepages of the IOs that operate on Chios; in particular the websites of training units and thematic units related to mixed migration. I also followed references from the interviewees and within the training documents themselves: If they referred to other guidelines as central tools, I looked for those. Further, in accordance with the research logic outlined so far, I traced the practices from the field: For example, since IOM staff provided psychosocial support, I searched for IOM training documents on psychosocial support. If several versions of a handbook were available, I chose the one which I deemed the most relevant according to the following criteria: (a) time (the most recent one), (b) geography (the one pertaining to Europe), (c) theme (the one most explicitly addressing mixed movements), or (d) addressees (the one addressing fieldworkers rather than program officers or managers). Most of the documents could be downloaded from the organizations' homepages. Where they have not been available to the general public, I was able to obtain some upon request, mostly following an interview. Some documents, however, could not be examined first hand due to security or copyright issues. Despite these limitations, I was able to gather different training documents for all organizations and practices reconstructed on Chios—119 in total.

In sum, I have triangulated different sources and research methods. I use observational and interview data from the field and the headquarters, NGO and IGO reports as well as training material and manuals to reconstruct the complex patterns of organizing mixed migration governing through practice in the field.

Analytical Process

Writing is the "linchpin of ethnographic inquiry" (Wolfinger 2002: 86) or as Wanda Vrasti (2008: 282) summarizes: "Schematically speaking, ethnography refers to the textual transcription/translation of holistic descriptions and experiences gathered through fieldwork." During desk and text work, experience-near knowledge needs to be translated into experience-distant concepts. And yet, as Christian Bueger (2014: 7) explains, this "does not necessarily implicate forcing meaning upon the practices studied. The solution [...] is to attempt to identify moments in which participants in a practice tend to articulate implicit meaning themselves." This in turn, does not imply that writing ethnography is a purely descriptive endeavor which only aims at reproducing the "native's point of view." Rather, in order to reconstruct meaning-making processes, an emic perspective (i.e. the description of the perspective of the insider) needs to be counterbalanced with an etic perspective (i.e. the fieldworker's analysis), which draws on pre-acquired theoretical knowledge and allows the application of concepts and tools to the empirical material (Lie 2013: 210). When it came to writing the organizational ethnography, I thus sought to distance myself from the field (geographically and intellectually) and used the theoretical knowledge described in Chapters 1 and 2 to structure, analyze, and interpret the empirical material while striving to avoid the inherent danger of losing the emic perspective (see Moeran 2009: 154).

To do that, as a first step, I systematically organized my field notes, interview transcripts, and other textual and material artifacts (i.e. *indexing*) to find specific details easily and see emerging patterns in the information (van der Waal 2009: 35). As a second step, I went through the field notes repeatedly to produce themes. King and Horrocks (2010: 150) define themes as: "recurrent and distinctive features of participants' accounts, characterizing particular perceptions and/or experiences, which the researcher sees as relevant to the research question." The main themes I have identified and used to structure the data are (1) practices, (2) institutional-political contexts, and (3) interorganizational dynamics. These three main themes have also been used to code the interviews (cp. below). As a third step, I further refined these themes by adding sub-themes such as "policy gaps," "improvisation," or "interpersonal relations" and (re)clustering those under the three main themes as well as specifying them in terms of possible arguments (Neyland 2008: 126; King and Horrocks 2010: 149–51).

This process of ordering and thematic analysis has been embedded in writing, a process throughout which I was constantly asking myself "how do I know what I know?" That way, I have been forced to provide evidence for my interpretations and arguments and look for instances where it openly deviates from the practitioners' own interpretations (Schwartz-Shea and Yanow 2009: 61–2). For the final account in the book, however, the rich and layered descriptions of objects, events, actors, and interactions of the organizational life of Chios, were condensed to provide a more tailored empirical illustration of the key arguments presented in the book.

In addition to ethnographic writing and thematic analysis, I used qualitative content analysis for the recorded expert interviews and documents (Saldana 2009). I first identified initial descriptive codes in the interview transcripts and organizational documents, which I then used to label, sort, and synthesize the data, using the computer software MAXQDA. The main objective at this stage of the analytic process has been to reduce the data and make it more manageable. For instance, I used the practices identified in the thematic analysis of the field notes such as "protection," "search and rescue," "interviewing," or "border guarding" as descriptive codes to mark all the passages in the training documents that describe which competences are required to perform these practices. During the following iterative process of description and interpretation, I used the synthesized data to refine the descriptive codes or group them together into clusters such "skills and competences" and to define interpretative codes such as "authority gap," "learning-by-doing," or "interorganizational competition." Going back and forth between the reduced data and the interpretive codes, I used those codes to further structure and analyze the data and to refine the codes at the same time.

For the analysis of stabilization processes, I have devised two, related, coding schemes. As mentioned before, the interviews mainly serve to reconstruct how training documents are created and, accordingly, their analysis focuses on reasons and processes of designing learning material. With regard to the training documents themselves, the analysis focuses on the content of learning. Generally, I have asked the headquarters material three main sets of questions during the analysis: "Why do IOs create handbooks and other learning products?," "How do they devise them and how do they teach?," and "What do they teach in terms of practical skills and know-how?." The first set of questions regarding the reasons then translates into the code "motives/rationales" for creating training material to which I assigned, after an initial round of coding, sub-codes such as "setting professional standards." This sub-code, in turn, has been used to code sections in the handbooks and interviews like this one:

> Frontex's mission in the field of training is to support the Member States to achieve an efficient, high and uniform level of border and coast guarding. To fulfil this mission, we strive to establish common standards and build up the knowledge, skills and competences of the law enforcement officers with border and coast guarding responsibilities.

In sum, these iterative steps of descriptive and interpretive coding ultimately led me toward detecting the patterns described in the empirical chapters (see King and Horrocks 2010: 152–8).

Research Ethics

Since organizational ethnographers rely on close social relationships and trust to gain access and insight into organizing processes, I was highly aware of the harm I could cause and was never deceptive about my research intentions, obtained (either written or verbal) informed consent from the participants, and protected my informants through confidentiality and anonymity (see Christians 2005: 144–5). This is why I usually only identify them using generic descriptors such as "humanitarian professional." I also gave participants the opportunity to withdraw from the research project at any time (see Neyland 2008: 144–6; King and Horrocks 2010: 115). Finally, I always depict what people did and said as accurately as possible.

ANNEX II

List of Interview Partners

The interviews listed below were conducted during the following research stays:

March 26 to May 9, 2016: Chios Island, Greece
January 30 to February 8, and February 13 to 17, 2017: Geneva, Switzerland
February 9 to 12, 2017: Brussels, Belgium
February 18 to 26, 2017: Valletta, Malta
May 29 to June 4, 2017: Warsaw, Poland

All interviews were conducted in English, except where indicated otherwise.

Interview number	Date	Function	Place	Duration
I-1 (telephone interview)	Oct. 12, 2016	Asylum expert, EASO	Skype	65 min.
I-2 (telephone interview)	Oct. 10, 2016	Field staff, IOM	Skype	47 min.
I-3 (telephone interview)	Jun. 14, 2016	Field staff, UNHCR	Skype	61 min.
I-4 (personal interview)	Apr. 28, 2016	Field staff, UNHCR	Chios	61 min.
I-5 (personal interview)	Apr. 20, 2016	Field staff, humanitarian NGO	Chios	38 min.
I-6 (personal interview)	Apr. 10, 2016	Coordinator, transnational volunteer team	Chios	55 min.
I-7 (personal interview)	May 6, 2016	Rescue professional, SAR NGO	Chios	57 min.
I-8 (personal interview)	May 1, 2016	Rescue professional, SAR NGO	Chios	55 min.
I-9 (personal interview)	Apr. 25, 2016	Field staff, humanitarian NGO	Chios	83 min.
I-10 (personal interview)	Apr. 24, 2016	Field staff, humanitarian NGO	Chios	50 min.
I-11 (personal interview)	Apr. 23, 2016	Field staff, humanitarian NGO	Chios	30 min.
I-12 (personal interview)	May 5, 2016	Field staff, humanitarian NGO	Chios	45 min.

Interview number	Date	Function	Place	Duration
I-13 (personal interview)	Apr. 26, 2016	Field staff, Frontex	Chios	ca. 20 min.
I-14 (personal interview)	May 3, 2016	Field staff, humanitarian NGO	Chios	ca. 60 min.
I-15 (personal interview)	May 8, 2016	Field staff, EASO	Chios	ca. 60 min.
I-16 (telephone interview, German)	Jun. 6, 2018	Field coordinator, legal NGO	Skype	55 min.
I-17 (personal interview)	May 30, 2017	Principal training project coordinator, training unit, Capacity-Building Division, Frontex	Frontex HQ, Warsaw	57 min.
I-18 (personal interview)	Jun. 2, 2017	Staff member, training unit, Capacity-Building Division, Frontex	Frontex HQ, Warsaw	25 min.
I-19 (personal interview)	Jun. 1, 2017	Head, press office, Frontex	Frontex HQ, Warsaw	28 min.
I-20 (personal interview)	May 29, 2017	Fundamental rights officer, Frontex	Frontex HQ, Warsaw	62 min.
I-21 (personal interview)	Jun. 2, 2017	UNHCR liaison officer to Frontex	UNHCR liaison office to Frontex, Warsaw	70 min.
I-22 (personal interview)	Feb. 9, 2017	EASO liaison officer to EU institutions, former head of training unit, Department of Asylum Support	EASO liaison office to EU institutions, Brussels	61 min.
I-23 (personal interview)	Feb. 20, 2017	Staff member, Department of Asylum Support, EASO	EASO HQ, Valletta	25 min.
I-24 (personal interview)	Feb. 24, 2017	Head, Department of Operations, EASO	EASO HQ, Valletta	55 min.
I-25 (personal interview)	Feb. 21, 2017	UNHCR senior liaison associate to EASO, former learning officer, Protection Unit GLC Budapest	UNHCR liaison office to EASO, Valletta	70 min.
I-26 (personal interview)	Feb. 10, 2017	Staff member, DMM, IOM	IOM HQ, Geneva	50 min.
I-27 (personal interview, German)	Feb. 14, 2017	Staff member, DMM, IOM	IOM HQ, Geneva	52 min.
I-28 (personal interview)	Feb. 17, 2017	Two staff members, DMM, IOM	IOM HQ, Geneva	39 min.

Interview number	Date	Function	Place	Duration
I-29 (personal interview)	Feb. 14, 2017	Staff member, Migration Policy Research Division, IOM	IOM HQ, Geneva	17 min.
I-30 (telephone interview)	Apr. 27, 2017	Trainer, Sphere	Skype	29 min.
I-31 (personal interview, German)	Feb. 2, 2017	Staff member, Division of International Protection, UNHCR	UNHCR HQ, Geneva	53 min.
I-32 (personal interview, German)	Feb. 4, 2017	Consultant, Division of International Protection, UNHCR	UNHCR HQ, Geneva	93 min.
I-33 (personal interview)	Feb. 3, 2017	Staff member, Division of International Protection, UNHCR	UNHCR HQ, Geneva	45 min.
I-34 (telephone interview)	Mar. 10, 2017	Staff member, Global Learning Centre, UNHCR	Skype	48 min.
I-35 (telephone interview)	Feb. 21, 2017	Staff member, Global Learning Centre, UNHCR	Skype	39 min.
I-36 (telephone interview)	May 22, 2017	Staff member, NRC	Skype	38 min.
I-37 (telephone interview)	Mar. 7, 2017	Staff member, DRC	Skype	28 min.
I-38 (telephone interview)	May 23, 2017	Global learning director, HLA	Skype	30 min.
I-39 (telephone interview)	Feb. 8, 2017	Humanitarian learning manager, HLA	Skype	54 min.
I-40 (personal interview)	Feb. 7, 2017	Membership coordinator, PHAP	PHAP Office, Geneva	54 min.

Intergovernmental Organization and Non-Governmental Organization Training Programs

Frontex's Learning Program

Frontex is equipped with an explicit training mandate. Its regulation tasks the agency to develop training tools on border guarding and to assist the European member states in training their national border officers, in particular those who will be seconded to Frontex operations as part of the European Border and Coast Guard Teams or as return escorts. Frontex has a training unit at its headquarters in Warsaw, which is part of the Capacity-Building Division and provides pre-deployment training on tasks such as screening, debriefing, and fingerprinting as well as thematic training on issues such as false document detection. It coordinates national training academies and develops training standards to be applied across Europe.

Frontex's main training principle is "interoperability" (I-17), which means that its training unit works toward training all coast- and border guards in European member states and Schengen associated countries according to the same standards and practices in order for them to be able to effectively work together. Since Frontex largely depends on member states to second personnel to its operations, training is often oriented toward national coast- and border guards but, under the new Frontex regulation, a standing corps with up to 10,000 operational staff will be set up over the course of the next eight years (see Chapter 6). Training will then increasingly focus on Frontex's own fieldworkers and, importantly, Frontex also trains third country nationals, i.e. coast- and border guards of non-EU states. It has started training operations in Turkey, the West Balkans, and West Africa (Frontex 2017c: 3).

With regards to training courses and learning material, Frontex has a highly integrated and standardized approach: It has developed a "Common Core Curriculum for Border and Coast Guard Training in the EU" as well as a "Sectoral Qualifications Framework for Border Guarding." These two documents constitute the baseline for all training activities. They are to "ensure an integrated platform for a coherent strategy which connects all Frontex training products" (Frontex 2013b: vol. 1, 19). They establish clear learning outcomes and job competence profiles according to which concrete training tools are developed.

EASO's Learning Program

EASO, like Frontex, has a specific training mandate. Its regulation states that EASO "shall establish and develop training available to members of all national administrations and courts and tribunals, and national services responsible for asylum matters in the Member States" (European Parliament and The Council 2010: Art. 6, 1). EASO has a training unit in its headquarters in Valletta, which is located within the Department of Asylum Support. The training unit develops training courses and carries out training sessions for caseworkers in national asylum administrations as well as for asylum officers to be deployed in EASO operations in the hotspots. Since December 2016, EASO can employ so-called "interim caseworkers" who are not seconded by the member states but directly hired by EASO. These caseworkers also receive pre-deployment training before they start working in EASO operations at the European external border: EASO hence employs and trains its own operational staff (see Chapter 5).

Training modules and handbooks are developed under the roof of EASO's Training Strategy and the European Asylum Curriculum (EAC). The EAC sets out a specific learning pathway for case officers and asylum practitioners. They are to be trained in three core modules on the application of the United Nations (UN) Refugee Convention, interview techniques, and evidence assessment. In addition to these core modules, they can continue their training in more advanced or specific areas such as interviewing children or vulnerable persons. Similar to Frontex, EASO thus has a rather coherent approach to training as all its courses are part of a specific module of the EAC. However, EASO can also develop additional training material, especially with regard to operational training needs, such as the training package for EASO asylum experts deployed in the hotspots (EASO 2017: 1).

IOM's Learning Program

IOM is a highly projectized and decentralized organization and, accordingly, its training and learning is also divided among the different thematic departments and divisions. The two main operational departments at IOM headquarters are the Department of Operations and Emergencies (DOE) and the Department of Migration Management (DMM). Within DOE, the Preparedness and Response Division, for instance, is in charge of shelter and camp management. In this specific thematic area, IOM is part of the Global Camp Coordination and Camp Management (CCCM) Cluster, an interagency initiative which the IOM runs together with the UNHCR and the Norwegian Refugee Council (NRC). The Global CCCM Cluster coordinates different actors who provide services to displaced communities in camps, urban settings, and informal settlements. Next to operational support and setting standards through gathering best practices, its main activity is capacity-building and training. It has established an interagency roster of international trainers and develops training material on camp management. It provides training to fieldworkers on issues such as protection in camps, coordination in camps, and settlement design to support CCCM's operations on the ground (CCCM 2015: 1–2).

Another useful example to illustrate how the IOM provides training and learning to its operational staff and other fieldworkers is from the DMM, which is, *inter alia*, responsible for the topic of "Migration Health." Within "Migration Health," IOM provides capacity-building on mental health and psychosocial support to "professionals, governments, agencies and IOM departments through: assessments, analysis and research; knowledge dissemination initiatives, including conferences; workshops, summer schools, masters programmes; development of policy papers and guidelines" (IOM 2019c). It also develops practical tools for implementing psychosocial support in emergencies and trains humanitarians, health professionals, and border officials in psychological first aid. The IOM is also part of the Inter-Agency Standing Committee (IASC) and its working groups which serve as a coordination forum for UN agencies and other IOs that provide humanitarian assistance. The IASC Reference Group for Mental Health and Psycho-Social Support in Emergency Settings has developed guidelines on mental health and psychosocial support to which the IOM has contributed and which it uses in its training.

Training and capacity-building in the IOM is hence dispersed across the organization and located within the different thematic divisions and sub-units rather than being a standalone training unit. The heads of the sub-units in the different departments are responsible for organizing training for their in-house colleagues and they develop training courses and material for government officials and practitioners employed by other IOs (I-28, I-29).

UNHCR's Learning Program

In 2009, the UNHCR established a Global Learning Centre (GLC), which is part of the Division of Human Resources Management and located in Budapest. GLC is intended to "provide a unified training strategy and structure to UNHCR" (Ralston n.d.: 2) and centralizes training activities within the organization. It develops training on protection and humanitarian assistance and, with regard to its internal organizational structure, basically mirrors the main thematic divisions at UNHCR headquarters in Geneva. Together with their thematic counterparts in Geneva, staff members in the GLC develop and deliver training on issues such as emergency management, protection in camps, and refugee status determination. They develop and update handbooks, tools, and guidelines for fieldworkers on issues such as operational protection in camps, prevention of sexual and gender-based violence, and participatory assessments in refugee settlements.

Similar to the IOM, the UNHCR also forms part of several interagency initiatives that have a strong focus on training. For example, UNHCR is the lead agency of the Global Protection Cluster on internally displaced persons (IDPs) which includes a Task Team on Learning that coordinates training among different field missions and different intergovernmental organizations (IGOs) and non-governmental organizations (NGOs). The task team provides an online training repository where it makes available training manuals and materials on issues such as protection in camps or child protection and it offers several training programs such as "Training of Trainers on Protection in Practice."

Humanitarian Learning Programs: ProCap, HLA, Sphere, PHAP, and IMRF

Humanitarian NGOs offer training to their in-house staff and join forces with other organizations to develop learning programs for the entire humanitarian sector. Similar to umbrella NGOs that unite advocacy organizations to increase their voice in multilateral negotiations, several humanitarian NGOs have pooled resources to devise joint training programs for humanitarian and protection professionals. The NRC, for example is a member in the Global Protection Cluster and the Global CCCM Cluster and it hosts the Protection Standby Capacity Project (ProCap) which deploys protection experts to field missions, and regional and global offices to assist other IOs that work in emergency settings. Next to deploying experts, ProCap trains staff from UN agencies, IGOs, and NGOs working on protection in emergencies:

> The field-focused and skills-based ProCap Protection Training has already provided more than 200 participants from standby rosters, through training events, with the skills to undertake context-specific protection analysis, establish priorities, design and plan inter-agency responses and advocate for protection. It complements issue- and agency-specific protection training. (NRC n.d.)

In a similar vein, the Humanitarian Leadership Academy (HLA), which shares an office with Save the Children in London, provides training programs and an online training platform for different NGOs such as NRC, Save the Children, and the International Rescue Committee. Its main purpose is to develop and provide humanitarian training to different IOs and individual practitioners, especially first responders at the frontlines of humanitarian crises. They offer training on food security and health in humanitarian emergencies as well as tools for implementing humanitarian action such as needs assessment and decision-making skills in crisis settings.

The most prominent example of interorganizational training, learning, and standard-setting in humanitarian assistance is the Sphere Project. Initially started by a group of humanitarian professionals from different NGOs, it has developed into a sector-wide movement that develops reference tools for NGOs, IGOs, and UN agencies. Its core document is the *Sphere Handbook* which defines and operationalizes humanitarian standards and principles. The *Sphere Handbook* is regularly updated and includes a training package for volunteers and practitioners from different IOs to learn how to work with the standards in practice. The *Sphere Handbook* is also used in training by other IOs, for example by the CCCM Cluster.

Next to such joint organizational initiatives on training in humanitarian practice, an individual-based professional organization has been established in the humanitarian sector that also provides training to its members: Professionals in Humanitarian Assistance and Protection (PHAP). PHAP is a professional association that seeks to connect humanitarian practitioners as they switch positions between different IOs, countries, and operations. It is not tied to employment in a specific IO as membership is explicitly individual. The aim of PHAP is to foster "concrete, practical measures to enhance the availability, experiences, skills, competencies, professional networks, and both formal and informal support structures of humanitarian personnel at all levels and in all parts of the system" (PHAP n.d.). As part of this mission, PHAP organizes webinars and training courses on different thematic issues, and provides certification and credentialing schemes for specific professional skills and competencies. Many of these schemes and programs are linked: Either the NGOs use handbooks and training material that have been developed in joint initiatives or they collaborate directly. HLA, for instance, provides the training infrastructure for learning and practicing the competences that PHAP certifies (I-39, I-40). ProCap experts function as trainers for PHAP webinars and PHAP has organized webinars and surveys to contribute to updating the *Sphere Handbook*.

Finally, there are also umbrella organizations that link thematically more specific humanitarian NGOs such as the International Maritime Rescue Federation (IMRF) that connects maritime search and rescue (SAR) organizations like SOS Méditerranée, Migrant Offshore Aid Station (MOAS), the Danish Sea Rescue Society, and the German Lifesaving Society. They, too, function as a type of global office or headquarters because they connect smaller organizations and operations across the globe. IMRF's mission is to "develop and improve maritime SAR capacity around the world, preventing loss of life in the world's waters" and to that end, it organizes "training in maritime search and rescue operational skills" (IMRF n.d.). It facilitates exchange between single SAR NGOs and develops and distributes training guidelines. It also hosts the Mixed Migration Safety Project and develops codes of conduct for NGOs operating in this context, specifically in the Mediterranean Sea.

References

Abbott, A. (1988), *The System of Professions: An Essay on the Division of Expert Labor* (Chicago: University of Chicago Press).

Abbott, K. W. (2012), "Engaging the Public and the Private in Global Sustainability Governance," *International Affairs*, 88/3: 543–64.

Abbott, K. W., and Faude, B. (2021), "Choosing Low-Cost Institutions in Global Governance," *International Theory*, 13/3: 397–426.

Abbott, K. W., and Snidal, D. (2001), "International "Standards" and International Governance," *Journal of European Public Policy*, 8/3: 345–70.

Abbott, K. W., Keohane, R. O., Moravcsik, A. et al. (2000), "The Concept of Legalization," *International Organization*, 54/3: 401–19.

Abbott, K. W., Genschel, P., Snidal, D., Zangl, B. (Hg.) (2015), *International Organizations as Orchestrators* (Cambridge: Cambridge University Press).

Acharya, A. (2004), "How Ideas Spread: Whose Norms Matter? Norm Localization and Institutional Change in Asian Regionalism," *International Organization*, 58/2: 239–75.

Acharya, A. (2016), "Rethinking Demand, Purpose and Progress in Global Governance: An Introduction," in A. Acharya (ed.), *Why Govern? Rethinking Demand and Progress in Global Governance* (Cambridge: Cambridge University Press), 1–28.

Acuto, M. (2014), "Everyday International Relations: Garbage, Grand Designs, and Mundane Matters," *International Political Sociology*, 8/4: 345–62.

Adler, E. (2005), *Communitarian International Relations: The Epistemic Foundations of International Relations* (London: Routledge).

Adler, E. (2008), "The Spread of Security Communities: Communities of Practice, Self-Restraint, and NATO's Post-Cold War Transformation," *European Journal of International Relations*, 14/2: 195–230.

Adler, E., and Pouliot, V. (2011), "International Practices," *International Theory*, 3/1: 1–36.

Adler, P. S., Kwon, S.-W., and Heckscher, C. (2008), "Professional Work: The Emergence of Collaborative Community," *Organization Science*, 19/2: 359–76.

Adler-Nissen, R., and Drieschova, A. (2019), "Track-Change Diplomacy. Technology, Affordances, and the Practice of International Negotiations," *International Studies Quarterly*, 63/3: 531–45.

Adler-Nissen, R., and Eggeling, K. A. (2022), "Blended Diplomacy. The Entanglement and Contestation of Digital Technologies in Everyday Diplomatic Practice," *European Journal of International Relations*, 28/3: 640–66.

Adler-Nissen, R., and Pouliot, V. (2014), "Power in Practice. Negotiating the International Intervention in Libya," *European Journal of International Relations*, 20/4: 889–911.

Aegean Boat Report (2022), "Chios Push-Back No. 99" <https://aegeanboatreport.com/2022/01/06/chios-pushback-nr-99/>, accessed Jan 23, 2023.

Agné, H., Dellmuth, L. M., and Tallberg, J. (2015), "Does Stakeholder Involvement Foster Democratic Legitimacy in International Organizations? An Empirical Assessment of a Normative Theory," *The Review of International Organizations*, 10/4: 465–88.

Agnew, J. (1994), "The Territorial Trap: The Geographical Assumptions of International Relations Theory," *Review of International Political Economy*, 1/1: 53–80.

Aldrich, H. E., and Pfeffer, J. (1976), "Environments of Organizations," *Annual Review of Sociology*, 2: 79–105.

Allan, B. B. (2017), “Producing the Climate. States, Scientists, and the Constitution of Global Governance Objects,” *International Organization*, 71/1: 131–62.

Allen, W., Anderson, B., van Hear, N. et al. (2018), “Who Counts in Crises? The New Geopolitics of International Migration and Refugee Governance,” *Geopolitics*, 23/1: 217–43.

Alter, K., and Meunier, S. (2009), “The Politics of Regime Complexity,” *Perspective on Politics*, 7/1: 13–24.

Anderl, F. (2016), “The Myth of the Local,” *The Review of International Organizations*, 11/2: 197–218.

Anderl, F., Daphi, P., and Deitelhoff, N. (2021), “‘Keeping Your Enemies Close? The Variety of Social Movements’ Reactions to International Organizations’ Opening Up,” *International Studies Review*, 23/4: 1273–99.

Anderson, B. (1991), *Imagined Communities: Reflections on the Origin and Spread of Nationalism* (2nd rev. ed., London: Verso).

Anderson, B., and Ruhs, M. (2010), “Researching Illegality and Labour Migration,” *Population, Space and Place*, 16/3: 175–9.

Andersson, R. (2016), “Hardwiring the Frontier? The Politics of Security Technology in Europes ‘Fight against Illegal Migration,’” *Security Dialogue*, 47/1: 22–39.

Andonova, L. B. (2017), *Governance Entrepreneurs: International Organizations and the Rise of Global Public-Private Partnerships* (Cambridge: Cambridge University Press).

Ansell, C., Sørensen, E., and Torfing, J. (2021), “The COVID-19 Pandemic as a Game Changer for Public Administration and Leadership? The Need for Robust Governance Responses to Turbulent Problems,” *Public Management Review*, 23/7: 949–60.

Antonakaki, M., Kasparek, B., and Maniatis, G. (2016), “Counting, Channeling, and Detaining: The Hotspot Center Vial in Chios, Greece,” *Society & Space*, Forum “Governing Mobility through European Hotspot Centres,” 1–19.

Argote, L. (1999), *Organizational Learning: Creating, Retaining, and Transferring Knowledge* (Boston: Kluwer Academic).

Autesserre, S. (2014), *Peaceland: Conflict Resolution and the Everyday Politics of International Intervention* (Cambridge: Cambridge University Press).

Avant, D. D., Finnemore, M., and Sell, S. K. (2010a) (eds.), *Who Governs the Globe?* (Cambridge: Cambridge University Press).

Avant, D. D., Finnemore, M., and Sell, S. K. (2010b), “Who Governs the Globe?,” in D. D. Avant, M. Finnemore, and S. K. Sell (eds.), *Who Governs the Globe?* (Cambridge: Cambridge University Press), 1–32.

Avramopoulos, D. (2015), “EU Commissioner for Migration, Home Affairs and Citizenship: Explanatory Note on the ‘Hotspot’ Approach” <http://www.statewatch.org/news/2015/jul/eu-com-hotsposts.pdf>, accessed May 4, 2018.

Babb, S. L. (2009), *Behind the Development Banks: Washington Politics, World Poverty, and the Wealth of Nations* (Chicago: University of Chicago Press).

Babb, S. L., and Buira, A. (2005), “Mission Creep, Mission Push and Discretion: The Case of IMF Conditionality,” in A. Buira (ed.), *The IMF and the World Bank at Sixty* (London: Anthem), 59–83.

Ban, C., Seabrooke, L., and Freitas, S. (2016), “Grey Matter in Shadow Banking: International Organizations and Expert Strategies in Global Financial Governance,” *Review of International Political Economy*, 23/6: 1001–33.

Banai, A., Moore, M., Miller, D. et al. (2014), “Symposium ‘Theories of Territory beyond Westphalia,’” *International Theory*, 6/1: 98–104.

Banulescu-Bogdan, N. (2018), “When Facts Don’t Matter: How to Communicate More Effectively about Immigration’s Costs and Benefits.” MPI Reports (Washington, DC: MPI).

Barnett, L. (2002), “Global Governance and the Evolution of the International Refugee Regime,” *International Journal of Refugee Law*, 14/2 and 3: 238–62.

Barnett, M. N., and Finnemore, M. (1999), "The Politics, Power, and Pathologies of International Organizations," *International Organization*, 53/4: 699–732.

Barnett, M., and Finnemore, M. (2004), *Rules for the World: International Organizations in Global Politics* (Ithaca, NY: Cornell University Press).

Bartley, T. (2018), *Rules without Rights: Land, Labor, and Private Authority in the Global Economy* (Oxford: Oxford University Press).

Bauböck, R., Mourão Permoser, J., and Ruhs, M. (2022), "The Ethics of Migration Policy Dilemmas," *Migration Studies*, 10/3: 427–41.

Bauer, M. W., Knill, C., and Eckhard, S. (2017) (eds.), *International Bureaucracy: Challenges and Lessons for Public Administration Research* (London: Palgrave Macmillan).

Baumann, R., and Dingwerth, K. (2015), "Global Governance vs Empire: Why World Order Moves towards Heterarchy and Hierarchy," *Journal of International Relations and Development*, 18/1: 104–28.

Bayard de Volo, L., and Schatz, E. (2004), "From the Inside Out: Ethnographic Methods in Political Research," *Political Science & Politics*, 37/2: 267–72.

Beer, C. T., Bartley, T., and Roberts, W. T. (2012), "NGOs: Between Advocacy, Service Provision, and Regulation," in D. Levi-Faur (ed.), *The Oxford Handbook of Governance* (Oxford: Oxford University Press), 325–38.

Beerli, M. J. (2018), "Saving the Saviors: Security Practices and Professional Struggles in the Humanitarian Space," *International Political Sociology*, 12/1: 70–87.

Benner, T., and Rotmann, P. (2008), "Learning to Learn? UN Peacebuilding and the Challenges of Building a Learning Organization," *Journal of Intervention and Statebuilding*, 2/1: 43–62.

Benner, T., Mergenthaler, S., and Rotmann, P. (2011), *The New World of UN Peace Operations: Learning to Build Peace?* (Oxford: Oxford University Press).

Bernstein, S., and van der Ven, H. (2017), "Best Practices in Global Governance," *Review of International Studies*, 43/3: 534–56.

Best, J. (2012), "Ambiguity and Uncertainty in International Organizations: A History of Debating IMF Conditionality," *International Studies Quarterly*, 56/4: 674–88.

Best, J. (2014), *Governing Failure: Provisional Expertise and the Transformation of Global Development Finance* (New York: Cambridge University Press).

Best, J., and Gheciu, A. (2014), "Theorizing the Public as Practices. Transformations of the Public in Historical Context," in J. Best and A. Gheciu (eds.), *The Return of the Public in Global Governance* (Cambridge: Cambridge University Press), 15–43.

Betsill, M. M., and Corell, E. (2008), *NGO Diplomacy: The Influence of Nongovernmental Organizations in International Environmental Negotiations* (Cambridge, MA: MIT Press).

Betts, A. (2010), "Towards a 'Soft Law' Framework for the Protection of Vulnerable Irregular Migrants," *International Journal of Refugee Law*, 22/2: 209–36.

Betts, A. (2011), "Introduction: Global Migration Governance," in A. Betts (ed.), *Global Migration Governance* (Oxford: Oxford University Press), 1–33.

Betts, A. (2013), "Regime Complexity and International Organizations: UNHCR as a Challenged Institution," *Global Governance*, 19/1: 69–81.

Betts, A., and Cerna, L. (2011), "High-Skilled Labour Migration," in A. Betts (ed.), *Global Migration Governance* (Oxford: Oxford University Press), 60–77.

Betts, A., and Orchard, P. (2014) (eds.), *Implementation and World Politics: How International Norms Change Practice* (Oxford: Oxford University Press).

Betts, A., Milner, J., and Loescher, G. (2012), *UNHCR: The Politics and Practice of Refugee Protection into the 21st Century* (Routledge Global Institutions Series; 2nd ed., Abingdon: Routledge).

Bicchi, F. (2011), "The EU as a Community of Practice: Foreign Policy Communications in the COREU Network," *Journal of European Public Policy*, 18/8: 1115–32.

Bicchi, F. (2022), "Communities of Practice and What They Can Do for International Relations," *Review of International Studies*, 48/1: 24–43.

Biermann, F., and Siebenhüner, B. (2009a) (eds.), *Managers of Global Change: The Influence of International Environmental Bureaucracies* (Cambridge, MA: MIT Press).

Biermann, F., and Siebenhüner, B. (2009b), "The Influence of International Bureaucracies in World Politics: Findings from the MANUS Research Programm," in F. Biermann and B. Siebenhüner (eds.), *Managers of Global Change: The Influence of International Environmental Bureaucracies* (Cambridge, MA: MIT Press), 319–50.

Biermann, R., and Koops, J. A. (2017), "Studying Relations among International Organizations in World Politics. Core Concepts and Challenges," in R. Biermann and J. A. Koops (eds.), *Palgrave Handbook of Inter-Organizational Relations in World Politics* (London: Palgrave Macmillan), 1–46.

Björkdahl, A., and Buckley-Zistel, S. (2022), "Space for Peace: A Research Agenda," *Journal of Intervention and Statebuilding*, 16/5: 659–76.

Blackler, F. (1995), "Knowledge, Knowledge Work and Organizations: An Overview and Interpretation," *Organization Studies*, 16/6: 1021–46.

Block-Lieb, S., and Halliday, T. C. (2017), *Global Lawmakers: International Organizations in the Crafting of World Markets* (Cambridge: Cambridge University Press).

Bode, I. (2015), *Individual Agency and Policy Change at the United Nations: The People of the United Nations* (London: Routledge).

Bode, I. (2018), "Reflective Practices at the Security Council: Children and Armed Conflict and the Three United Nations," *European Journal of International Relations*, 24/2: 293–318.

Bode, I., and Karlsrud, J. (2018), "Implementation in Practice: The Use of Force to Protect Civilians in United Nations Peacekeeping," *European Journal of International Relations*, 25/2: 458–85.

Bojar, A., and Kriesi, H. (2023), "Policymaking in the EU under Crisis Conditions: Covid and Refugee Crises Compared," *Comparative European Politics*, 21/4: 427–47.

Borton, J., and Collison, S. (2017), *Responses to Mixed Migration in Europe: Implications for the Humanitarian Sector*, Network Paper, No. 81.

Börzel, T. A., and Risse, T. (2018), "From the Euro to the Schengen Crises: European Integration Theories, Politicization, and Identity Politics," *Journal of European Public Policy*, 25/1: 83–108.

Boswell, C. (2003), "The 'External Dimension' of EU Immigration and Asylum Policy," *International Affairs*, 79/3: 619–38.

Boswell, C. (2008), "The Political Functions of Expert Knowledge: Knowledge and Legitimation in European Union Immigration Policy," *Journal of European Public Policy*, 15/4: 471–88.

Boswell, C. (2012), *The Political Uses of Expert Knowledge: Immigration Policy and Social Research* (Cambridge: Cambridge University Press).

Boswell, C. (2017), "The Role of Expert Knowledge in International Organizations," in A. Littoz-Monnet (ed.), *The Politics of Expertise in International Organizations* (Abingdon: Routledge), 19–36.

Bousiou, A., and Papada, E. (2020), "Introducing the EC Hotspot Approach: A Framing Analysis of EU's Most Authoritative Crisis Policy Response," *International Migration*, 58/6: 139–52.

Bove, V., Ruffa, C., and Ruggeri, A. (2020), *Composing Peace: Mission Composition in UN Peacekeeping* (Oxford: Oxford University Press).

Bradley, M. (2021), "Joining the UN Family? Explaining the Evolution of IOM-UN Relations," *Global Governance*, 27/2: 251–74.

Bradley, M., Costello, C., and Sherwood, A. (2022), "IOM Unbound? Obligations and Accountability of the International Organization for Migration in an Era of Expansion," in

C. Costello, M. Bradley, and A. Sherwood (eds.), *IOM Unbound? Obligations and Accountability of the International Organization for Migration in an Era of Expansion* (Cambridge: Cambridge University Press), 1–41.
Brassett, J., Richardson, B., and Smith, W. (2012), "Private Experiments in Global Governance: Primary Commodity Roundtables and the Politics of Deliberation," *International Theory*, 4/3: 367–99.
Brian, T., and Laczko, F. (2014), *Fatal Journeys: Tracking Lives Lost during Migration* (Geneva: IOM).
Brigg, M., and George, N. (2020), "Emplacing the Spatial Turn in Peace and Conflict Studies," *Cooperation and Conflict*, 55/4: 409–20.
Broome, A., and Seabrooke, L. (2012), "Seeing Like an International Organisation," *New Political Economy*, 17/1: 1–16.
Broome, A., and Seabrooke, L. (2015), "Shaping Policy Curves. Cognitive Authority in Transnational Capacity-Building," *Public Administration*, 93/4: 956–72.
Broome, A., Clegg, L., and Rethel, L. (2015) (eds.), *Global Governance in Crisis* (London: Routledge).
Broome, A., Homolar, A., and Kranke, M. (2017), "Bad Science: International Organizations and the Indirect Power of Global Benchmarking," *European Journal of International Relations*, 24/3: 514–39.
Brunnée, J., and Toope, S. J. (2010), *Legitimacy and Legality in International Law* (Cambridge: Cambridge University Press).
Buchanan, A., and Keohane, R. O. (2006), "The Legitimacy of Global Governance Institutions," *Ethics and International Affairs*, 20/4: 405–37.
Bueger, C. (2014), "Pathways to Practice: Praxiography and International Politics," *European Political Science Review*, 6/3: 383–406.
Bueger, C. (2015), "Making Things Known: Epistemic Practices, the United Nations, and the Translation of Piracy," *International Political Sociology*, 9/1: 1–18.
Bueger, C., and Edmunds, T. (2021), "Pragmatic Ordering: Informality, Experimentation, and the Maritime Security Agenda," *Review of International Studies*, 47/2: 171–91.
Bueger, C., and Gadinger, F. (2014), *International Practice Theory: Core Approaches* (London: Palgrave Pivot).
Bueger, C., and Gadinger, F. (2015), "The Play of International Practice," *International Studies Quarterly*, 59/3: 449–60.
Buitelaar, T. (2023), "Just Leaves in the Wind? Using Agent-Level Factors to Explain Variation in Human Rights Promotion Strategies," *Journal of Intervention and Statebuilding*, 17/3: 273–93.
Búrca, G. de, Keohane, R. O., and Sabel, C. (2014), "Global Experimentalist Governance," *British Journal of Political Science*, 44/3: 477–86.
Busch, P.-O., and Liese, A. (2017), "The Authority of International Public Administrations," in M. W. Bauer, C. Knill, and S. Eckhard (eds.), *International Bureaucracy: Challenges and Lessons for Public Administration Research* (London: Palgrave Macmillan), 97–122.
Büthe, T., and Mattli, W. (2011), *The New Global Rulers: The Privatization of Regulation in the World Economy* (Princeton, NJ: Princeton University Press).
Búzás, Z. I., and Graham, E. R. (2020), "Emergent Flexibility in Institutional Development: How International Rules Really Change," *International Studies Quarterly*, 64/4: 821–33.
Campbell, S. P. (2008), "When Process Matters: The Potential Implications of Organisational Learning for Peacebuilding Success," *Journal of Peacebuilding & Development*, 4/2: 20–32.
Campbell, S. P. (2018), *Global Governance and Local Peace* (Cambridge: Cambridge University Press).
Cantat, C., Pécoud, A., and Thiollet, H. (2023), "Migration as Crisis," *American Behavioral Scientist*, forthcoming.

Carling, J. (2018), "Three Reasons for Rejecting a 'Global Compact for Most Migration'" <https://jorgencarling.org/2018/03/11/three-reasons-for-rejecting-a-global-compact-for-most-migration/>, accessed May 18, 2018.

Carpenter, R. C. (2003), "'Women and Children First': Gender, Norms, and Humanitarian Evacuation in the Balkans 1991–95," *International Organization*, 57/4: 661–94.

Carpenter, R. C. (2010), "Governing the Global Agenda: 'Gatekeepers' and 'Issue Adoption' in Transnational Advocacy Networks," in D. D. Avant, M. Finnemore, and S. K. Sell (eds.), *Who Governs the Globe?* (Cambridge: Cambridge University Press), 202–37.

Carvalho, B. d., Leira, H., and Hobson, J. M. (2011), "The Big Bangs of IR: The Myths That Your Teachers Still Tell You about 1648 and 1919," *Millennium—Journal of International Studies*, 39/3: 735–58.

Castles, S., and van Hear, N. (2011), "Root Causes," in A. Betts (ed.), *Global Migration Governance* (Oxford: Oxford University Press), 287–306.

CCCM (2015), *Camp Management Toolkit.*

CCCM (2015), *CCCM Capacity Development Evaluation: Final Report.*

CCCM (2015a), *CCCM Capacity Development Evaluation: Final Report.*

CCCM (2015b), *Master Trainer Workshop Report: Turin, 27 April–1 May 2015.*

Cerny, P. G. (1995), "Globalization and the Changing Logic of Collective Action," *International Organization*, 49/4: 595–625.

Chorev, N. (2013), "Restructuring Neoliberalism at the World Health Organization," *Review of International Political Economy*, 20/4: 627–66.

Christians, C. G. (2005), "Ethics and Politics in Qualitative Research," in N. K. Denzin and Y. S. Lincoln (eds.), *The SAGE Handbook of Qualitative Research* (3rd ed., Thousand Oaks, CA: SAGE), 139–64.

Chwieroth, J. M. (2013), "'The Silent Revolution': How the Staff Exercise Informal Governance over IMF Lending," *The Review of International Organizations*, 8/2: 265–90.

Collins, H. M. (2001), "What is Tacit Knowledge?," in T. Schatzki, K. Knorr Cetina, and E. v. Savigny (eds.), *The Practice Turn in Contemporary Theory* (London: Routledge), 115–28.

Conceição-Heldt, E. d., and Mueller, T. (2021), "The (Self-)Empowerment of the European Central Bank during the Sovereign Debt Crisis," *Journal of European Integration*, 43/1: 83–98.

Coning, C. de (2010), "Mediaton and Peacebuilding: SRSGs and DSRSGs in Integrated Missions," *Global Governance*, 16/2: 281–99.

Cook, S. D. N., and Seely-Brown, J. (1999), "Bridging Epistemologies: The Generative Dance between Organizational Knowledge and Organizational Knowing," *Organization Science*, 10/4: 381–400.

Cooley, A. (2010), "Outsourcing Authority: How Project Contracts Transform Global Governance Networks," in D. D. Avant, M. Finnemore, and S. K. Sell (eds.), *Who Governs the Globe?* (Cambridge: Cambridge University Press), 238–65.

Cooley, A., and Ron, J. (2002), "The NGO Scramble: Organizational Insecurity and the Political Economy of Transnational Action," *International Security*, 27/1: 5–39.

Cooper, A. F., and Cornut, J. (2019), "The Changing Practices of Frontline Diplomacy: New Directions for Inquiry," *Review of International Studies*, 45/2: 300–19.

Cornut, J. (2015), "To be a Diplomat Abroad: Diplomatic Practice at Embassies," *Cooperation and Conflict*, 50/3: 385–401.

Cornut, J. (2018), "Diplomacy, Agency, and the Logic of Improvisation and Virtuosity in Practice," *European Journal of International Relations*, 24/3: 712–36.

Corradi, J., Gherardi, S., and Verzelloni, L. (2010), "Through the Practice Lens: Where is the Bandwagon of Practice-Based Studies Heading?," *Management Learning*, 41/3: 265–83.

Costello, C. (2018), "Refugees and (Other) Migrants: Will the Global Compacts Ensure Safe Flight and Onward Mobility for Refugees?," *International Journal of Refugee Law*, 30/4: 643–49.

Côté-Boucher, K., Infantino, F., and Salter, M. B. (2014), "Border Security as Practice: An Agenda for Research," *Security Dialogue*, 45/3: 195–208.

Council of the EU (2016), "EU-Turkey Statement" <http://www.consilium.europa.eu/en/press/press-releases/2016/03/18/eu-turkey-statement/pdf>, accessed May 4, 2018.

Cox, R. W., and Jacobson, H. K. (1974), *The Anatomy of Influence: Decision Making in International Organization* (New Haven, CT: Yale University Press).

Crawley, H., and Skleparis, D. (2017), "Refugees, Migrants, Neither, Both: Categorical Fetishism and the Politics of Bounding in Europe's 'Migration Crisis,'" *Journal of Ethnic and Migration Studies*, 44/1: 48–64.

Crawley, H., Düvell, F., Jones, K. et al. (2018), *Unravelling Europe's "Migration Crisis": Journeys over Land and Sea* (Bristol: Policy Press).

Crisp, J. (2008), *Beyond the Nexus: UNCHR's Evolving Perspective on Refugee Protection and International Migration*, New Issues in Refugee Research, Research Paper No. 155, Geneva.

Crisp, J. (2009), "Refugees, Persons of Concern, and People on the Move: The Broadening Boundaries of UNHCR," *Refuge: Canada's Journal of Refugees*, 26/1: 73–6.

Cusumano, E. (2019), "Migrant Rescue as Organized Hypocrisy: EU Maritime Missions Offshore Libya between Humanitarianism and Border Control," *Cooperation and Conflict*, 54/1: 3–24.

Cusumano, E. (2021), "United to Rescue? Humanitarian Role Conceptions and NGO-NGO Interactions in the Mediterranean Sea," *European Security*, 30/4: 547–68.

Cusumano, E., and Bell, F. (2021), "Guilt by Association? The Criminalisation of Sea Rescue NGOs in Italian Media," *Journal of Ethnic and Migration Studies*, 47/19: 4285–307.

Cuttitta, P. (2017), "Repoliticization through Search and Rescue? Humanitarian NGOs and Migration Management in the Central Mediterranean," *Geopolitics*, 23/3: 632–60.

Czaika, M., and Haas, H. de (2015), "The Globalization of Migration: Has the World Become More Migratory?," *International Migration Review*, 48/2: 283–323.

Czaika, M., and Hobolth, M. (2016), "Do Restrictive Asylum and Visa Policies Increase Irregular Migration into Europe?," *European Union Politics*, 17/3: 345–65.

Czarniawska, B. (2007), *Shadowing: And other Techniques for Doing Fieldwork in Modern Societies* (Malmö: Liber; Copenhagen Business School Press).

Czarniawska-Joerges, B. (1992), *Exploring Complex Organizations: Toward an Anthropological Perspective* (Thousand Oaks, CA: SAGE).

da Conceição-Heldt, E. (2010), "Who Controls Whom? Dynamics of Power Delegation and Agency Losses in EU Trade Politics," *Journal of Common Market Studies*, 48/4: 1107–26.

da Conceição-Heldt, E. (2017), "Regaining Control of Errant Agents? Agency Slack at the European Commission and the World Health Organization," *Cooperation and Conflict*, 52/4: 469–84.

da Costa, D. F., and Karlsrud, J. (2013), "'Bending the Rules': The Space between HQ Policy and Local Action in UN Civilian Peacekeeping," *Journal of International Peacekeeping*, 17/3–4: 293–312.

Daho, G., Duclos, N., and Jouhanneau, C. (2019), "Political Sociology of International Interventions: Peacebuilders and the Ground," *Journal of Intervention and Statebuilding*, 13/3: 249–62.

Dairon, E., and Badache, F. (2021), "Understanding International Organizations' Headquarters as Ecosystems: The Case of Geneva," *Global Policy*, 12/S7: 24–33.

Danish Refugee Council (DRC) (2017), *Fundamental Rights and the EU Hotspot Approach* (Copenhagen: DRC).

Davis Cross, M. K. (2013), "Rethinking Epistemic Communities Twenty Years later," *Review of International Studies*, 39/1: 137–60.

DeBono, D. (2019), "Plastic Hospitality. The Empty Signifier at the EU's Mediterranean Border," *Migration Studies*, 35/2: 1–22.

Deitelhoff, N. (2009), "The Discursive Process of Legalization: Charting Islands of Persuasion in the ICC Case," *International Organization*, 63/1: 33–65.

Deitelhoff, N., and Daase, C. (2021), "Rule and Resistance in Global Governance," *International Theory*, 13/1: 122–30.

Deleixhe, M., and Duez, D. (2019), "The New European Border and Coast Guard Agency: Pooling Sovereignty or Giving It Up?," *Journal of European Integration*, 41/7: 921–36.

Deloffre, M. Z. (2016), "Global Accountability Communities: NGO Self-Regulation in the Humanitarian Sector," *Review of International Studies*, 42/4: 724–47.

Deutsche Welle (2023), "EU Border Pushbacks: A 'Shadow' Migration Policy?" <https://www.infomigrants.net/en/post/50484/eu-border-pushbacks-a-shadow-migration-policy>, accessed Jul 27, 2023.

Devault, M. L., and McCoy, L. (2002), "Institutional Ethnography: Using Interviews to Investigate Ruling Relations," in J. F. Gubrium and J. A. Holstein (eds.), *Handbook of Interview Research; Context and Method* (Thousand Oaks, CA: SAGE), 751–75.

Dijkstra, H., Petrov, P., and Mahr, E. (2019), "Learning to Deploy Civilian Capabilities: How the United Nations, Organization for Security and Co-operation in Europe and European Union Have Changed Their Crisis Management Institutions," *Cooperation and Conflict*, 54/4: 524–43.

Dingwerth, K. (2007), *The New Transnationalism: Transnational Governance and Democratic Legitimacy* (New York: Palgrave Macmillan).

Dingwerth, K., and Pattberg, P. (2006), "Global Governance as a Perspective on World Politics," *Global Governance*, 12/2: 185–203.

Duvall, R., and Chowdhury, A. (2011), "Practices of Theory," in E. Adler and V. Pouliot (eds.), *International Practices* (Cambridge: Cambridge University Press), 335–54.

Düvell, F. (2008), "Clandestine Migration in Europe," *Social Science Information*, 47/4: 479–97.

Düvell, F. (2011), "Irregular Migration," in A. Betts (ed.), *Global Migration Governance* (Oxford: Oxford University Press), 78–108.

Düvell, F. (2012), "Transit Migration. A Blurred and Politicised Concept," *Population, Space and Place*, 18/4: 415–27.

EASO (2014), *Practical Guide: Personal Interview*, EASO Practical Guide Series (Valletta Harbour: EASO).

EASO (2015), *Practical Guide: Evidence Assessment*, EASO Practical Guide Series (Valletta Harbour: EASO).

EASO (2016), "EASO Special Operating Plan to Greece (Valletta Harbour and Athens)." EASO/DOP/OU/2016/1812. <https://www.easo.europa.eu/sites/default/files/EASO%20Special%20Operating%20Plan%20to%20Greece%202017_%2014122016.pdf>, accessed Jun 25, 2018.

EASO (2017), *Terms of Reference for the EASO Training Curriculum: EASO/DAS/2017/107* (Valletta Harbour: EASO).

EASO (2017a), *Annual Training Report* (Valletta Harbour: EASO).

EASO (2017b), *Training Curriculum* (Valletta Harbour: EASO).

EASO (2018a), *Practical Guide: Qualification for Interntional Protection*, EASO Practical Guide Series (Valletta Harbour: EASO).

EASO (2018b), *Training Catalogue* (Valletta Harbour: EASO).

EASO (n.d.a), "Quality Assurance Tool: Module 1 Personal Interview" (Valletta Harbour: EASO).

EASO (n.d.b), "Tool for Identification of Persons with Special Needs" <https://ipsn.easo.europa.eu/easo-tool-identification-persons-special-needs>, accessed Jun 12, 2019.

EC (2015a), *European Commission. A European Agenda on Migration*, COM(2015) 240 final.

EC (2015b), *European Commission: Managing the Refugee Crisis: State of Play of the Implementation of the Priority Actions under the European Agenda on Migration*, COM(2015) 510 final.

EC (2016), *Management of the Migration Crisis in Greece since October 2015: Implementation of the EU-Turkey Statement since 20 March 2016* <https://ec.europa.eu/home-affairs/migration_en, accessed Jun 30, 2022.

EC (2017), *European Commission: Hotspot State of Play* <https://ec.europa.eu/home-affairs/sites/homeaffairs/files/what-we-do/policies/european-agenda-migration/press-material/docs/state_of_play_-_hotspots_en.pdf>, accessed May 22, 2018.

ECCHR (2017), "EASO Case Report" <https://www.ecchr.eu/fileadmin/Fallbeschreibungen/CaseReport_Greece_EASO_2017April.pdf>, accessed Jun 20, 2022.

Eckhard, S., and Parizek, M. (2020), "Policy Implementation by International Organizations: A Comparative Analysis of Strengths and Weaknesses of National and International Staff," *Journal of Comparative Policy Analysis: Research and Practice*, 24/3: 254–70.

Eckl, J. (2021), "Zooming in Dissolves the Taken-For-Granted. Towards a Political Anthropology of International Organisations," in S. Biecker and K. Schlichte (eds.), *The Political Anthropology of Internationalized Politics* (London: Rowman & Littlefield Publishers), 67–93.

Eckl, J., and Hanrieder, T. (2023), "The Political Economy of Consulting Firms in Reform Processes: The Case of the World Health Organization," *Review of International Political Economy*, 30/6: 2309–32.

Edelman, L. B., Uggen, C., and Erlanger, H. S. (1999), "The Endogeneity of Legal Regulation: Grievance Procedures as Rational Myth," *American Journal of Sociology*, 105/2: 406–54.

Egger, C. (2017), "Just Part-Time Lovers? Competition, Coercive Coordination, and Friendship among International INGOs," *Cambridge Review of International Affairs*, 30/4: 394–414.

Eilstrup-Sangiovanni, M., and Bondaroff, T. N. P. (2014), "From Advocacy to Confrontation: Direct Enforcement by Environmental NGOs," *International Studies Quarterly*, 58/2: 348–61.

Eilstrup-Sangiovanni, Mette, and Hofmann, Stephanie C. (2024), "Accountability in Densely Institutionalized Governance Spaces," *Global Policy*, 15: 103–13.

Eilstrup-Sangiovanni, M., and Sharman, J. C. (2022), *Vigilantes beyond Borders: NGOs as Enforcers of International Law* (Princeton, NJ: Princeton University Press).

Emerson, R. M., Fretz, R. I., and Shaw, L. L. (1995), *Writing Ethnographic Fieldnotes* (Chicago: The University of Chicago Press).

Endres de Oliveira, P. (2016), "Legaler Zugang zu internationalem Schutz. Zur Gretchenfrage im Flüchtlingsrecht," *Kritsische Justiz*, 49/2: 167–79.

Equal Rights Beyond Borders, HIAS Greece, and Refugee Support Aegean (2022), *The State of the Border Procedure on the Greek Islands* <https://rsaegean.org/wp-content/uploads/2022/10/BorderProcedure_Greek_islands_report.pdf>, accessed Jan 11, 2024.

Eriksen, S. S., and Sending, O. J. (2013), "There Is No Global Public. The Idea of the Public and the Legitimation of Governance," *International Theory*, 5/2: 213–37.

Esguerra, A., and van der Hel, S. (2021), "Participatory Designs and Epistemic Authority in Knowledge Platforms for Sustainability," *Global Environmental Politics*, 21/1: 130–51.

EUAA (2022), "New EU Agency for Asylum Starts Work with Reinforced Mandate: Press Release" <https://www.euaa.europa.eu/news-events/new-eu-agency-asylum-starts-work-reinforced-mandate>, accessed Feb 8, 2022.

European Ombudsman (2013), *Special Report of the European Ombudsman in Own-Initiative Inquiry OI/5/2012/BEH-MHZ Concerning Frontex* <https://www.ombudsman.europa.eu/en/special-report/en/52465>, accessed Dec 4, 2023.

European Parliament (2016), *Directorate General for Internal Policies Policy Department C: Citizens' Rights and Constitutional Affairs: On the Frontline. The Hotspot Approach to Managing Migration* (Brussels: European Parliament).

European Parliament and the Council (2010), *Regulation No. 439/2010: Establishing a European Asylum Support Office*. Brussels: European Parliament and the Council.

European Parliament and the Council (2013), *Regulation No. 603/2013 of 26 June 2013 on the Establishment of "Eurodac" for the Comparison of Fingerprints for the Effective Application of Regulation (EU) No 604/2013 Establishing the Criteria and Mechanisms for Determining the Member State Responsible for Examining an Application for International Protection Lodged in one of the Member States by a Third-Country National or a Stateless Person and on Requests for the Comparison with Eurodac Data by Member States' Law Enforcement Authorities and Europol for Law Enforcement Purposes, and Amending Regulation (EU) No 1077/2011 Establishing a European Agency for the Operational Management of Large-Scale IT Systems in the Area of Freedom, Security and Justice (Recast)*. Brussels: European Parliament and the Council.

Evetts, J. (2003), "The Sociological Analysis of Professionalism. Occupational Change in the Modern World," *International Sociology*, 18/2: 395–415.

Eyal, G., and Pok, G. (2015), "What is Security Expertise? From the Sociology of the Professions to the Analysis of Networks of Expertise," in T. V. Berling and C. Bueger (eds.), *Security Expertise: Practice, Power, Responsibility* (PRIO New Security Studies, London and New York: Routledge, Taylor & Francis Group), 37–59.

Fargues, P. (2009), "Work, Refuge, Transit: An Emerging Pattern of Irregular Immigration South and East of the Mediterranean," *International Migration Review*, 43/3: 544–77.

Faulconbridge, J. R., and Muzio, D. (2012), "Professions in a Globalizing World: Towards a Transnational Sociology of the Professions," *International Sociology*, 27/1: 136–52.

Fechter, A.-M., and Hindman, H. (2011) (eds.), *Inside the Everyday Lives of Development Workers: The Challenges and Futures of Aidland* (Sterling: Kumarian Press).

Feller, E. (2005), "Refugees Are Not Migrants," *Refugee Survey Quarterly*, 24/4: 27–35.

Ferris, E. G., and Donato, K. M. (2020), *Refugees, Migration and Global Governance: Negotiating the Global Compacts* (Abingdon: Routledge).

Fine, S. (2017), "Liaisons, Labelling and Laws: International Organization for Migration Bordercratic Interventions in Turkey," *Journal of Ethnic and Migration Studies*, 28/6: 1–13.

Fine, S. (2018), "Liaisons, Labelling and Laws: International Organization for Migration Bordercratic Interventions in Turkey," *Journal of Ethnic and Migration Studies*, 44/10: 1743–55.

Fjørtoft, T. N. (2022), "More Power, More Control: The Legitimizing Role of Expertise in Frontex after the Refugee Crisis," *Regulation & Governance*, 16/2: 557–71.

Florini, A. M. (2000), "Who Does What? Collective Action and the Changing Nature of Authority," in R. D. Higgott and Geoffrey Underhill, and Andreas Bieler (eds.), *Non-State Actors and Authority in the Global System* (London: Routledge), 15–30.

Flyvbjerg, B. (2006), "Five Misunderstandings about Case-Study Research," *Qualitative Inquiry*, 12/2: 219–45.

Fox, S. (2000), "Communities of Practice, Foucault and Actor-Network Theory," *Journal of Management Studies*, 37/6: 853–68.

Friesendorf, C. (2018), *How Western Soldiers Fight: Organizational Routines in Multinational Missions* (Cambridge: Cambridge University Press).

Froitzheim, M., Schierenbeck, I., and Söderbaum, F. (2022), "Peace Research Meets Implementation Studies: The Role of Implementing Actors," *International Relations*, 36/2: 285–306.

Frontex (2013a), *Fundamental Rights Training for Border Guards: Trainers' Manual* (Warsaw: Frontex).

Frontex (2013b), *Sectoral Qualifications Framework for Border Guarding* (Warsaw: Frontex).

Frontex (2014a), *12 Seconds to Decide: In Search of Excellence: Frontex and the Principle of Best Practice* (Warsaw: Frontex).

Frontex (2014b), *Handbook to the Operational Plan: Joint Maritime Operations* (Warsaw: Frontex).

Frontex (2015), *Training Catalogue* (Warsaw: Frontex).

Frontex (2016a), *Annual Risk Analysis for 2016* (Warsaw: Frontex).

Frontex (2016b), *FRAN Quarterly Q1: Quarter 1 January-March 2016* (Warsaw: Frontex).

Frontex (2016c, *Guide for Joint Return Operations by Air coordinated by Frontex* (Warsaw: Frontex).

Frontex (2016d), *FRAN Quarterly Q2: Quarter 2 April–June 2016* (Warsaw: Frontex).

Frontex (2017a), *Common Core Curriculum for Border and Coast Guard Basic Training in the EU: Learning and Working Together at the Borders* (Warsaw: Frontex).

Frontex (2017b), *Handbook to the Operational Plan: Joint Maritime Operations* (Warsaw: Frontex).

Frontex (2017c), *A Year in Review: First 12 Months of European Border and Coast Guard Agency* <https://frontex.europa.eu/assets/Publications/General/A_Year_in_Review.pdf>, accessed May 7, 2019.

Frontex (2017d), *FRAN Quarterly Q1: January–March 2017* (Warsaw: Frontex).

Frontex (2018a), *Code of Conduct: For Return Operations and Return Interventions Coordinated or Organised by Frontex* (Warsaw: Frontex).

Frontex (2018b), *Course Catalogue* (Warsaw: Frontex).

Furnari, S. (2014), "Interstitial Spaces: Microinteraction Settings and the Genesis of New Practices between Institutional Fields," *Academy of Management Review*, 39/4: 439–62.

Furrusten, S. (2017), "Organizing Expertise though Improvising," in S. Furrusten and A. Werr (eds.), *The Organization of the Expert Society* (Routledge studies in management, organizations and society, New York: Routledge), 133–45.

Gammeltoft-Hansen, T. (2014), "International Refugee Law and Refugee Policy. The Case of Deterrence Policies," *Journal of Refugee Studies*, 27/4: 574–95.

Gammeltoft-Hansen, T. (2019), "The Normative Impact of the Global Compact on Refugees," *International Journal of Refugee Law*, 30/4: 605–10.

Gazit, O. (2018), "A Simmelian Approach to Space in World Politics," *International Theory*, 10/2: 219–52.

GCM (2018), *Global Compact for Safe, Orderly and Regular Migration: Intergovernmentally Negotiated and Agreed Outcome* <https://refugeesmigrants.un.org/sites/default/files/180713_agreed_outcome_global_compact_for_migration.pdf>, accessed Jul 1, 2019.

Geddes, A. (2021), *Governing Migration beyond the State: Europe, North America, South America, and Southeast Asia in a Global Context* (Oxford: Oxford University Press).

Geddes, A., and Boswell, C. (2011), *Migration and Mobility in the European Union* (Basingstoke: Palgrave Macmillan).

Geertz, C. (2000), "Thick Description: Toward an Interpretive Theory of Culture," in C. Geertz (ed.), *The Interpretation of Cultures: Selected Essays* (3rd ed., New York: Basic Books), 3–35.

Gehring, T., and Faude, B. (2013), "The Dynamics of Regime Complexes. Microfoundations and Systemic Effects," *Global Governance*, 19/1: 119–30.

Gent, S. E., Crescenzi, M. J. C., Menninga, E. J. et al. (2015), "The Reputation Trap of NGO Accountability," *International Theory*, 7/3: 426–63.

Gherardi, S. (2000), "Practice-Based Theorizing on Learning and Knowing in Organizations," *Organization*, 7/2: 211–23.

Gherardi, S., and Nicolini, D. (2016), "To Transfer is to Transform. The Circulation of Safety Knowledge," *Organization*, 7/2: 329–48.

Ghosh, B. (2007), "Managing Migration: Towards the Missing Regime?," in A. Pécoud and P. d. Guchteneire (eds.), *Migration without Borders: Essays on the Free Movement of People* (Social Science Studies Series, Paris and New York: UNESCO Pub and Berghahn Books), 97–118.

Glouftsios, G. (2023), "Performing Secrecy: Hiding and Obfuscation in Frontex's Pushbacks Scandal," *Journal of Ethnic and Migration Studies*, forthcoming.

Glyniadaki, K. (2021), "Toward Street-Level Communities of Practice? The Implications of Actor Diversification in Migration Management in Athens and Berlin," *Journal of Immigrant & Refugee Studies*, 19/3: 258–71.

Goddard, S. E. (2009), "Brokering Change: Networks and Entrepreneurs in International Politics," *International Theory*, 1/2: 249–81.

Goetze, C. (2017), *The Distinction of Peace: A Social Analysis of Peacebuilding* (Configurations, Ann Arbor, MI: University of Michigan Press).

Goetze, C. (2019), "Learning in Peacebuilding: Mission Impossible?," *Journal of Intervention and Statebuilding*, 13/3: 340–56.

Gómez-Mera, L. (2016), "Regime Complexity and Global Governance: The Case of Trafficking in Persons," *European Journal of International Relations*, 22/3: 566–95.

Græger, N. (2016), "European Security as Practice: EU–NATO Communities of Practice in the Making?," *European Security*, 25/4: 478–501.

Graham, E. R. (2014), "International Organizations as Collective Agents: Fragmentation and the Limits of Principal Control at the World Health Organization," *European Journal of International Relations*, 20/2: 366–90.

Graham, E. R (2015), "Money and Multilateralism: How Funding Rules constitute IO Governance," *International Theory*, 7/1: 162–94.

Graham, E. R. (2017), "The Institutional Design of Funding Rules at International Organizations: Explaining the Transformation in Financing the United Nations," *European Journal of International Relations*, 23/2: 365–90.

Grant, R. W., and Keohane, R. O. (2005), "Accountability and the Abuses of Power in World Politics," *American Political Science Review*, 99/1: 29–43.

Greek Law (2016), "Greece Law No. 4375 of 2016 on the Organization and Operation of the Asylum Service, the Appeals Authority, the Reception and Identification Service, the Establishment of the General Secretariat for Reception." The Transposition into Greek Legislation of the Provisions of Directive 2013/32/EC.

Greek Ombudsman for Human Rights, The (2017), "Migration Flows and Refugee Protection: Administrative Challenges and Human Rights." Special Report.

Green, J. F. (2013), *Rethinking Private Authority: Agents and Entrepreneurs in Global Environmental Governance* (Princeton, NJ: Princeton University Press).

Green, J. F. (2018), "Transnational Delegation in Global Environmental Governance: When Do Non-State Actors Govern?," *Regulation & Governance*, 12/2: 263–76.

Green, J. F. (2022), "Hierarchy in Regime Complexes: Understanding Authority in Antarctic Governance," *International Studies Quarterly*, 66/1.

Green, J. F., and Hadden, J. (2021), "How Did Environmental Governance Become Complex? Understanding Mutualism between Environmental NGOs and International Organizations," *International Studies Review*, 23/4: 1792–821.

Grigorescu, A. (2020), *The Ebb and Flow of Global Governance. Intergovernmentalism versus Nongovernmentalism in World Politics* (Cambridge: Cambridge University Press).
Gross Stein, J. (2011), "Background Knowledge in the Foreground: Conversations about Competent Practice in 'Sacred Space,'" in E. Adler and V. Pouliot (eds.), *International Practices* (Cambridge: Cambridge University Press), 87–107.
Guardian (2016), "Syrian Refugee Wins Appeal Against Forced Return to Turkey" <https://www.theguardian.com/world/2016/may/20/syrian-refugee-wins-appeal-against-forced-return-to-turkey>, accessed Apr 13, 2023.
Guevara, B. B. de, and Kostić, R. (2017), "Knowledge Production in/about Conflict and Intervention. Finding 'Facts', Telling 'Truth,'" *Journal of Intervention and Statebuilding*, 11/1: 1–20.
Guild, E. (2022), *What Monitoring for Fundamental Rights at EU Borders?* <https://verfassungsblog.de/what-monitoring-for-fundamental-rights-at-eu-borders/>, accessed Apr 13, 2023.
Guild, E., Grant, S., and Groenendijk, K. (2017), *IOM and the UN: Unfinished Business*, Queen Mary School of Law Legal Studies Research Paper No. 255/2017.
Gutner, T. (2005), "Explaining the Gaps between Mandate and Performance: Agency Theory and World Bank Environmental Reform," *Global Environmental Politics*, 5/2: 10–37.
Gutner, T., and Thompson, A. (2010), "The Politics of IO Performance: A Framework," *Review of International Organizations*, 5/3: 227–48.
Haas, E. B. (1990), *When Knowledge Is Power: Three Models of Change in International Organizations* (Berkeley, CA: University of California Press).
Haas, E. B., and Haas, P. M. (1995), "Learning to Learn: Improving International Governance," *Global Governance*, 1/3: 255–84.
Haas, H. de (2008), "The Myth of Invasion: The Inconvenient Realities of African Migration to Europe," *Third World Quarterly*, 29/7: 1305–22.
Haas, H. de, Castles, S., and Miller, M. J. (2019), *The Age of Migration: International Population Movements in the Modern World* (6. ed., rev. and updated, Basingstoke: Palgrave Macmillan).
Haas, P. M. (1992), "Introduction: Epistemic Communities and International Policy Coordination," *International Organization*, 46/1: 1–35.
Hall, N. (2015), "Money or Mandate? Why International Organizations Engage with the Climate Change Regime," *Global Environmental Politics*, 15/2: 79–97.
Hall, N. (2016), *Displacement, Development, and Climate Change: International Organizations Moving Beyond their Mandates* (Global institutions series, 120, Abingdon: Routledge).
Hall, N. (2022), *Transnational Advocacy in the Digital Era* (Oxford: Oxford University Press).
Halliday, T. C., and Carruthers, B. G. (2007), "The Recursivity of Law: Global Norm Making and National Lawmaking in the Globalization of Corporate Insolvency Regimes," *American Journal of Sociology*, 112/4: 1135–202.
Hanrieder, T. (2014), "Local Orders in International Organisations: The World Health Organization's Global Programme on AIDS," *Journal of International Relations and Development*, 17/2: 220–41.
Hanrieder, T (2015), *International Organization in Time: Fragmentation and Reform* (Oxford: Oxford University Press).
Hanrieder, T. (2019), "How Do Professions Globalize? Lessons from the Global South in US Medical Education," *International Political Sociology*, 8/3: 143–62.
Hardt, H. (2018), *NATO's Lessons in Crisis: Institutional Memory in International Organizations* (Oxford: Oxford University Press).
Hawkins, D. G., Lake, D. A., Nielson, D. L. et al. (2006a) (eds.), *Delegation and Agency in International Organizations* (Cambridge: Cambridge University Press).

Hawkins, D. G., Lake, D. A., Nielson, D. L. et al. (2006b), "Delegation Under Anarchy. States, International Organizations, and Principal-Agent Theory," in D. G. Hawkins, D. A. Lake, D. L. Nielson et al. (eds.), *Delegation and Agency in International Organizations* (Cambridge: Cambridge University Press), 3–38.

Heinzel, M. (2022), "International Bureaucrats and Organizational Performance: Country-Specific Knowledge and Sectoral Knowledge in World Bank Projects," *International Studies Quarterly*, 66/2: forthcoming.

Henriksen, L. F., and Seabrooke, L. (2017), "Issue Professionals and Transnational Organizing," in L. Seabrooke and L. F. Henriksen (eds.), *Professional Networks in Transnational Governance* (Cambridge: Cambridge University Press), 286–99.

Herold, J., Liese, A., Busch, P.-O. et al. (2021), "Why National Ministries Consider the Policy Advice of International Bureaucracies: Survey Evidence from 106 Countries," *International Studies Quarterly*, 65/3: 669–82.

Hess, S. (2010), "'We are Facilitating States!' An Ethnographic Analysis of the ICMPD," in M. Geiger and A. Pécoud (eds.), *The Politics of International Migration Management* (Basingstoke: Palgrave Macmillan), 96–118.

Heupel, M., Hirschmann, G., and Zürn, M. (2018), "International Organisations and Human Rights: What Direct Authority Needs for its Legitimation," *Review of International Studies*, 44/2: 343–66.

Heupel, M., Koenig-Archibugi, M., Kreuder-Sonnen, C. et al. (2021), "Emergency Politics after Globalization," *International Studies Review*, 23/4: 1959–87.

Hirschmann, G. (2012), "Organizational Learning in United Nations' Peacekeeping Exit Strategies," *Cooperation and Conflict*, 47/3: 368–85.

Hirschmann, G. (2019), "Guarding the Guards: Pluralist Accountability for Human Rights Violations by International Organisations," *Review of International Studies*, 45/1: 20–38.

Hirschmann, G. (2020), *Accountability in Global Governance* (Oxford: Oxford University Press).

Hofius, M. (2016), "Community at the Border or the Boundaries of Community? The Case of EU Field Diplomats," *Review of International Studies*, 42/5: 939–67.

Hollifield, J. F. (2000), "Migration and the 'New' International Order. The Missing Regime," in B. Ghosh (ed.), *Managing Migration: Time for a New International Regime?* (Oxford: Oxford University Press), 75–109.

Holmes, G. (2019), "Situating Agency, Embodied Practices and Norm Implementation in Peacekeeping Training," *International Peacekeeping*, 26/1: 55–84.

Honig, D. (2018), *Navigation by Judgment: Why and When Top-Down Management of Foreign Aid Doesn't Work* (New York: Oxford University Press).

Honig, D. (2019), "When Reporting Undermines Performance: The Costs of Politically Constrained Organizational Autonomy in Foreign Aid Implementation," *International Organization*, 73/1: 171–201.

Honig, D. (2020), "Information, Power, and Location: World Bank Staff Decentralization and Aid Project Success," *Governance*, 33/4: 749–69.

Hooghe, L., Marks, G., and Lenz, T. (2019), *A Theory of International Organization* (Oxford: Oxford University Press).

Hooghe, L., Marks, G., Lenz, T. et al. (2017), *Measuring International Authority: A Postfunctionalist Theory of Governance* (Oxford: Oxford University Press).

Hopf, T. (2018), "Change in International Practices," *European Journal of International Relations*, 24/3: 687–711.

Hor, A. J. Y. (2022), "The Everyday Emotional Lives of Aid Workers: How Humanitarian Anxiety gets in the Way of Meaningful Local Participation," *International Theory*, 14/2: 358–87.

Horii, S. (2012), "It Is About More Than Just Training: The Effect of Frontex Border Guard Training," *Refugee Survey Quarterly*, 31/4: 158–77.

Howard, L. M. (2008), *UN Peacekeeping in Civil Wars* (Cambridge: Cambridge University Press).

Human Rights at Sea et al. (2017), *Voluntary Code of Conduct for Search and Rescue Operations Undertaken by Civil Society Non-Government Organisations in the Mediterranean Sea.*

Hupe, P. L., Hill, M., and Buffat, A. (2015) (eds.), *Understanding Street-Level Bureaucracy* (Bristol: Policy Press).

Hurd, I. (1999), "Legitimacy and Authority in International Politics," *International Organization*, 53/2: 379–408.

Huysmans, J. (2000), "The European Union and the Securitization of Migration," *Journal of Common Market Studies*, 38/5: 751–77.

IASC (2007), *Guidelines on Mental Health and Psychosocial Support in Emergency Settings: IASC Reference Group on Mental Health and Psychosocial Support in Emergency Settings.*

IASC (2008), "Guidelines on Mental Health and Psychosocial Support in Emergency Settings. Check List for Field Use."

IASC (2017), *Field Handbook on Unacommpanied and Separated Children: Inter-Agency Working Group on Unaccompanied and Separated Children.*

IASC and CCCM (2014), *Mental Health and Psychosocial Support in Emergency Settings: What Should Camp Coordination and Camp Management Actors Know?*

ICMPD (2007), *Arab and European Partner States Working Document on the Joint Management of Mixed Migration Flows: Mediterranean Transit Migration (MTM) Dialogue: Towards a Comprehensive Response to Mixed Migration Flows.*

Ikenberry, G. J. (2018), "The End of Liberal International Order?" *International Affairs*, 94/1: 7–23.

ILO (2004), *Towards a Fair Deal for Migrant Workers in the Global Economy: International Labour Conference, 92nd Session, Report VI, Sixth Item on the Agenda* (Geneva: ILO).

ILO (2016), *Towards Comprehensive Labour Migration Governance within Broader Labour Market Governance: With Particular Attention to Jordanization, Fair Migration and Decent Work for Refugees*, Project Leaflet: Research and Advocacy Initiative for Mixed Migration Strategies in Jordan <http://www.ilo.org/wcmsp5/groups/public/—arabstates/—ro-beirut/documents/projectdocumentation/wcms_518989.pdf>, accessed Sep 5, 2017.

IMO (2015), "UN Agencies to Deliver as One on Mixed Migration by Sea. Press Briefing 5" <http://www.imo.org/fr/MediaCentre/PressBriefings/Pages/05-migrantsends.aspx>, accessed Aug 18, 2019.

IMO, UNHCR, and International Chamber of Shipping (2015), *Rescue at Sea: A Guide to Principle and Practice as Applied to Refugees and Migrants.*

IMRF (2011), *A Common Standard of Training for Maritime SAR Unit Coxswains, Mechanics & Crew Members.* Pool: IMRF.

IMRF (n.d.), "The IMRF and Our Mission" <https://www.international-maritime-rescue.org/vision-and-mission>, accessed May 14, 2019.

Infantino, F. (2021), "How Does Policy Change at the Street Level? Local Knowledge, a Community of Practice and EU Visa Policy Implementation in Morocco," *Journal of Ethnic and Migration Studies*, 47/5: 1028–46.

IOM (2008), *International Dialogue on Migration 2008: Challenges of Irregular Migration: Addressing Mixed Migration Flows*, Ninety-Sixth Session, MC/INF/294 (Geneva: IOM) <https://www.iom.int/jahia/webdav/shared/shared/mainsite/microsites/IDM/workshops/return_migration_challenges_120208/mixed_migration_flows.pdf>, accessed Jan 2, 2019.

IOM (2009a), *Irregular Migration and Mixed Flows: IOM's Approach*, Ninety-Eight Session, MC/INF/297.

IOM (2009b), *Psychosocial Needs Assessment in Emergency, Displacement, Early Recovery and Return: IOM Tools* (Geneva).

IOM (2015), *Addressing Complex Migration Flows in the Mediterranean.*

IOM (2016), "IOM Niger Opens Migrant Information Office in Agadez. Press Release" <https://www.iom.int/news/iom-niger-opens-migrant-information-office-agadez>, accessed Jul 3, 2019.

IOM (2017a), *Migrant Vulnerability to Human Trafficking and Exploitation: Evidence from the Central and Eastern Mediterranean Migration Routes* (Geneva).

IOM (2017b), "Regional Migration Response Centres: Network in the Horn of Africa. Fact Sheet—Annual Overview" <https://reliefweb.int/sites/reliefweb.int/files/resources/IOM%20MRCs%20Fact%20Sheet_2017.pdf>, accessed Jul 3, 2019.

IOM (2017c) (ed.), *World Migration Report 2018.*

IOM (2019a), *Glossary on Migration,* International Migration Law (Geneva: IOM).

IOM (2019b), "Missing Migrants Project: Spotlight on the Mediterranean" <http://missingmigrants.iom.int/region/mediterranean>, accessed Jan 9, 2019.

IOM (2019c), "Mental Health, Psychosocial Response and Intercultural Communication. Homepage of the MHPSS Section" <https://www.iom.int/mental-health-psychosocial-response-and-intercultural-communication>, accessed May 8, 2019.

IOM DTM (2018), *Mixed Migration Flows in the Mediterranean: Compilation of Available Data and Information* (Geneva: IOM).

IOM Nairobi (n.d.), "Mixed Migration Brochure" <https://www.iom.int/files/live/sites/iom/files/Country/docs/Mixed-Migration-HOA.pdf>, accessed Jul 3, 2019.

IOM Regional Office for West and Central Africa (2018), *Mixed Migration and Protection in West Africa* (Dakar: IOM).

Jeandesboz, J., and Pallister-Wilkins, P. (2015), "Crisis, Routine, Consolidation: The Politics of the Mediterranean Migration Crisis," *Mediterranean Politics*, 21/2: 316–20.

Jenne, N. (2023), "Who Leads Peace Operations? A New Dataset on Leadership Positions in UN Peace Operations, 1948–2019," *Journal of Peace Research*, 60/3: 532–44.

Jepsen, H., Lundgren, M., Monheim, K. et al. (2021) (eds.), *Negotiating the Paris Agreement: The Insider Stories* (Cambridge: Cambridge University Press).

Joachim, J. (2003), "Framing Issues and Seizing Opportunities: The UN, NGOs, and Women's Rights," *International Studies Quarterly*, 47/2: 247–74.

Joachim, J. M., Reinalda, B., and Verbeek, B. (2010), *International Organizations and Implementation: Enforcers, Managers, Authorities?* (London: Routledge).

Johnson, T. (2014), *Organizational Progeny: Why Governments Are Losing Control over the Proliferating Structures of Global Governance* (Oxford: Oxford University Press).

Johnson, T., and Urpelainen, J. (2014), "International Bureaucrats and the Formation of Intergovernmental Organizations: Institutional Design Discretion Sweetens the Pot," *International Organization*, 68/1: 177–209.

Johnstone, I. (2005), "The Power of Interpretative Communities," in M. N. Barnett and R. Duvall (eds.), *Power in Global Governance* (Cambridge: Cambridge University Press), 185–204.

Jönsson, C., and Tallberg, J. (2010) (eds.), *Transnational Actors in Global Governance: Patterns, Explanations and Implications* (Basingstoke: Palgrave Macmillan).

Julian, R., Bliesemann de Guevara, B., and Redhead, R. (2019), "From Expert to Experiential Knowledge: Exploring the Inclusion of Local Experiences in Understanding Violence in Conflict," *Peacebuilding*, 7/2: 210–25.

Kahler, M., and Lake, D. A. (2003), "Globalization and Changing Patterns of Political Authority," in M. Kahler and D. A. Lake (eds.), *Governance in a Global Economy: Political Authority in Transition* (Princeton, NJ: Princeton University Press), 412–39.

Kainz, L., and Betts, A. (2021), "Power and Proliferation: Explaining the Fragmentation of Global Migration Governance," *Migration Studies*, 9/1: 65–89.

Kalkman, J. P. (2021), "Frontex: A Literature Review," *Int Migration*, 59/1: 165–81.

Kalkman, J. P., and Groenewegen, P. (2018), "On Frontline Workers as Bureau-Political Actors. The Case of Civil-Military Crisis Management," *Administration & Society*, 51/7: 1148–70.

Kalm, S. (2010a), "Liberalizing Movements? The Political Rationality of Global Migrations Management," in M. Geiger and A. Pécoud (eds.), *The Politics of International Migration Management* (Basingstoke: Palgrave Macmillan), 21–44.

Kalm, S. (2010b), "Limits to Transnational Participation: The Global Governance of Migration," in C. Jönsson and J. Tallberg (eds.), *Transnational Actors in Global Governance: Patterns, Explanations and Implications* (Basingstoke: Palgrave Macmillan), 134–54.

Kamradt-Scott, A. (2016), "WHO's to Blame? The World Health Organization and the 2014 Ebola Outbreak in West Africa," *Third World Quarterly*, 37/3: 401–18.

Kanie, N., and Biermann, F. (2017) (eds.), *Governing Through Goals: Sustainable Development Goals as Governance Innovation* (Cambridge, MA: The MIT Press).

Karatani, R. (2005), "How History Separated Refugee and Migrant Regimes. In Search of Their Institutional Origins," *International Journal of Refugee Law*, 17/3: 517–41.

Karlsrud, J. (2013), "Special Representatives of the Secretary-General as Norm Arbitrators? Understanding Bottom-Up Authority in UN Peacekeeping," *Global Governance*, 19/4: 525–44.

Karlsrud, J. (2015), "The UN at War: Examining the Consequences of Peace-Enforcement Mandates for the UN Peacekeeping Operations in the CAR, the DRC and Mali," *Third World Quarterly*, 36/1: 40–54.

Karlsrud, J. (2018), *Norm Change in International Relations: Linked Ecologies in UN Peacekeeping Operations* (London and New York: Routledge and Taylor Francis Group).

Katzenstein, P. J., and Seybert, L. A. (2017) (eds.), *Protean Power: Exploring the Uncertain and Unexpected in World Politics* (Cambridge: Cambridge University Press).

Katzenstein, P. J., and Seybert, L. A. (2018), "Protean Power and Uncertainty: Exploring the Unexpected in World Politics," *International Studies Quarterly*, 62/1: 80–93.

Keck, M., and Sikkink, K. (1998), *Activists Beyond Borders: Advocacy Networks in International Politics* (Ithaca, NY: Cornell University Press).

Kelley, J., and Simmons, B. A. (2020) (eds.), *The Power of Global Performance Indicators* (Cambridge: Cambridge University Press).

Kennedy, D. (2016), *A World of Struggle: How Power, Law, and Expertise Shape Global Political Economy* (Princeton, NJ: Princeton University Press).

Kentikelenis, A. E., and Babb, S. (2019), "The Making of Neoliberal Globalization: Norm Substitution and the Politics of Clandestine Institutional Change," *American Journal of Sociology*, 124/6: 1720–62.

Kentikelenis, A. E., and Seabrooke, L. (2017), "The Politics of World Polity: Script-writing in International Organizations," *American Sociological Review*, 82/5: 1065–92.

Kimber, L. R., and Maertens, L. (2021), "Experiencing Time and Space within the United Nations," *Global Policy*, 12/S7: 14–23.

King, N., and Horrocks, C. (2010), *Interviews in Qualitative Research* (London: SAGE).

Kingsley, P. (2016), *The New Odyssey: The Story of the European Refugee Crisis* (London: Guardian Books; Faber & Faber Limited).

Kleine, M. (2013), *Informal Governance in the European Union: How Governments Make International Organizations Work* (Ithaca, NY: Cornell University Press).

Kneebone, S. (2014), "The Bali Process and Global Refugee Policy in the Asia-Pacific Region," *Journal of Refugee Studies*, 27/4: 596–618.

Koch, A. (2013), "The Politics and Discourse of Migrant Return: The Role of UNHCR and IOM in the Governance of Return," *Journal of Ethnic and Migration Studies*, 40/6: 905–23.

Koenig-Archibugi, M. (2017), "How to Diagnose Democratic Deficits in Global Politics: The Use of the "All-Affected Principle"," *International Theory*, 9/2: 171–202.

Koinova, M., Deloffre, M. Z., Gadinger, F. et al. (2021), "It's Ordered Chaos: What Really Makes Polycentrism Work," *International Studies Review*, 23/4: 1988–2018.

Koremenos, B. (2013), "What's Left Out and Why? Informal Provisions in Formal International Law," *The Review of International Organizations*, 8/2: 137–62.

Koremenos, B., Lipson, C., and Snidal, D. (2001), "The Rational Design of International Institutions," *International Organization*, 55/4: 761–99.

Kortendiek, N. (2021), "How to Govern Mixed Migration in Europe: Transnational Expert Networks and Knowledge Creation in International Organizations," *Global Networks*, 21/2: 320–38.

Kortendiek, N., and Oertel, J. (2023), "Caught between Vulnerability and Competence—UNHCR's Visual Framing of Refugees, Economic Threat Perceptions and Attitudes toward Asylum Seekers in Germany," *Journal of Immigrant & Refugee Studies*, forthcoming.

Koser, K. (2009), "Dimensions and Dynamics of Irregular Migration," *Population, Space and Place*, 16/3: 181–93.

Koser, K. (2010), "Introduction: International Migration and Global Governance," *Global Governance*, 16/3: 301–15.

Koslowski, R. (2011a), "Gobal Mobility Regimes: A Conceptual Framework," in R. Koslowski (ed.), *Global Mobility Regimes* (New York: Palgrave Macmillan), 1–25.

Koslowski, R. (2011b), "International Travel," in A. Betts (ed.), *Global Migration Governance* (Oxford: Oxford University Press), 109–32.

Koslowski, R. (2011c), *The Evolution of Border Controls as a Mechanism to Prevent Illegal Immigration* (Washington, DC).

Kranke, M. (2022), "Exclusive Expertise: The Boundary Work of International Organizations," *Review of International Political Economy*, 29/2: 453–76.

Krause, M. (2014), *The Good Project: Humanitarian Relief NGOs and the Fragmentation of Reason* (Chicago: The University of Chicago Press).

Kreuder-Sonnen, C. (2019), *Emergency Powers of International Organizations: Between Normalization and Containment* (Oxford: Oxford University Press).

Kreuder-Sonnen, C., and Tantow, P. (2022), "Crisis and Change at IOM: Critical Juncture, Precedent, and Task Expansion," in C. Costello, M. Bradley, and A. Sherwood (eds.), *IOM Unbound? Obligations and Accountability of the International Organization for Migration in an Era of Expansion* (Cambridge: Cambridge University Press), 187–212.

Kriesi, H., Altiparmakis, A., Bojar, A. et al. (2024), *Coming to Terms with the European Refugee Crisis* (Cambridge: Cambridge University Press).

Krisch, N. (2017), "Liquid Authority in Global Governance," *International Theory*, 9/2: 237–60.

Kuptsch, C., and Martin, P. (2011), "Low-Skilled Labour Migration," in A. Betts (ed.), *Global Migration Governance* (Oxford: Oxford University Press), 34–59.

Kurowska, X. (2014), "Practicality by Judgement: Transnational Interpreters of Local Ownership in the Polish-Ukrainian Border Reform Encounter," *Journal of International Relations and Development*, 17/4: 545–65.

Kustermans, J. (2016), "Parsing the Practice Turn: Practice, Practical Knowledge, Practices," *Millennium—Journal of International Studies*, 44/2: 175–96.

Lake, D. A. (2010), "Rightful Rules: Authority, Order, and the Foundations of Global Governance," *International Studies Quarterly*, 54/3: 587–613.

Lam, A. (2000), "Tacit Knowledge, Organizational Learning and Societal Institutions: An Integrated Framework," *Organization Studies*, 21/3: 487–513.

Lambach, D. (2022), "Space, Scale, and Global Politics: Towards a Critical Approach to Space in International Relations," *Review of International Studies*, 48/2: 282–300.

Lasswell, H. D. (1936), *Politics: Who Gets What, When, and How* (New York: Whittlesey House).

Laurence, M. (2019), "An 'Impartial' Force? Normative Ambiguity and Practice Change in UN Peace Operations," *International Peacekeeping*, 26/3: 256–80.

Lave, J., and Wenger, E. (1991), *Situated Learning: Legitimate Peripheral Participation* (Cambridge: Cambridge University Press).

Lavenex, S. (2004), "The External Dimension of Europeanization: The Case of Immigration Policies," *Cooperation and Conflict*, 39/4: 417–43.

Lavenex, S. (2015), "Multilevelling EU External Governance: The Role of International Organizations in the Diffusion of EU Migration Policies," *Journal of Ethnic and Migration Studies*, 42/4: 554–70.

Lavenex, S. (2020), "The UN Global Compacts on Migration and Refugees: A Case for Experimentalist Governance?," *Global Governance*, 26/4: 673–96.

Lavenex, S., and Piper, N. (2019), "Regional Migration Governance: Perspectives from 'Above' and 'Below,'" in A. Geddes, M. Vera Espinoza, L. Hadj Abdou et al. (eds.), *The Dynamics of Regional Migration Governance* (Elgaronline, Cheltenham: Edward Elgar Publishing), 15–35.

Lenz, A., and Eckhard, S. (2022), "Conceptualizing and Explaining Flexibility in Administrative Crisis Management: A Cross-district Analysis in Germany," *Journal of Public Administration Research and Theory*, 33/3: 485–97.

Léonard, S. (2010), "EU Border Security and Migration into the European Union: FRONTEX and Securitisation through Practices," *European Security*, 19/2: 231–54.

Lesch, M. (2023), "Contested Facts: The Politics and Practice of International Fact-Finding Missions," *International Studies Review*, 25/3.

Lesch, M., and Loh, D. M. H. (2022), "Field Overlaps, Normativity, and the Contestation of Practices in China's Belt and Road Initiative," *Global Studies Quarterly*, 2/4: 1–12.

Lesch, M., and Reiners, N. (2023), "Informal Human Rights Law-Making: How Treaty Bodies use General Comments to Develop International Law," *Global Constitutionalism*, 12/2: 378–401.

LeVoy, M., and Geddie, E. (2010), "Irregular Migration: Challenges, Limits and Remedies," *Refugee Survey Quarterly*, 28/4: 87–113.

Lie, J. H. S. (2013), "Challenging Anthropology: Anthropological Reflections on the Ethnograpic Turn in International Relations," *Millennium—Journal of International Studies*, 41/2: 201–20.

Lie, J. H. S. (2015), "Developmentality. Indirect Governance in the World Bank-Uganda Partnership," *Third World Quarterly*, 36/4: 723–40.

Liese, A., Herold, J., Feil, H. et al. (2021), "The Heart of Bureaucratic Power: Explaining International Bureaucracies' Expert Authority," *Review of International Studies*, 47/3: 353–76.

Lipsky, M. (1980), *Street-Level Bureaucracy: Dilemmas of the Individual in Public Service* (New York: Russel Sage Foundation).

Lipson, C. (1991), "Why Are Some International Agreements Informal?," *International Organization*, 45/4: 495–538.

Liste, P. (2016), "Geographical Knowledge at Work: Human Rights Litigation and Transnational Territoriality," *European Journal of International Relations*, 22/1: 217–39.

Littig, B. (2009), "Interviewing the Elite—Interviewing Experts: Is There a Difference?," in A. Bogner, B. Littig, and W. Menz (eds.), *Interviewing Experts* (Research Methods Series, Basingstoke: Palgrave Macmillan), 98–113.

Little, A., and Vaughan-Williams, N. (2017), "Stopping Boats, Saving Lives, Securing Sub jects. Humanitarian Borders in Europe and Australia," *European Journal of International Relations*, 23/3: 533–56.

Littoz-Monnet, A. (2017a), "Expert Knowledge as a Strategic Resource: International Bureaucrats and the Shaping of Bioethical Standards," *International Studies Quarterly*, 61/3: 584–95.

Littoz-Monnet, A. (2017b), "Production and Uses of Expertise by International Bureaucracies," in A. Littoz-Monnet (ed.), *The Politics of Expertise in International Organizations* (Abingdon: Routledge), 1–18.

Littoz-Monnet, A. (2017c) (ed.), *The Politics of Expertise in International Organizations* (Abingdon: Routledge).

Littoz-Monnet, A. (2020), *Governing through Expertise: The Politics of Bioethics* (Cambridge: Cambridge University Press).

Littoz-Monnet, A. (2021), "Expanding Without Much Ado: International Bureaucratic Expansion Tactics in the Case of Bioethics," *Journal of European Public Policy*, 28/6: 858–79.

Littoz-Monnet, A. (2022), "Exclusivity and Circularity in the Production of Global Governance Expertise: The Making of 'Global Mental Health' Knowledge," *International Political Sociology*, 16/2: Forthcoming.

Loescher, G., and Milner, J. (2011), "UNHCR and the Global Governance of Refugees," in A. Betts (ed.), *Global Migration Governance* (Oxford: Oxford University Press), 189–209.

Long, K. (2013), "When Refugees Stopped Being Migrants: Movement, Labour and Humanitarian Protection," *Migration Studies*, 1/1: 4–26.

Loschi, C., and Slominski, P. (2022), "The EU Hotspot Approach in Italy: Strengthening Agency Governance in the Wake of the Migration Crisis?," *Journal of European Integration*, 44/6: 769–86.

Louis, M., and Maertens, L. (2021), *Why International Organizations Hate Politics* (Global Institutions Series, Abingdon: Routledge, 2021).

Lundgren, M., Oksamytna, K., and Bove, V. (2021), "Politics or Performance? Leadership Accountability in UN Peacekeeping," *Journal of Conflict Resolution*, 66/1: 32–60.

Lutterbeck, D. (2006), "Policing Migration in the Mediterranean," *Mediterranean Politics*, 11/1: 59–82.

Macdonald, T. (2015), "Political Legitimacy in International Border Governance Institutions," *European Journal of Political Theory*, 14/4: 409–28.

MacKay, J., and Levin, J. (2015), "Hanging Out in International Politics: Two Kinds of Explanatory Political Ethnography for IR," *International Studies Review*, 17/2: 163–88.

Maertens, L. (2018), "Depoliticisation as a Securitising Move: The Case of the United Nations Environment Programme," *European Journal of International Security*, 3/3: 344–63.

Maertens, L. (2019), "From Blue to Green? Environmentalization and Securitization in UN Peacekeeping Practices," *International Peacekeeping*, 26/3: 302–26.

Mainwaring, Ċ. (2019), *At Europe's Edge: Migration and Crisis in the Mediterranean* (Oxford: Oxford University Press).

Marchetti, C. (2010), "Expanded Borders: Policies and Practices of Preventive Refoulement in Italy," in M. Geiger and A. Pécoud (eds.), *The Politics of International Migration Management* (Basingstoke: Palgrave Macmillan), 160–83.

Markard, N., and Heuser, H. (2016), *Möglichkeiten und Grenzen einer menschenrechtskonformen Ausgestaltung von sogenannten ,Hotspot' an den europäischen Außengrenzen: Gutachten* (Hamburg: Universität Hamburg).

Marshall, N., and Rollinson, J. (2004), "Maybe Bacon Had a Point: The Politics of Interpretation in Collective Sensemaking," *British Journal of Management*, 15/S1: 71–86.

Martin, P., and Martin, S. (2006), "GCIM: A New Global Migration Facility," *International Migration*, 44/1: 5–12.

Martin, P. L., Abella, M. I., and Kuptsch, C. (2006), *Managing Labor Migration in the Twenty-First Century* (New Haven, CT: Yale University Press).

Martin, S., and Callaway, A. (2011), "Human Trafficking and Smuggling," in A. Betts (ed.), *Global Migration Governance* (Oxford: Oxford University Press), 224–41.

Martin de Almagro, M. (2021), "Indicators and Success Stories: The UN Sustaining Peace Agenda, Bureaucratic Power, and Knowledge Production in Post-War Settings," *International Studies Quarterly*, 65/3: 699–711.

Mattli, W. (2001), "The Politics and Economics of International Institutional Standards Setting: An Introduction," *Journal of European Public Policy*, 8/3: 328–44.

Maynard-Moody, S., and Portillo, S. (2011), "Street-Level Bureaucracy Theory," in R. F. Durant (ed.), *The Oxford Handbook of American Bureaucracy* (The Oxford Handbooks of American Politics, Oxford: Oxford University Press), 252–77.

McAuliffe, M., and Triandafyllidou, A. (2021) (eds.), *World Migration Report 2022* (Geneva: IOM).

Menjívar, C., Ruiz, M., and Ness, I. (2019), *The Oxford Handbook of Migration Crises* (Oxford: Oxford University Press).

Meyer, C. C., and Boll, S. (2018), "Categorising Migrants: Standards, Complexities, and Politics. Editorial. Special Issue Irregular Migrants, Refugees or Trafficked Persons?," *Anti-Trafficking Review*, 11: 1–14.

Micinski, N. R. (2019), "Everyday Coordination in EU Migration Management: Civil Society Responses in Greece," *International Studies Perspectives*, 20/2: 129–48.

Micinski, N. R. (2021), *UN Global Compacts: Governing Migrants and Refugees* (Abingdon: Routledge).

Micinski, N. R., and Weiss, T. G. (2017), "Global Migration Governance: Beyond Coordination and Crises," in G. Ziccardi Capaldo (ed.), *The Global Yearbook of International Law and Jurisprudence* (Oxford: Oxford University Press), 175–98.

Miettinen, R., Samra-Fredericks, D., and Yanow, D. (2009), "Re-Turn to Practice: An Introductory Essay," *Organization Studies*, 30/12: 1309–27.

MMC Asia (2019), *Quarterly Mixed Migration Update: Asia*, Quarter 1.

MMC East Africa & Yemen (2019), *Quarterly Mixed Migration Update: East Africa and Yemen*, Quarter 1.

MMTF Somalia (2008), *Mixed Migration through Somalia and across the Gulf of Aden.*

Moeran, B. (2009), "From Particpant Observation to Observant Participation," in S. Ybema, D. Yanow, H. Wels et al. (eds.), *Organizational Ethnography: Studying the Complexities of Everyday Life* (London: SAGE), 139–55.

Momani, B. (2005), "Recruiting and Diversifying IMF Technocrats," *Global Society*, 19/2: 167–87.

Moreno-Lax, V. (2017), *Accessing Asylum in Europe: Extraterritorial Border Controls and Refugee Rights under EU Law* (Oxford: Oxford University Press).

Mørk, B. E., Hoholm, T., Ellingsen, G. et al. (2010), "Challenging Expertise: On Power Relations Within and Across Communities of Practice in Medical Innovation," *Management Learning*, 41/5: 575–92.

Moschella, M. (2011), "Lagged Learning and the Response to Equilibrium Shock: The Global Financial Crisis and IMF Surveillance," *Journal of Public Policy*, 31/2: 121–41.

Moschella, M. (2015), "The Institutional Roots of Incremental Ideational Change: The IMF and Capital Controls after the Global Financial Crisis," *The British Journal of Politics and International Relations*, 17/3: 442–60.

Moschella, M., and Tsingou, E. (2013), "Regulating Finance after the Crisis: Unveiling the Different Dynamics of the Regulatory Process," *Regulation & Governance*, 7/4: 407–16.

Mosse, D. (2011a) (ed.), *Adventures in Aidland: The Anthropology of Professionals in International Development* (New York, Oxford: Berghahn).

Mosse, D (2011b), "Introduction. The Anthropology of Expertise and Professionals in International Development," in D. Mosse (ed.), *Adventures in Aidland: The Anthropology of Professionals in International Development* (New York: Berghahn), 1–32.

Mourad, L., and Norman, K. P. (2020), "Transforming Refugees into Migrants: Institutional Change and the Politics of International Protection," *European Journal of International Relations*, 26/3: 687–713.

Müller, B. (2013) (ed.), *The Gloss of Harmony: The Politics of Policy-Making in Multilateral Organisations* (London: Pluto Press).

Murtaza, N. (2012), "Putting the Lasts First: The Case for Community-Focused and Peer-Managed NGO Accountability Mechanisms," *Voluntas*, 23/1: 109–25.

Nair, D. (2020), "Emotional Labor and the Power of International Bureaucrats," *International Studies Quarterly*, 64/3: 573–87.

Nair, D. (2021), "'Hanging Out' while Studying 'Up': Doing Ethnographic Fieldwork in International Relations," *International Studies Review*, 23/4: 1300–27.

Nasiritousi, N., Hjerpe, M., and Bäckstrand, K. (2016), "Normative Arguments for Non-State Actor Participation in International Policymaking Processes: Functionalism, Neocorporatism or Democratic Pluralism?," *European Journal of International Relations*, 22/4: 920–43.

Natorski, M. (2016), "Epistemic (Un)Certainty in Times of Crisis: The Role of Coherence as a Social Convention in the European Neighbourhood Policy after the Arab Spring," *European Journal of International Relations*, 22/3: 646–70.

Neumann, I. B. (2005), "To Be a Diplomat," *International Studies Perspectives*, 6/1: 72–93.

Neumann, I. B. (2007), "'A Speech That the Entire Ministry May Stand for' or: Why Diplomats Never Produce Anything New," *International Political Sociology*, 1/2: 183–200.

Neumann, I. B., and Sending, O. J. (2010), *Governing the Global Polity: Practice, Mentality, Rationality* (Ann Arbor, MI: University of Michigan Press).

Newland, K. (2010), "The Governance of International Migration: Mechanisms, Processes, and Institutions," *Global Governance*, 16/3: 331–43.

Newland, K. (2018), "The Global Compact for Safe, Orderly and Regular Migration: An Unlikely Achievement," *International Journal of Refugee Law*, 30/4: 657–60.

Newland, K., and Riester, A. (2018), *Welcome to Work? Legal Migration Pathways for Low-Skilled Workers*, MPI Policy Briefs, Issue No. 3 (Washington, DC: MPI).

Neyland, D. (2008), *Organizational Ethnography* (London: SAGE).

Nicolini, D. (2009a), "Zooming In and Out: A Package of Method and Theory to Study Work Practices," in S. Ybema, D. Yanow, H. Wels et al. (eds.), *Organizational Ethnography. Studying the Complexities of Everyday Life* (London: SAGE), 120–38.

Nicolini, D. (2009b), "Zooming In and Out: Studying Practices by Switching Theoretical Lenses and Trailing Connections," *Organization Studies*, 30/12: 1391–418.

Nicolini, D. (2013), *Practice Theory, Work and Organization* (Oxford: Oxford University Press).

Nicolini, D., and Monteiro, P. (2016), "The Practice Approach: For a Praxeology of Organisational and Management Studies," in A. Langley and H. Tsoukas (eds.), *The SAGE Handbook of Process Organization Studies* (London: SAGE), 110–26.

Nicolini, D., Gherardi, S., and Yanow, D. (2003), "Towards a Practice-Based View of Knowing and Learning in Organizations," in D. Nicolini, S. Gherardi, and D. Yanow (eds.), *Knowing in Organizations: A Practice-Based Approach* (Armonk, NY: M.E. Sharpe), 3–31.

Nielson, D. L., and Tierney, M. J. (2003), "Delegation to International Organizations: Agency Theory and World Bank Environmental Reform," *International Organization*, 57/2: 241–76.

Niemann, A., and Speyer, J. (2018), "A Neofunctionalist Perspective on the 'European Refugee Crisis': The Case of the European Border and Coast Guard," *Journal of Common Market Studies*, 56/1: 23–43.

Niemann, A., and Zaun, N. (2018), "EU Refugee Policies and Politics in Times of Crisis: Theoretical and Empirical Perspectives," *Journal of Common Market Studies*, 56/1: 3–22.

Niezen, R., and Sapignoli, M. (2017), *Palaces of Hope* (Cambridge: Cambridge University Press).

Nonaka, I. (1994), "A Dynamic Theory of Organizational Knowledge Creation," *Organization Science*, 5/1: 14–37.

Nonaka, I., and Takeuchi, H. (1995), *The Knowledge-Creating Company: How Japanese Companies Create the Dynamics of Innovation* (Oxford: Oxford University Press).

Norwegian Refugee Council et al. (2016), *More than Six Months Stranded—What Now? A Joint Policy Brief on the Situation for Displaced Persons in Greece* <https://www.nrc.no/resources/reports/more-than-six-months-stranded/>, accessed Jun 18, 2018.

NRC (2016), *Dignified Reception Guidelines: Key Essentials to Dignified Reception of Refugees and Asylum-Seekers in Europe* (Oslo: NRC).

NRC (n.d.), "ProCap: What We Do" <https://www.humanitarianresponse.info/en/coordination/procap/procap-what-we-do>, accessed May 13, 2019.

NT (2023), "Greece Border Abuses Highlight Europe's Clashing Priorities on Migration." *New York Times*, Feb 14 <https://www.nytimes.com/2023/02/14/world/europe/eu-greece-border-abuses.html#:~:text=the%20main%20story-,Greece%20Border%20Abuses%20Highlight%20Europe's%20Clashing%20Priorities%20on%20Migration, there%20were%20mistreating%20asylum%20seekers.>, accessed Apr 13, 2023.

Obendiek, A. (2021), "What Are We Actually Talking About? Conceptualizing Data as a Governable Object in Overlapping Jurisdictions," *International Studies Quarterly*, 66/1: 1–13.

Oelgemöller, C. (2021), "The Global Compacts, Mixed Migration and the Transformation of Protection," *Interventions*, 23/2: 183–90.

Oksamytna, K., Bove, V., and Lundgren, M. (2021), "Leadership Selection in United Nations Peacekeeping," *International Studies Quarterly*, 65/1: 16–28.

Oliver, C. (2011), "Lifestyle Migration," in A. Betts (ed.), *Global Migration Governance* (Oxford: Oxford University Press), 133–52.

Orlikowski, W. J. (2002), "Knowing in Practice: Enacting a Collective Capability in Distributed Organizing," *Organization Science*, 13/3: 249–73.

Painter, J., Papoutsi, A., Papada, E. et al. (2018), "Flags Flying Up a Trail Mast: Reflections on the Hotspot Mechanism in Mytilene," *Society & Space*, 2018: 1–15.

Pantzerhielm, L., Holzscheiter, A., and Bahr, T. (2020), "Power in Relations of International Organisations: The Productive Effects of 'Good' Governance Norms in Global Health," *Review of International Studies*, 46/3: 395–414.

Papada, E., Papoutsi, A., Painter, J. et al. (2020), "Pop-Up Governance: Transforming the Management of Migrant Populations through Humanitarian and Security Practices in Lesbos, Greece, 2015–2017," *Environment and Planning D: Society and Space*, 38/6: 1028–45.

Park, S., and Vetterlein, A. (2012) (eds.), *Owning Development: Creating Policy Norms in the IMF and the World Bank* (Cambridge: Cambridge University Press).

Patriotta, G. (2003), *Organizational Knowledge in the Making: How Firms Create, Use, and Institutionalize Knowledge* (Oxford: Oxford University Press).

Patz, R., and Goetz, K. H. (2019), *Managing Money and Discord in the UN: Budgeting and Bureaucracy* (Oxford: Oxford University Press).

Pavlin, S., Svetlik, I., and Evetts, J. (2010), "Revisiting the Role of Formal and Practical Knowledge from a Sociology of the Professions Perspective," *Current Sociology*, 58/1: 94–118.

Pécoud, A. (2010), "Informing Migrants to Manage Migration? An Anlysis of IOM's Information Campaigns," in M. Geiger and A. Pécoud (eds.), *The Politics of International Migration Management* (Basingstoke: Palgrave Macmillan), 184–201.

Pécoud, A., and Thiollet, H. (2023), "Introduction: The Institutions of Global Migration Governance," in A. Pécoud and H. Thiollet (eds.), *Research Handbook on the Institutions of Global Migration Governance* (Elgar Handbooks in Migration, Cheltenham: Edward Elgar Publishing), 1–17.

Perkowski, N. (2019), "'There Are Voices in Every Direction': Organizational Decoupling in Frontex*," *Journal of Common Market Studies*, 57/5: 1182–99.

PHAP (n.d.), "Homepage: Themes. Macro Trends. Migration" <https://phap.org/PHAP/Sector_Monitoring/Themes/Macro_trends/Migration/PHAP/Themes/Migration.aspx>, accessed Apr 30, 2019.

Pillinger, M., Hurd, I., and Barnett, M. N. (2016), "How to Get Away with Cholera: The UN, Haiti, and International Law," *Perspectives on Politics*, 14/1: 70–86.

Pincock, K., Betts, A., and Easton-Calabria, E. (2020), *The Global Governed? Refugees as Providers of Protection and Assistance* (Cambridge: Cambridge University Press).

Piper, N. (2017), "Global Governance of Labour Migration: From 'Management' of Migration to an Integrated Rights-Based Approach," in P. Drahos (ed.), *Regulatory Theory: Foundations and Applications* (Canberra: ANU Press), 377–94.

Polanyi, M. (2009 [1958]), *The Tacit Dimension* (Reissued, with a new foreword by Amartya Sen, Chicago: University of Chicago Press).

Pollozek, S., and Passoth, J. H. (2019), "Infrastructuring European Migration and Border Control: The Logistics of Registration and Identification at Moria Hotspot," *Environment and Planning D: Society and Space*, 37/4: 606–24.

Pouliot, V. (2007), "Sobjectivism: Toward a Constructivist Methodology," *International Studies Quarterly*, 51/2: 359–84.

Pouliot, V. (2008), "The Logic of Practicality: A Theory of Practice of Security Communities," *International Organization*, 62/2: 257–88.

Pouliot, V. (2021), "The Gray Area of Institutional Change: How the Security Council Transforms Its Practices on the Fly," *Journal of Global Security Studies*, 6/3: Forthcoming.

Pouliot, V., and Thérien, J.-P. (2018), "Global Governance in Practice," *Global Policy*, 9/2: 163–72.

Pouliot, V., and Thérien, J.-P. (2023), *Global Policymaking: The Patchwork of Global Governance* (Cambridge: Cambridge University Press).

Powell, W. W., and Clemens, E. (1998) (eds.), *Private Action and the Public Good* (New Haven, CT: Yale University Press).

Price, R. (1998), “Reversing the Gun Sights: Transnational Civil Society Targets Land Mines,” *International Organization*, 52/3: 613–44.

Price, R. (2003), “Transnational Civil Society and Advocacy in World Politics,” *World Politics*, 55/4: 579–606.

Quack, S. (2007), “Legal Professionals and Transnational Law-Making: A Case of Distributed Agency,” *Organization*, 14/5: 643–66.

Ralston, A. (n.d.), “UNHCR Global Learning Centre (GLC) Division of Human Resources Management: Interactive Learning Strategies for Mobile Learning” <http://www.unesco.org/new/fileadmin/MULTIMEDIA/HQ/ED/ICT/pdf/Ralston.pdf>, accessed May 8, 2019.

Rankin, M. (2022), *De Facto International Prosecutors in a Global Era: With My Own Eyes* (Cambridge: Cambridge University Press).

Rasche, L., Welfens, N., and Engler, M. (2022), *The EU Migration Pact at Two: What Remains of the Fresh Start?* Policy Brief (Berlin: Hertie School Jacques Delors Centre).

Reckwitz, A. (2002), “Toward a Theory of Social Practices: A Development in Culturalist Theorizing,” *European Journal in Social Theory*, 5/2: 243–63.

Refugee Support Aegean and Pro Asyl (2023), “What Is Happening Today in the Refugee Structures on the Aegean Islands” <https://rsaegean.org/wp-content/uploads/2023/05/ccac-aegean-islands-greece.pdf>, accessed Jan 11, 2024.

Reinalda, B., and Verbeek, B. (1998) (eds.), *Autonomous Policy Making by International Organizations* (London: Routledge).

Reinalda, B., and Verbeek, B (2006), *Decision-Making within International Organizations* (New York: Routledge).

Reiners, N. (2022), *Transnational Lawmaking Coalitions for Human Rights* (Cambridge: Cambridge University Press).

Reuters (2018), “U.N. Members Adopt Global Migration Pact Rejected by U.S. and Others” <https://www.reuters.com/article/us-europe-migrants-un-pact/u-n-members-adopt-global-migration-pact-rejected-by-u-s-and-others-idUSKBN1O90YS>, accessed Jun 30, 2019.

Rietig, K. (2021), *Learning in Governance: Climate Policy Integration in the European Union* (Cambridge, MA: MIT Press).

Risse, T (2018), “Hierarchical and Non-Hierarchical Coordination,” in A. Draude, T. A. Börzel, and T. Risse (eds.), *The Oxford Handbook of Governance and Limited Statehood* (Oxford: Oxford University Press), 311–32.

Risse, T. (2000), “‘Let’s Argue!’ Communicative Action in World Politics,” *International Organization*, 54/1: 1–39.

Roberts, J. (2006), “Limits to Communities of Practice,” *Journal of Management Studies*, 43/3: 623–39.

Robinson, C. (2018), “Making Migration Knowable and Governable: Benchmarking Practices as Technologies of Global Migration Governance,” *International Political Sociology*, 12/4: 418–37.

Rodenhäuser, T. (2014), “Another Brick in the Wall: Carrier Sanctions and the Privatization of Immigration Control,” *International Journal of Refugee Law*, 26/2: 223–47.

Roger, C. B. (2020), *The Origins of Informality: Why the Legal Foundations of Global Governance are Shifting, and Why It Matters* (Oxford: Oxford University Press).

Rosenau, J. (1990), *Turbulence in World Politics: A Theory of Change and Continuity* (Princeton, NJ: Princeton University Press).

Rosenau, J. (1992), “Governance, Order, and Change in World Politics,” in J. N. Rosenau and E.-O. Czempiel (eds.), *Governance without Government: Order and Change in World Politics* (Cambridge: Cambridge University Press), 1–29.

Rosenau, J. (1997), *Along the Domestic-Foreign Frontier: Exploring Governance in a Turbulent World* (Cambridge: Cambridge University Press).

Rosenau, J. (2002), "Governance in a New Global Order," in D. M. Held (ed.), *Governing Globalization. Power, Authority and Global Governance* (Cambridge: Polity Press), 70–86.

Rother, S. (2009), "'Inside-Outside' or 'Outsiders by Choice'. Civil Society Strategies towards the 2nd Global Forum on Migration and Development (GFMD) in Manila," *ASIEN*, 111: 95–107.

Rother, S., and Steinhilper, E. (2019), "Tokens or Stakeholders in Global Migration Governance? The Role of Affected Communities and Civil Society in the Global Compacts on Migration and Refugees," *International Migration*, 57/6: 243–57.

Ruffa, C., and Rietjens, S. (2022), "Meaning Making in Peacekeeping Missions: Mandate Interpretation and Multinational Collaboration in the UN Mission in Mali," *European Journal of International Relations*, 29/1: 53–78.

Ruggie, J. G. (1993), "Territoriality and Beyond: Problematizing Modernity in International Relations," *International Organization*, 47/1: 139–74.

Ruggie, J. G. (2004), "Reconstituting the Global Public Domain: Issues, Actors, and Practices," *European Journal of International Relations*, 10/4: 499–531.

Ruhs, M. (2017), *The Price of Rights: Regulating International Labor Migration* (Princeton, NJ: Princeton University Press) <https://ebookcentral.proquest.com/lib/kxp/detail.action?docID=1205617>.

Ruhs, M., and Martin, P. (2008), "Numbers vs. Rights. Trade-Offs and Guest Worker Programs," *International Migration Review*, 42/1: 249–65.

Saldana, J. (2009), *The Coding Manual for Qualitative Researchers* (London: SAGE).

Schettler, L., Heucher, A., and Liese, A. (2018), "International Organizations' Modes of Governance in Areas of Limited Statehood: The Case of Food Security," SFB-Governance Working Paper Series, No. 73.

Schimmelfennig, F. (2018), "European Integration (Theory) in Times of Crisis: A Comparison of the Euro and Schengen Crises," *Journal of European Public Policy*, 25/7: 969–89.

Schindler, S., and Wille, T. (2015), "Change in and through Practice: Pierre Bourdieu, Vincent Pouliot, and the End of the Cold War," *International Theory*, 7/2: 330–59.

Schindler, S., and Wille, T. (2019), "How Can We Criticize International Practices?," *International Studies Quarterly*, 63/4: 1014–24.

Schmitz, H. P., Raggo, P., and Bruno-van Vijfeijken, T. (2012), "Accountability of Transnational NGOs," *Nonprofit and Voluntary Sector Quarterly*, 41/6: 1175–94.

Schneiker, A., and Joachim, J. (2021), "Linking Pins as Drivers of Interagency Cooperation: Humanitarian NGOs and Security Networks," *Globalizations*, 18/4: 600–16.

Scholte, J. A. (2021), "Beyond Institutionalism: Toward a Transformed Global Governance Theory," *International Theory*, 13/1: 179–91.

Schön, D. A. (1983), *The Reflective Practitioner: How Professionals Think in Action* (Farnham: Ashgate).

Schwartz-Shea, P., and Yanow, D. (2009), "Reading and Writing as a Method: In Search of Trustworthy Texts," in S. Ybema, D. Yanow, H. Wels et al. (eds.), *Organizational Ethnography. Studying the Complexities of Everyday Life* (London: SAGE), 56–82.

Schwartz-Shea, P., and Yanow, D (2012), *Interpretive Research Design: Concepts and Processes* (Routledge Series on Interpretive Methods, New York: Routledge).

Scott, W. R., and Davis, G. F. (2007), *Organizations and Organizing: Rational, Natural, and Open System Perspectives* (Upper Saddle River, NJ: Pearson Prentice Hall).

Seabrooke, L. (2014), "Epistemic Arbitrage: Transnational Professional Knowledge in Action," *Journal of Professions and Organization*, 1/1: 49–64.

Seabrooke, L., and Henriksen, L. F. (2017a), "Issue Control in Transnational Professional and Organizational Networks," in L. Seabrooke and L. F. Henriksen (eds.), *Professional Networks in Transnational Governance* (Cambridge: Cambridge University Press), 3–24.

Seabrooke, L., and Henriksen, L. F (2017b) (eds.), *Professional Networks in Transnational Governance* (Cambridge: Cambridge University Press).

Seabrooke, L., and Sending, O. J. (2019), "Contracting Development. Managerialism and Consultants in Intergovernmental Organizations," *Review of International Political Economy*, 8/2: 1–26.

Seabrooke, L., and Tsingou, E. (2014), "Distinctions, Affiliations, and Professional Knowledge in Financial Reform Expert Groups," *Journal of European Public Policy*, 21/3: 389–407.

Seabrooke, L., and Tsingou, E (2015), "Professional Emergence on Transnational Issues: Linked Ecologies on Demographic Change," *Journal of Professions and Organization*, 2/1: 1–18.

Seabrooke, L., and Tsingou, E (2019), "Europe's Fast- and Slow-Burning Crises," *Journal of European Public Policy*, 26/3: 468–81.

Seabrooke, L., and Tsingou, E. (2021), "Revolving Doors in International Financial Governance," *Global Networks*, 21/2: 294–319.

Seabrooke, L., and Wigan, D. (2015), "Powering Ideas through Expertise: Professionals in Global Tax Battles," *Journal of European Public Policy*, 23/3: 357–74.

Seely-Brown, J., and Duguid, P. (1991), "Organizational Learning and Communities-of-Practice. Toward a Unified View of Working, Learning and Innovation," *Organization Science*, 2/1: 40–57.

Seely Brown, J., and Duguid, P. (2001), "Knowledge and Organization: A Social-Practice Perspective," *Organization Science*, 12/2: 198–213.

Selee, A., Bolter, J., Muñoz-Pogossian, B. et al. (2019), *Creativity amid Crisis: Legal Pathways for Venezuelan Migrants in Latin America*, MPI Policy Briefs (Washington, DC: MPI).

Sell, S. K. (2003), *Private Power, Public Law: The Globalization of Intellectual Property Rights* (Cambridge: Cambridge University Press).

Sending, O. J. (2015a), "Diplomats and Humanitarians in Crisis Governance," in O. J. Sending, V. Pouliot, and I. B. Neuman (eds.), *Diplomacy and the Making of World Politics* (Cambridge: Cambridge University Press), 256–83.

Sending, O. J. (2015b), *The Politics of Expertise: Competing for Authority in Global Governance* (Ann Arbor, MI: University of Michigan Press).

Sending, O. J., and Lie, J. H. S. (2015), "The Limits of Global Authority: World Bank Benchmarks in Ethiopia and Malawi," *Review of International Studies*, 41/5: 993–1010.

Sending, O. J., and Neumann, I. B. (2011), "Banking on Power: How Some Practices in an International Organization Anchor Others," in E. Adler and V. Pouliot (eds.), *International Practices* (Cambridge: Cambridge University Press), 231–54.

Sending, O. J., Pouliot, V., and Neuman, I. B. (2015) (eds.), *Diplomacy and the Making of World Politics* (Cambridge: Cambridge University Press).

Sharpe, M. (2018), "Mixed Up: International Law and the Meaning(s) of 'Mixed Migration,'" *Refugee Survey Quarterly*, 37/1: 116–38.

Slaughter, A.-M. (2009), *A New World Order* (Princeton, NJ: Princeton University Press).

Smirl, L. (2015), *Spaces of Aid: How Cars, Compounds and Hotels Shape Humanitarianism* (London: Zed Books).

Solomon, T., and Steele, B. J. (2016), "Micro-Moves in International Relations Theory," *European Journal of International Relations*, 23/2: 267–91.

Sondarjee, M. (2021a), "Change and Stability at the World Bank: Inclusive Practices and Neoliberal Technocratic Rationality," *Third World Quarterly*, 42/2: 348–65.

Sondarjee, M. (2021b), "Collective Learning at the Boundaries of Communities of Practice: Inclusive Policymaking at the World Bank," *Global Society*, 35/3: 307–26.

SOS Méditerranée (2019), "Search and Rescue Competency-Based Training by SOS MEDITERRANEE" https://sosmediterranee.com/search-and-rescue-competence-based-training/>, updated Jun 7, 2019.

SOS Méditerranée (2019), "Search and Rescue Competency-based Training by SOS MEDITERRANEE" https://sosmediterranee.com/search-and-rescue-competence-based-training/>, updated Jun 7, 2019.

Sphere (2018), *The Sphere Handbook: Humanitarian Charter and Minimum Standards in Humanitarian Response* (London: Sphere).

Squire, V. (2017), "Governing Migration through Death in Europe and the US: Identification, Burial and the Crisis of Modern Humanism," *European Journal of International Relations*, 23/3: 513–32.

Srivastava, S. (2022), *Hybrid Sovereignty in World Politics* (Cambridge: Cambridge University Press).

Stappert, N. (2020), "Practice Theory and Change in International Law: Theorizing the Development of Legal Meaning through the Interpretive Practices of International Criminal Courts," *International Theory*, 12/1: 33–58.

Stasavage, D. (2004), "Open-Door or Closed-Door? Transparency in Domestic and International Bargaining," *International Organization*, 58/4: 667–703.

Steffek, J. (2007), "Legitimacy in International Relations: From State Compliance to Citizen Consensus," in A. S. S. Hurrelmann (ed.), *Legitimacy in an Age of Global Politics* (Basingstoke: Palgrave Macmillan), 175–92.

Steffek, J. (2010), "Public Accountability and the Public Sphere of International Governance," *Ethics & International Affairs*, 24/1: 45–68.

Steffek, J. (2013), "Explaining Cooperation between IGOs and NGOs: Push factors, Pull Factors, and the Policy Cycle," *Review of International Studies*, 39/4: 993–1013.

Steffek, J. (2015), "The Output Legitimacy of International Organizations and the Global Public Interest," *International Theory*, 7/2: 263–93.

Steffek, J. (2021), *International Organization as Technocratic Utopia* (Oxford: Oxford University Press).

Steinhilper, E. (2021), *Migrant Protest: Interactive Dynamics in Precarious Mobilizations* (Amsterdam: Amsterdam University Press).

Stierl, M. (2023), "Rebel Spirits at Sea: Disrupting EUrope's Weaponizing of Time in Maritime Migration Governance," *Security Dialogue*, 54/4: 356–73.

Stone, R. W (2013), "Informal Governance in International Organizations: Introduction to the Special Issue," *The Review of International Organizations*, 8/2: 121–36.

Stone, R. W. (2011), *Controlling Institutions: International Organizations and the Global Economy* (Cambridge: Cambridge University Press).

Strange, S. (1996), *The Retreat of the State: The Diffusion of Power in the World Economy* (New York: Cambridge University Press).

Stroup, S. S., and Wong, W. H. (2017), *The Authority Trap: Strategic Choices of International NGOs* (Ithaca, NY: Cornell University Press).

Stürner-Siovitz, J. (2023), *Curtains Up: City Diplomacy in Global Migration Governance* (Wiesbaden: Springer).

Svenson, N. (2017), *The United Nations as a Knowledge System* (Abingdon: Routledge).

Tallberg, J., Sommerer, T., Squatrito, T. et al. (2013), *The Opening up of International Organizations: Transnational Access in Global Governance* (Cambridge: Cambridge University Press).

Tazzioli, M. (2018), "Crimes of Solidarity: Migration and Containment Through Rescue," *Radical Philosophy*, 2/1: 4–10.

Tazzioli, M., and Garelli, G. (2018), "Containment beyond Detention: The Hotspot System and Disrupted Migration Movements across Europe," *Environment and Planning D: Society and Space*, 48/1: 1–19.

Thorvaldsdottir, S., and Patz, R. (2021), "Explaining Sentiment Shifts in UN System Annual Reporting: A Longitudinal Comparison of UNHCR, UNRWA and IOM," *International Review of Administrative Sciences*, 87/4: 794–812.

Thouez, C. (2003), *The Role of Civil Society in Shaping International Migration Policy* (Durham, NC: Duke University).

Thym, D. (2022) (ed.), *Reforming the Common European Asylum System: Opportunities, Pitfalls, and Downsides of the Commission Proposals for a New Pact on Migration and Asylum* (Baden-Baden: Nomos).

Toksöz, G. (2018), "Irregular Migration and Migrants' Informal Employment: A Discussion Theme in International Migration Governance," *Globalizations*, 15/6: 779–94.

Trauner, F. (2016), "Asylum Policy: The EU's 'Crises' and the Looming Policy Regime Failure," *Journal of European Integration*, 38/3: 311–25.

Triandafyllidou, A. (2017), "Beyond Irregular Migration Governance: Zooming in on Migrants' Agency," *European Journal of Migration and Law*, 19/1: 1–11.

Triandafyllidou, A. (2018), "Migrant Smuggling: Novel Insights and Implications for Migration Control Policies," *The Annals of the American Academy of Political and Social Science*, 676/1: 212–21.

Triandafyllidou, A., and Maroukis, T. (2012), *Migrant Smuggling: Irregular Migration from Asia and Africa to Europe* (Migration, Diasporas and Citizenship, Basingstoke: Palgrave Macmillan).

Tsourapas, G., and Zartaloudis, S. (2022), "Leveraging the European Refugee Crisis: Forced Displacement and Bargaining in Greece's Bailout Negotiations," *Journal of Common Market Studies*, 60/2: 245–63.

Tsourdi, E. (2020), "Holding the European Asylum Support Office Accountable for Its Role in Asylum Decision-Making: Mission Impossible?" *German Law Journal*, 21/3: 506–31.

Türk, V. (2002), "UNHCR's Global Consultations on International Protection: Progress and Outlook," *Refugee Survey Quarterly*, 21/3: 217–21.

Turner, S. (2006), "Negotiating Authority between UNHCR and 'The People'," *Development & Change*, 37/4: 759–78.

UN DESA (2020), *International Migration 2020: Highlights* (New York: UN).

UN General Assembly (2016), "New York Declaration for Refugees and Migrants." A/RES/71/1 (New York: UN).

UN General Assembly (2017), "Unlawful Death of Refugees and Migrants: Report of the Special Rapporteur of the Human Rights Council on Extrajudicial, Summary or Arbitrary Executions." A/72/335. (New York: UN)

UN Secretary-General Ban Ki-Moon (2016), "In Safety and Dignity: Addressing the Large Movements of Refugees and Migrants." A/70/59 (New York: UN).

UNDP (2010), "Mobility and Migration: A Guidance Note for Human Development Report Teams." <http://hdr.undp.org/sites/default/files/nhdr_migration_gn.pdf>, accessed Mar 5, 2017.

UNHCR (2006a), *Operational Protection in Camps and Settlements: Reference Guide of Good Practices* (Geneva: UNHCR).

UNHCR (2006b), *Tool for Participatory Assessment in Operations* (Geneva: UNHCR).

UNHCR (2007a), *Refugee Protection and Mixed Migration: A 10-Point Plan of Action* (Geneva: UNHCR).

UNHCR (2007b), *UNHCR, Refugee Protection and International Migration* (Geneva: UNHCR).

UNHCR (2014), *Global Initiative on Protection at Sea* (Geneva: UNHCR).

UNHCR (2015), *Global Learning Centre: Training Catalogue* (Geneva: UNHCR).

UNHCR (2016a), "Chios Data Snapshot 17 March 2016." <https://data.unhcr.org/en/documents/details/47194>, accessed Jan 24, 2024.

UNHCR (2016b), "Chios Island Snapshot 21 March 2016." UNHCR Data Portal Greece <https://data2.unhcr.org/en/documents/download/47219>, accessed May 23, 2018.

UNHCR (2016c), "CHIOS: Who Is Doing What and Where (3W), as of 1 June 2016." <https://reliefweb.int/report/greece/chios-who-doing-what-and-where-3w-01-june-2016>, accessed Jan 24, 2024.

UNHCR (2017), *Pocket Guide for Emergency Responders* (Geneva: UNHCR).

UNHCR (2018), *Guidelines on Assessing and Determining the Best Interests of the Child* (Geneva: UNHCR).

UNHCR (2019), *Handbook on Procedures and Criteria for Determining Refugee Status and Guidelines on International Protection: Under the 1951 Convention and the 1967 Protocol Relating to the Status of Refugees* (Geneva: UNHCR).

UNHCR (2020a), *Aide-Memoire & Glossary of Case Processing Modalities, Terms and Concepts Applicable to RSD under UNHCR's Mandate* (Geneva: UNHCR).

UNHCR (2020b), *Procedural Standards for Refugee Status Determination under UNHCR's Mandate* (Geneva: UNHCR).

UNHCR (2020c), "Returns from Greece to Turkey (under EU-Turkey Statement) as of 31 January 2020" <https://data.unhcr.org/en/documents/details/74125>, accessed Dec 5, 2022.

UNHCR (2022), *Global Trends: Forced Displacement in 2022* (Geneva: UNHCR).

UNHCR Regional Bureau for Europe (2016), "Refugees and Migrants Sea Arrivals in Europe (Brussels)" <https://data2.unhcr.org/ar/documents/download/49921>, accessed Feb 7, 2018.

UNHCR and IDC (2016), *Vulnerability Screening Tool: Identifying and Addressing Vulnerability: A Tool for Asylum and Migration Systems* (Geneva: UNHCR and IDC).

UNHCR and ILO (2001), "The Asylum-Migration Nexus: Refugee Protection and Migration Perspectives from ILO." Presented to the UNHCR Global Consultations on International Protection, Geneva.

UNHCR and IOM (2001), "Global Consultations on International Protection / Third Track: Refugee Protection and Migration Control. Perspectives from UNHCR and IOM." EC/GC/01/11 (Geneva: UNHCR).

UNHCR and IOM (2016), *Regional Refugee and Migrant Response Plan for Europe: Eastern Mediterranean and Western Balkans Route* (Geneva: UNHCR and IOM).

UNHCR, IOM, and IIHL (2016), "Workshop on Search and Rescue of Refugees and Migrants in the Mediterranean: Practitioners' Perspectives," Sanremo.

UNSMIL and OHCHR (2018), *Desperate and Dangerous: Report on the Human Rights Situation of Migrants and Refugees in Libya* (New York: UNSMIL and OHCHR).

Vabulas, F., and Snidal, D. (2013), "Organization without Delegation: Informal Intergovernmental Organizations (IIGOs) and the Spectrum of Intergovernmental Arrangements," *The Review of International Organizations*, 8/2: 193–220.

van der Kist, J., Dijstelbloem, H., and Goede, M. de (2019), "In the Shadow of Asylum Decision-Making. The Knowledge Politics of Country-of-Origin Information," *International Political Sociology*, 13/1: 68–85.

van der Klaauw, J. (2010), "Refugee Rights in Times of Mixed Migration: Evolving Status and Protection Issues," *Refugee Survey Quarterly*, 28/4: 59–86.

van der Waal, K. (2009), "Getting Going: Organizing Ethnographic Fieldwork," in S. Ybema, D. Yanow, H. Wels et al. (eds.), *Organizational Ethnography: Studying the Complexities of Everyday Life* (London: SAGE), 23–39.

van Hear, N. (1998), *New Diasporas: The Mass Exodus, Dispersal and Regrouping of Migrant Communities* (Seattle, WA: UCL Press).

van Hear, N. (2011), *Mixed Migration: Policy Challenges* (Policy Primer, Oxford: The Migration Observatory).

van Maanen, J. (1988), *Tales of the Field: On Writing Ethnography* (2nd ed., Chicago: University of Chicago Press).

Venzke, I. (2011), "The Role of International Courts as Interpreters and Developers of the Law: Working out the Jurisgenerative Practice of Interpretation," *Loyola of Los Angeles International and Comparative Law Review*, 34/1: 99–131.

Vespe, M., Natale, F., and Pappalardo (2017), "Data Sets on Irregular Migration and Irregular Migrants in the European Union," *Migration Policy Practice*, 7/2: 26–33.

Voeten, E. (2008), "Delegation and the Nature of Security Council Authority," in B. Cronin and I. Hurd (eds.), *The UN Security Council and the Politics of International Authority* (London: Routledge), 43–56.

Vollmer, B. A. (2011), *Irregular Migration in the UK: Definitions, Pathways and Scale* (Oxford: The Migration Observatory Briefing).

Vrasti, W. (2008), "The Strange Case of Ethnography and International Relations," *Millennium—Journal of International Studies*, 37/2: 279–301.

Wagenaar, H. (2004), "'Knowing' the Rules. Administrative Work as Practice," *Public Administration Review*, 64/6: 643–56.

Weaver, C. (2008), *Hypocrisy Trap: The World Bank and the Poverty of Reform* (Princeton, NJ: Princeton University Press).

Welfens, N. (2023), "'Promising Victimhood': Contrasting Deservingness Requirements in Refugee Resettlement," *Journal of Ethnic and Migration Studies*, 49/5: 1103–24.

Welfens, N., and Bekyol, Y. (2021), "The Politics of Vulnerability in Refugee Admissions under the EU-Turkey Statement," *Frontiers in Political Science*, 3: 1–7.

Wenger, E. (1998), *Communities of Practice: Learning, Meaning, and Identity* (Cambridge: Cambridge University Press).

Westerwinter, O., Abbott, K. W., and Biersteker, T. (2021), "Informal Governance in World Politics," *The Review of International Organizations*, 16/1: 1–27.

White, J. (2022), "The De-Institutionalisation of Power beyond the State," *European Journal of International Relations*, 28/1: 187–208.

Wihtol de Wenden, C. (2012), "Globalization and International Migration Governance," in M. Geiger and A. Pécoud (eds.), *The New Politics of International Mobility: Migration Management and Its Discontents* (Osnabrück: IMIS), 75–86.

Williams, J., and Boyce, G. A. (2013), "Fear, Loathing and the Everyday Geopolitics of Encounter in the Arizona Borderlands," *Geopolitics*, 18/4: 895–916.

Winch, C. (2014), "Know-How and Knowledge in the Professional Curriculum," in M. Young and J. Muller (eds.), *Knowledge, Expertise and the Professions* (London: Routledge).

Witt, A. (2022), "Beyond Formal Powers: Understanding the African Union's Authority on the Ground," *Review of International Studies*, 48/4: 626–45.

Wolfinger, N. H. (2002), "On Writing Fieldnotes: Collection Strategies and Background Expectancies," *Qualitative Research*, 2/1: 85–93.

Yang, H. (2021), "Contesting Legitimacy of Global Governance Institutions: The Case of the World Health Organization during the Coronavirus Pandemic," *International Studies Review*, 23/4: 1813–34.

Yanow, D. (2000), "Seeing Organizational Learning: A 'Cultural' View," *Organization*, 7/2: 247–68.

Yanow, D. (2004), "Translating Local Knowledge at Organizational Peripheries," *British Journal of Management*, 15/S1: 9–25.

Yanow, D (2009), "Organizational Ethnography and Methodological Angst: Myths and Challenges in the Field," *Qualitative Research in Organizations and Management*, 4/2: 186–99.

Yanow, D., Ybema, S., and van Hulst, M. (2012), "Practicing Organisational Ethnography," in C. Cassell and G. Symon (eds.), *Qualitative Organizational Research* (London: SAGE), 331–50.

Ybema, S., Yanow, D., Wels, H. et al. (2009), "Studying Everyday Organizational Life," in S. Ybema, D. Yanow, H. Wels et al. (eds.), *Organizational Ethnography: Studying the Complexities of Everyday Life* (London: SAGE), 1–20.

Yildiz, E. (2023), *Between Forbearance and Audacity: The European Court of Human Rights and the Norm against Torture* (Cambridge: Cambridge University Press).

Young, M., and Muller, J. (2014), "From the Sociology of the Professions to the Sociology of Professional Knowledge," in M. Young and J. Muller (eds.), *Knowledge, Expertise and the Professions* (London: Routledge), 3–17.

Zahle, J. (2012), "Practical Knowledge and Participant Observation," *Inquiry*, 55/1: 50–65.

Zaiotti, R. (2016a) (ed.), *Externalizing Migration Management: Europe, North America and the Spread of "Remote Control" Practices* (Abingdon: Routledge).

Zaiotti, R. (2016b), "Mapping Remote Control: The Externalization of Migration Management in the 21st Century," in R. Zaiotti (ed.), *Externalizing Migration Management. Europe, North America and the Spread of "Remote Control" Practices* (Abingdon: Routledge), 3–30.

Zaum, D. (2013) (ed.), *Legitimating International Organizations* (Oxford: Oxford University Press).

Zaun, N. (2018), "States as Gatekeepers in EU Asylum Politics: Explaining the Non-Adoption of a Refugee Quota System," *Journal Common Market Studies*, 56/1: 44–62.

Zaun, N., Leroch, M., and Thielemann, E. (2023), "Why Courts are the Life Buoys of Migrant Rights: Anti-Immigrant Pressure, Variation in Judicial Independence, and Asylum Recognition Rates," *Journal of European Public Policy*, forthcoming.

Zetter, R. (2007), "More Labels, Fewer Refugees: Remaking the Refugee Label in an Era of Globalization," *Journal of Refugee Studies*, 20/2: 172–92.

Ziebritzki, C. (2020), "The Integrated EU Hotspot Administration and the Question of the EU's Liability," in M. Kotzur, D. Moya, Ü. S. Sözen et al. (eds.), *The External Dimension of EU Migration and Asylum Policies: Human Rights, Development and Neighbourhood Policies in the Mediterranean Area* (Baden-Baden: Nomos), 253–94.

Ziebritzki, C., and Nestler, R. (2017), "'Hotspots' an der EU-Außengrenze. Eine rechtliche Bestandsaufnahme. ['Hotspots' at the EU External Border. A Legal Survey)," Max Planck Institute for Comparative Public Law & International Law (MPIL) Research Paper No. 2017-17.

Zürn, M. (2017), "From Constitutional Rule to Loosely Coupled Spheres of Liquid Authority. A Reflexive Approach," *International Theory*, 9/2: 261–85.

Zürn, M. (2018), *A Theory of Global Governance: Authority, Legitimacy, and Contestation* (Oxford: Oxford University Press).

Zürn, M., Tokhi, A., and Binder, M. (2021), "The International Authority Database," *Global Policy*, 12/4: 430–42.

Index

For the benefit of digital users, indexed terms that span two pages (e.g., 52–53) may, on occasion, appear on only one of those pages.

N

O